INDIAN WOMEN NOVELISTS
CRITICAL DISCOURSES

Dr. M.F. Patel (b. 1974) achieved Bachelor Degree in English from Shri. & Smt. P.K. Kotawala Arts College, Patan in 1994 and Master Degree from Department of English, North Gujarat University, Patan in 1996. Presently he is discharging his duties as Prinicipal of Smt. C.C. Mahila Arts & Sheth C.N. Commerce College, Visnagar, Gujarat. He had also served as a NCC Officer with the rank of Lieutenant. He obtained his Ph.D. Degree from Hemchandracharya North Gujarat University, Patan on 7th August, 2007 on *The Novels of Anita Desai: A Multi-Dimensional Thematic Study*. Dr Patel's twenty articles have been published in books and various national & International journals. He has presented papers in State, National & International Level Seminars and participated in various workshops and International Symposium as well as International Writers Festival. He has completed a Minor Research Project entitled *Critical Study of the Novels of Anita Desai*, accorded by the UGC, New Delhi. His area of special interest is Indian Writing in English. He has to his credit seventeen voluminous books till date. He has launched a Refereed National Journal of English Language & Literary Writings entitled *The Literary Musing* (ISSN : 0976-4976) in June 2010.

INDIAN WOMEN NOVELISTS
CRITICAL DISCOURSES

Editor

Dr. M.F. Patel

Principal
Smt. C.C. Mahila Arts &
Sheth C.N. Commerce College
Visnagar, Gujarat

Aavishkar Publishers, Distributors
Jaipur 302 003 (Raj.) India

Published by
Prem C. Bakliwal for
Aavishkar Publishers, Distributors
807, Vyas Building, Chaura Rasta
Jaipur 302 003 (Raj.) India
Phone : 0141-2578159
e-mail : aavishkarbooks@hotmail.com

2017

ISBN 978-81-7910-331-9

Price : ₹ 1250.00

Printed at
Sheetal Printers
Jaipur (Raj.) India

Preface

Today Indian English Literature is an endeavour of showcasing the rare gems of Indian writing in English. From being a curious native explosion, Indian English has become a new form of Indian culture, and voice in which India speaks. Not only are the works of Indian writers writing in English soaring on the best-sellers list, they are also receiving a great deal of critical acclaim from Anita Desai, Kiran Desai, Jhumpa Lahiri, Arundhati Roy ... the parade of fine Indian women writers is long and lengthening. Here, you can explore the interesting history of Indian writing in English, and also experience its various facets, as expressed by Indian women Novelists.

Indian Women Novelists: Critical Discourses is a latest attempt to explore and criticise the major Indian Women Novelists. The book covers a unique collection of thirty scholarly papers from eminent scholars of India. The major Indian Women Novelists analysed in this book are: Arundhati Roy, Shashi Deshpande, Anita Desai, Kiran Desai, Kamala Markandaya, Jhumpa Lahiri, Bharati Mukherjee, Manju Kapur and Shobha De.

Women novelists have contributed a lot in the development of Indian English Literature. The present issue discusses various aspects of these women novelists. The first paper is by Dr. Mallikarjun Patil and he discusses the experiment of language in Arundhati Roy's *The God of Small Things*. The second paper is also on Booker Prize Winner novelist Arundhati by Dr. Saurabh Kumar Singh and his discourse is mainly focused on Commodification, Imperialism, Environmental

Feminism, Caste in Arundhati Roy's novels. Prashant Subhash Mothe also takes the novel *The God of Small Things* and he studies it through the marginal gender. V.S. Sankarao Rao Chinnam writes his paper on the narrative techniques in *The God of Small Things.* This book has seven papers on Arundhati Roy. Next paper by M. Ambikavathy and he discusses about socio-political situation in the novel. Satya Prakash Prasad discusses about the woes of women in *The God of Small Things.* Child abuse is the major problem in India and Dr. Anju Bala Agrawal discusses this problem in this novel. Shashi Deshpande is the another feminist writer who takes feminine issues. Dr. Anil Verma takes Sexual Contentment vs. Emotional Bond in Marriage in the novel *That Long Silence.* Dr. Arvind M. Nawale is also a young critic and scholar and in his paper he takes images and symbols in the novels of Anita Desai's *Fire on the Mountain.* Dr. Ashok Kumar takes all the works of Anita Desai and studies those in the context of Multi-Cultural Dimension of Contemporary Society in his paper. Next paper is by P. Roopana entitled Anita Desai's Novels as Women's Fiction. Maithry Shinde takes Anita Desai's three novels *Cry, the Peacock, Voices in the City* and *Fire on the Mountain* as study in her paper. Sarojini Sudha takes theme of loneliness in Kiran Desai's *The Inheritance of Loss.* Mrs. Smita A. Mujumdar takes Kiran Desai's novel *The Inheritance of Loss* from the study of post-modern perspective. Dr. T. Sasikanth Reddy takes innovative approach in his paper entitled Immigration is a Line of Attack to Scrutinize Individual Loss: A Bird's Eye View on Kiran Desai's *The Inheritance of Loss.* Dr. Datendra Kumar also studies *The Inheritence of Loss* in his paper entitled Kiran Desai's *The Inheritance of Loss* versus the Inheritance of Writing. Dr. Kanwar Dinesh Singh is a significant name among the scholars of India and he takes Alienation, Anger and Angst in Kiran Desai's *The Inheritance of Loss.* Dr. Shubha Mukherjee's main discourse is on the famous novelist Kamala Markandaya in her scholarly paper. Shishu Paul takes Kamala Markandaya's *Some Inner Fury* and he scrutinizes this novel through Human Relationships and Political Upheaval with special reference to Minor Characters. Dr. Pradnya Vijay Ghorpade and Dr. J.A. Shinde take Kamala Markandaya's *A Handful of Rice.* Rachel Irdaya Raj takes Kamala Markandaya's *Nectar in Sieve.* S. Rajiya Swami studies Kamala Markandaya's as A Crusading Spirit for the Welfare of Humanity and the Elevation of Human Suffering. Dr. Indu Goyal studies Jhumpa Lahiri's novels in her scholarly paper. Dr. Anju Bala Agrarwal studies Jhumpa Lahiri's

Unaccustomed Earth from the point of view of immigrant psyche. Arti Nirmal takes Jhumpa Lahiri's *The Namesake* as inheritance and exile. D. Balapriyadarshini in her paper studies on Bharati Mukherjee's Jasmine as Women and their Transformations. Dr. Ashok Kumar in his paper takes Manju Kapur's *Difficult Daughters* from the study of social web and cry of self. Dr. Sarika Dubey explores feministic visions in the novels of Manju Kapur. P. Madhurima and V. Saravanan take Nayantara Sahgal's novels from the point of feministic perspective. N. Jaishree takes the theme of feminism in the novels of Kiran Desai, Kamala Markandaya and Shobha De.

I have received great help and support in making of this book so it is my pleasure to record the obligations to all the contributors who contributed their tremendous co-operation for their scholarly papers.

On the whole the present book covers a fairy comprehensive ground. It is hoped that the anthology will be of great help to the students, researchers and teachers of English literature and will even appeal to those interested in Indian English literature.

I am also richly grateful to my better-half, Leela, without whose co-operation this book would not have been possible. I must not forget to express my thanks to my dear daughter Khyati and dear son Aryan who never disturbed me in my work inspite of being deprived of my love and affection.

Last but not least, I must express my heartfelt sense of gratitude to the publisher, Aavishkar Publishers, Distributors, Jaipur, India for publishing this book in a proper time.

Dr. M.F. Patel

Contents

Contributors

Agrawal, Anju Bala

Reader, Department of English, R.C.A. Girls' P.G. College, Mathura.

Ambikavathy, M.

Research Scholar, Department of English, Bharathiar University, Coimbatore-641 046, Tamilnadu.

Balapriyadarshini, D.

Department of English, Bharathiar University, Coimbatore-641046, Tamil Nadu.

Chinnam, V.S. Sankarao Rao

Assistant Professor, School of Humanities and Sciences, Vignan University, Vadlamudi, Guntur-522 213, AP.

Dubey, Sarika

Vidya College of Engineering, Vidya Knowledge Park, Meerut 250 002.

Ghorpade, Pradnya Vijay

Professor, Department of English, KRP Kanya Mahavidyalaya, Islampur, Maharashtra

Goyal, Indu

Department of English, Allahabad Degree College, Allahabad-211 001, U.P.

Jaishree, N.

Lecturer in English, Sri Eshwar College of Engineering, Kinathukadavu, Coimbatore, Tamil Nadu.

Kumar, Ashok

Department of English, Urdu & Other Languages, State Council of Educational Research & Training, Narendranagar, Tehri Garhwal-249 175, Uttarakhand.

Kumar, Lt. Satendra

Assistant Professor & Head, Department of English, Govt. P.G. College, Lansdowne, Dist. Pauri Garhwal, Uttarakhand.

Madhurima, P.

Assistant Professor in English, Chaitanya Bharathi Institute of Technology (CBIT), Hyderabad-500 075, Andhra Pradesh

Maithry Shinde

Head, Department of English, Aurora's Degree College, Chikkadpally, Hyderabad-500 020, Andhra Pradesh.

Mothe, Prashant Subhash

Adarsh Senior College, Omerga, Dist. Osmanabad, Maharashtra.

Mujumdar, Smita A.

Department of English, Shivraj College, Gadhinglaj-416 502, Dist. Kolhapur, Maharashtra.

Mukherjee, Shubha

GN Khalsa College, Matunga, Mumbai-700 019, Maharashtra.

Nawale, Arvind M.

Head, Dept. of English, Shivaji Mahavidyalaya, Udgir-413 517, Dist. Latur, Maharashtra.

Nirmal, Arti

Assistant Professor, Department of English, Vasanta College for Women, Banaras Hindu University, Rajghat, Varanasi, U.P.

Patil, Mallikarjun

Associate Professor, Department of English, Karnatak University, Dharwad-580 003, Karnataka.

Paul, Shishu

Sehgal Niwas, Gurudwara Road, Palampur-176 061, Himachal Pradesh.

Prasad, Satya Prakash

Research Scholar, Department of English, Banaras Hindu University, Varanasi, U.P.

Raj, Rachel Irdaya

Faculty, Department of English, Aurora's Degree College, Street No 12, Chikkadpally, Hyderabad-500 020, Andhra Pradesh.

Reddy, T. Sasikanth

Academic Consultant, Department of Humanities, Yogi Vemana University College of Engineering, Proddatur, YSR Kadapa Dist, Andhra Pradesh.

Roopana, P.

Assistant Professor in English, SSN College of Engineering, Old Mahabalipuram Road, Kalavakkam-603 110.

Saravanan, V.

Lecturer in English, Velammal Engineering College, Chennai-600 066, Tamil Nadu.

Shinde, J.A.

Former Head, Department of English, Shivaji University, Kolhapur, Maharashtra.

Singh, Kanwar Dinesh

Assistant Professor of English, Government Postgraduate College, Solan, Himachal Pradesh.

Singh, Saurabh Kumar

Assistant Professor of English, Vasanta College for Women, Banaras Hindu University, Rajght Fort, Varanasi-221 005, U.P.

Sudha, Sarojini

Associate Professor of English, PG Department of English, NSS College, Ottappalam-3, Palakkad Dist, Kerala.

Swamy, S. Rajiya

Assistant Professor of English, Gudlavalleru Engineering College, Gudlavalleru-521 356, Krishna Dt., Andhra Pradesh.

Verma, Anil

Senior Lecturer, Department of English, LPU, Punjab 144 001.

1

Arundhati Roy's *The God of Small Things* : An Experiment in Language

Mallikarjun Patil

John Berger cannot be fully accepted when he remarks "Never again will a single story be told as though it's the only one" in regard to Arundhati Roy's *The God of Small Things*. What bothers us is not the story of the novel but the way Roy tells it. No doubt, the story of the two lives that love each other and die loving is worthy of narration. Human strife ever since the dawn of man's rise has been nothing but a 'hideous grief', for the commonest reason -- 'love is a sweet poison'. This is applicable to the main characters of the novel here. "Dark of Heartness tiptoed into the Heart of Darkness" (306) of Ammukutty and Veluta, because "...they broke the Love Laws That lay down who should be loved. And how. And how much" (328). Man, it is sure while follows the ways unendorsed by his society, falls headlong into an unretrival ditch. This is what happens to Ammuktty, a gross-widow who falls in love with Velum, a down-trodden:

> Biology designed the dance. Terror timed it. Dictated the rhythm with which their bodies answered each other. As though they knew already that for each tremor of pleasure they would pay with an equal measure of pain. As though they knew that how far they went would be measured against how far they

> would be taken, so they held back. Tormented each other. Gave of each other slowly. But that only made it worse. It only raised the stakes, cost them more. Because it smoothed the wrinkles, the fumble and rush of unfamiliar love and roused them to fever pitch (p. 335).

However, Baby Kochamma says that it was 'a Small Price to Pay', it cost 'Two Lives'. In Arundhati Roy's words" it became a history lesson for future offender" (p. 336). No doubt they loved each other intensively, they violated the love-laws'. The result of the violation is nothing but the suffering and tragic end.

The novel *The God of Small Things* deals with a theme that is human suffering because of man's individual limitations and social codes. Ammu, the heroine undergoes untold misery and pain, for she erred beyond measure. Much against the parental wish, she married a clerk in Calcutta but returns home with Rahel and Estha (twins) divorced. Ammu comes to Ayemenem where her kindreds Baby Kochamma, Mammachi, Chacko lived together. Ammu finds herself amidst her family -- all Syrian Christians lived like Brahmins with caste-phobia. Soon Margaret, an English woman, having lost Joe, her second husband, comes to Ayemenem with Sophie Mol (her daughter born to Chacko before he was divorced by Margaret) just to get rid of the sorrowing. But in an accident, Sophie dies while Zebra-crossing and the Communist government of Kerala does not offset the loss though it had to. Already Chacko, her husband, had been in misery in India. So now his ex-wife Margaret loses all of her happiness. In Roy's words: "she had come to Ayemenem to heal her wounded world, and had lost all of it instead. She shattered like grass" (p.263). Similar is the case with Rahel and Estha. Rahel who finds substandard education at Ayemenem and later at Delhi, fails to make a career. Later she marries an American and goes to the USA. But like her mother, she too finds her husband indifferent to her wishes. Finally, as an enforced widow, she comes back to Ayemenem dismayed while Estha, her brother had already 're-Returned' from Calcutta. Likewise, due to the fetters of life Baby Kochamma and Mammachi live a life of penury. Besides, the whole family of these Syrian Christians is totally conservative almost blind to the new awakenings.

Arundhati Roy's *The God of Small Things* deals with a theme that is already dealt about but the depiction of her is excellent in so far as a few features of the art of writing are concerned. Roy has made an experiment in theme, language and treatment. Occasional incoherence, incongruity and lack of unity stem. Descriptions related to the lives of men and women come even after their death but as if they were still living. Titles of some chapters are misleading. Even the very title of the novel is not yet understood by a cross section of the reading public. Sophie is described as dead, but the latter part of the novel is interspersed with scenes in which she is depicted as living.

Arundhati Roy has made an experiment in language. *The God of Small Things* is full of new lines so far as the language is concerned. Some descriptions, in part due to the lively words, phrases and expressions, are splendid:

> May in Ayemenem is a hot, brooding month. The days are long and humid. The river shrinks and black crows gorge on bright mangoes in still, dustgreen trees. Red bananas ripen. Jackfruits burst. Dissolute blue bottles hum vacuously in the fruity air. Then they stun themselves against clear window panes and die, fatly baffled in the sun (p.1).

Another description related to Mammachi:

> Mammachi held a gleaming violin under her chin. Her opaque fifties sunglasses were black and slantyeyed, with rhinestones on the corners of the frames. Her sari was starched and perfumed. Off white and gold. Her dimond earrings shone in her ears like tiny chandeliers. Her ruby rings were loose. Her pale, fine skin was creased like cream on cooling milk and dusted with tiny red moles. She was beautiful. Old, unusual, regal (p.166).

Lively descriptions, meaningful statements, comic dialogues abound throughout the novel. Look at the statements: "It was a time uncles became fathers, mothers, lovers and cousins died and had funerals. It was a time when the unthinkable became thinkable and the impossible really happened" (p.31), "Sophie Mol died because she couldn't breathe. Her funeral killed her" (p.7), "Pappachi was dead by then. Chacko divorced. Paradise pickles was seven years old. Kerala was reeling in the aftermath of famine and a failed mansoon.

People were dying. Hunger had to be very high up on any government list of priorities" (p. 68). The descriptions related to love, life and death are still vivid:

> He could do only one thing at a time.
> If he held her, he couldn't kiss her.
> If he kissed her, he couldn't see her.
> If he saw her, he couldn't feel her (p.215).

Life had been lived. That her cup was full of dust' (p.222). Heartfelt expressions and sayings go in making the novel an interesting piece of art. The beauteous scenes like children's love for their mother (Ammu), Estha's waywardness at the talkie, tutorial exercises at home, Mol's death, the love making business and the disastrous repurcussions to the loving and loved etc., make the novel a very good reading. Lively expressions like 'May be and may be not' (p.115), 'So, she a glass bead, and he a green gram' (p.132), 'Sometimes', Sophie said. 'And sometimes not' (p.153), 'One for you and one for me', (p.142), 'Not old, not young, but a viable die-able age' (p.161), 'Her life had a size and a shape now' (p.155), 'He broke the egg but burned the omelette' (p.28!), 'The time for that had come and gone' (p.334) and finally the mysterious question:

> Who was he?
> Who would he have been?
> The God of Loss.
> The God of Small Things.
> The God of Goose Bumps and Sudden Smiles.
> He could do only one thing at a time.
> If he touched her, he couldn't talk to her,
> If he loved her, he couldn't leave, if he spoke
> He couldn't listen, if he fought he couldn't win.
> Ammu longed for him. Ached for him with the whole
> of her biology (p.330).

Arundhati Roy makes the inanimate things talk and act the way she desires. She tells: 'The silence was unsure of this compromise' (p.152) and 'Nights elbows rested on the water and watched them' (p.335). Music too bursts out like magic and drives the attention of us. Symbols like woman as earth, History as the rigid social code, Ayemenem House as the root of the Syrian Christian family and

'Anything'- as an indication of everlasting uncertainty are enough to assess Roy's maturity of thoughts. The concepts of Marxism, History, hideous grief and the sad white music of life are clearly expanded. Besides, no love description in the novel related to love or any carnal emotion looks either obscene or vulger. For instance the images of sex like 'melon in her blouse', 'he kissed her belly' or 'his love went deeper into hers', do not distort the readers' feelings. Typical words, phrases and sentences, like 'love-laws', 'teachrly', 'Cement Kangaroors', 'Jolly well Behave', 'hair oil darkness', 'nodder nodded', 'Man less Woman', 'Rabel Alone' and 'An Estha - shaped hole', contribute to the pleasure one gets out of his reading. Shortest sentences made of one word or two like 'Dum - dum' (p.119), 'A log'. 'A serene crocodile' (p.329). 'Her ashes,' 'The grit from her bones,' 'The teeth from her smile,' 'Receipt No. Q 498673' (p.163) etc, do not hurt our sense of propriety. As a diadem to all these are the songs interspersed in the description, some horizontally and others vertically, throughout the novel.

However, demerits go, with the merits of Roy's treatment of theme. Eccentric and unacceptable things are as abundant as those of the acceptable ones. Every para, every page, every chapter points out the linguistic as well as grammatical absurdities any ideal reader can dislike. No matter how grand the theme is and the novel has got a Booker Prize, *The God of Small Things* has unpardonable linguistic peculiarities such as typical words, phrases and sentences which are unacceptable. Words wrongly constructed, sentences either broken or ungrammatical, or verbal errors equally apparent, needless brackets, italics, structures of lines, syntactic inversions, reverse words, repetitions, words running into other words, cliche, distorted words, coinages, foreign words, obscure expressions, typical imagery and finally vague abstractions go together in degrading the standards of *The God of Small Things.* The errors listed above can be seen thus: clubbed words (Thiswayandthat'); reverse words (The serutnevda of eisus lerruqs' (p.60); typical imagery ('Rice-Christians', 'redsteps'); repetition ('Estha washed her face and hands and face and hands'); Coinages Amayrica'); cliche ('beige and pointy shoes'); ungrammatical sentences ('no, we can't not go to school'); lack of punctuations ('In Amayrica now, isn't it' (?); needless contracts (Further east. in a small country with similar landscapes (jungles, rivers, rice-fields, communists), vague abstractions ('Plymouth,' 'Little Elvis the pelvis'); obscure words and expressions ('Wash 'n' ever, No **Locusts stand**

I); distorted words (stoppit, porketmunny, Thang God, Never, The Less nevertheless); Indian words (namaste naale etc.,); hyphanated words (an honest-to-goodness Genuine Bourgeoise, trying-not-to-cry mouth); absurd songs; senseless sounds (verrry, Enee vee ee aar): typical wordy sentences (Is. That. Clear?); half- sentences (Like old roses in a breeze); needless italics (certain, inside (13)); needless capitals (LayTer, Hopes, Inbreeding, and others.

However grand the tale is, or might be, its errors in terms of language and style, another aspect of the novel, namely its complexion, is an admixture of cookery guide (p.195), a guide book and a travel-account, influenced by its author's architectural language. Certain linguistic experiment the way the story is narrated and interspersed with inconsistency of all-is striking enough to say 'Anything may get prize'.

WORK CITED

All the textual references are from Arundhati Roy's *The God of Small Things.*

2

Commodification, Imperialism, Environmental Feminism, Caste in Arundhati Roy's *The God of Small Things*

SAURABH KUMAR SINGH

Arundhati Roy's maiden text *The God of Small Things* has the capacity to address various issues which are, at present, the burning topics in the world of fertile academic discourses. It has immense bearings in the contemporary socio-political conditions. A number of readings of this novel have focused on the novel as subaltern history, feminist reading, and patriarchal oppression and so on so forth. Undoubtedly these critical readings have yielded to lots of fresh insights, but the issues like: devouring commodification, creeping imperialism, nasty dalitism and essential environmental feminism that constitute the very deep texture of this celebrated text concerning small but inevitable incidents, accidents, and *things* of life, have not been given proper placement. In a very important and vital move postcolonial feminists (in this case environmental feminists) have strongly advocated the view that political economy of imperialism affects a community's social interaction with nature and land and reduces that into mere commodity. Nature and land, once occupied a very sacred position in the psyche of people, has become the prey to the economical greed of common folk. These feminists/activists have suggested the possible understanding regarding the interconnections of gender, class, caste exploitation and environment destruction to a typical habit of capitalist accumulation that eventually yields to deeper form of commodification of natural resources.

In this article I am going to talk about these macros which are hidden but deeply embedded in the small lives (micros) of ours. The structural narrative of *The God of Small Things* allows us to develop greater insight into this commodification that in turn perpetuates the construction of typical patriarchal ideological constructions under the cultural logic of capitalism. Being written in the heyday of postcolonialism does not entail the impression that this novel is merely against western perception of the world, but it is strictly against that patriarchal ideology which is found everywhere (globally and locally) and directly links itself with the political economy of imperialism. This novel very aptly unearths the complicated issues of history and economics which are somehow concealed under the burden of dominant narratives and discourses of any sort.

The story primarily takes place in a town named Ayemenem now part of Kottyam in Kerala state of India. The temporal setting shifts back and forth from 1969, when Rahel and Estha, a set of fraternal twins are 7 years old, to 1993, when the twins are reunited at age 31. From the novel we come to know that the family derives its name from a prominent Syrian Christian descendant, father E. John Ipe, who in 1876 at the age of seven received blessings from the patriarch of Antioch. The family prospered well under British Empire as landowners and government bureaucrats, but since independence their fortunes have deteriorating. Shri Benaan John Ipe (referred to as Pappachi, which means grandfather), an imperial entomologist prior to his retirement, fathered Ammu and Chacko with his wife, Shoshamma Ipe (referred to as Mammachi, which means grandmother). Pappachi has been bitter since his discovery of a new species of moth was dismissed and then credited to someone else. His facade of being a perfect husband and father hides his abusive tendencies towards his family, especially Mammachi and Ammu. One night, while Pappachi is beating his wife, Chacko, Ammu's brother, a Rhodes Scholar home from Oxford University stops him and tells him never to do it again. From then on, till his death, Pappachi never hits nor speaks to Mammachi again. He also refuses to let Ammu continue with her college education, so she is forced to return home to Ayemenem.

Without sufficient dowry for a marriage proposal, Ammu becomes desperate to escape her ill-tempered father and bitter, long-suffering mother. Finally, she convinces her parents to let her spend a summer with a distant aunt in Calcutta. To avoid returning to Ayemenem, she marries a man who assists managing a tea estate (who she later discovers to be a heavy alcoholic, who beats her and attempts to prostitute her to his boss so that he can keep his job). She gives birth to two children, dizygotic twins Estha and Rahel, but ultimately leaves her husband and returns to live with her mother and brother in Ayemenem.

While studying at Oxford, Chacko had fallen in love and married an English woman named Margaret. Shortly after the birth of their daughter Sophie Mol (Mol means girl), Chacko and Margaret get a divorce (Margaret having fallen in love with another man, Joe, whilst pregnant). Unable to find a job, Chacko returns to India to teach. Chacko never stops loving Margaret, and the two of them keep in touch (even though she no longer sees him in a romantic light). After the death of Pappachi, Chacko returns to Ayemenem and expands his mother's pickling business into an ultimately unsuccessful pickle factory called Paradise Pickles and Preserves. Margaret remarries, but her husband Joe is killed in an accident. Chacko invites the grieving Margaret and Sophie to spend Christmas in Ayemenem. On the way to the airport, the family (Chacko, Ammu, Estha, Rahel, and Baby Kochamma) encounters a group of communist protesters. The protesters surround the family car and force Baby Kochamma to wave a red flag and chant a communist slogan. She is humiliated and begins to harbor a deep hatred towards Velutha (a man from the factory), who Rahel claims to have seen in the crowd. After this, the family visits a theatre playing "The Sound of Music", where Estha is molested by the "Orange drink Lemon drink man" (the food vendor).

Velutha is an untouchable (the lowest caste), a *dalit*. His family has been working for Chacko's for generations. Velutha is extremely gifted with his hands, an accomplished carpenter and mechanic. Unlike other untouchables, Velutha has a self-assured air. While his skills with repairing the machinery have made him indispensable at the pickle factory, there is a lot of hostility about the fact that he is an untouchable working in a factory of touchables who resent him. His self-assured air does not help. Rahel and Estha look up to Velutha and he becomes a father figure to them. This relationship is further solidified figuratively on the day of Margaret and Sophie's arrival. Ammu and Velutha realize that they are attracted to one another.

When her intimate relationship with Velutha is discovered,

Ammu is tricked and locked in her room and Velutha is banished. When the twins ask their mother why she has been locked up, Ammu (in her rage) blames them as the reason why she cannot be free and screams at them to go away. She says they are the two millstones around her neck, and she says she should have taken them to an orphanage the day they were born. Rahel and Estha decide to run away, and Sophie convinces them to take her with them. During the night, while trying to reach an abandoned house across the river, their boat capsizes and Sophie drowns. The twins cannot find her. Wearily, they fall asleep at the abandoned house where they had already been storing food and toys in preparation for their departure. They are unaware that Velutha is there as well, for it is where he secretly meets with Ammu.

When Sophie's body is discovered, Baby Kochamma, another member of the family, goes to the police and accuses Velutha of being responsible for Sophie's death. She claims that Velutha attempted to rape Ammu, threatened the family, and kidnapped the children. A group of policemen hunts Velutha down and savagely beats him for crossing caste lines. The twins witness this terrible scene, and are deeply affected.

When the twins reveal the truth of Sophie's death to the chief of police, he is alarmed. He knows that Velutha is a communist, and is afraid that the wrongful arrest and impending death of Velutha will cause a riot amongst the local communists. He threatens Baby Kochamma, telling her that unless she gets the children to change their story, she will be held responsible for falsely accusing Velutha of the crime. Baby Kochamma tricks Rahel and Estha into believing that unless they accuse Velutha of Sophie's death, they and Ammu will all be sent to jail. Estha bares an even heavier burden, when at the police station he is called in to respond "yes" to police questioning that will reveal Velutha as guilty. Not only does he carry the extra guilt of being forced into testifying against Velutha, but he also sees the aftermath of the police beating. Velutha dies from his injuries.

However, Baby Kochamma has underestimated Ammu's love for Velutha. Hearing of his arrest, Ammu comes to the station to tell the truth about their relationship. She is told by the police to leave the matter alone. Afraid of being exposed, Baby Kochamma convinces Chacko to feel that Ammu and the twins are responsible for his daughter's death. Chacko forces Ammu to leave the house. Ammu, unable to find a job, is forced to send Estha to live with his father. Estha never sees Ammu again, as she dies alone and impoverished a few years later.

Rahel, when grown up, leaves for the US, gets married, divorced and finally returns to Ayemenem after several years working as a waitress in an Indian restaurant and as a night clerk at a gas station. Rahel and Estha, both 31 at this time, are reunited for the first time since they were 7 years old. Both Estha and Rahel have been damaged by their past, and by this time Estha has become perpetually silent because of his traumatic childhood.

The commodification of things whether animate or inanimate can well be perceived from the very beginning of the novel. The very first chapter of the novel, "Paradise Pickles and Preserves," unmistakably refers to the just beginning of the commodification. The pickle business that Chacko has seized from his mother, Mammachi, and his adherence to reconstruct it according to new demands of patriarchal/imperial/market scenario which he has learnt from West, marks a painful deviation and shift in the mode of production from a simple house business to bigger factory labour that marginalizes middle class women in deep private, while at the same time imposing some more exploitative techniques that encompasses working class women and low caste labourers. Earlier this business was in the hand of women, so some power and authority, but now it has been snatched from them, and is being fully *enjoyed* by patriarchal forces. It also marks the subsequent degradation of middle class women to the level of proletariat class and further pushed into the direction of commodification. Women as merely a commodity. Useless. Here goes the vivid presentation of this shifting:

> Up to the time Chacko arrived, the factory had been a small but profitable enterprise. Mammachi just ran it like a large kitchen. Chacko had it registered as a partnership and informed Mammachi that she was the Sleeping partner. He invested in equipment (canning machines, cauldrons, cookers) and expanded the labor force (Roy: 1997: 55-56).

In an interesting observation regarding commodity fetishism, Karl Marx ponders, "a commodity is...a mysterious thing [because] a definite social relation between men...assumes, in their eyes, the fantastic form of a relation between things" (1978: 320-21). If we apply this on the moves of Chacko, it is quite possible to understand that his deliberate effort to craft a brand name for his business is in accordance with the new forms of productions.

> Until Chacko arrived in Ayemenem, Mammachi's factory had no name. It was Chacko who christened the factory Paradise Pickles & Preserves and had labels designed and printed at Comrade K.N.M. Piilai's press. At first he had wanted to call it Zeus Pickles & Preserves, but that idea was vetoed because everybody said that Zeus was too obscure and had no local relevance, whereas Paradise did (Roy: 1997: 56).

From the novel we can easily glean several other examples of subjects turning into merely a commodity. Baby Kochamma and the cook Kochu Maria are addicted to the temptation of satellite television. Accordingly they don't fail to assume the viewpoint of a white, middle class subject. Baby Kochamma, to the sheer height of absurdity, views ethnic cleansing, famine and genocide, as direct threats to her furniture (29). Rahel and Estha tragically compare themselves to the so called "clean children" in *The Sound of Music*, and as a result there is a formation of negative image of themselves which is intensified by the patriarchal stamp of Estha as deviant and dirty during the sexual assault by the Lemandrink man (100). As a result the children perpetually live in a world dominated by isolation and traumatized paralysis which shockingly affects the emotional plane. Estha internalizes profound colonial patriarchal assumptions that ditch him with the profound sense of shame, inferiority, and objectification. Even afterwards, he continually strives to wipe away these negative feelings by constantly cleaning and bathing. In this novel the woman's body is severely stripped of her animate and dynamic qualities and has been reduced to objects and things (commodity/property). Ammu's body is "jiggling and sliding". She compares herself as an object that is being consumed by marriage in the same way in which firewood is consumed by cremation. In the police station she is being humiliated by a police officer when he "tapped her breasts with his baton ... As though he was choosing mangoes from a basket" (9-10). This is nothing but a stark reminder of her status as a commodity.

Environmental feminism is that social and political movement which points to the co-existence of environment and feminism on considerable grounds. They voice their strong argument in the favour of impressive parallel between the oppression and subordination of women in family and society and the steadfast degradation of nature through the incessant construction of differences into conceptual binaries and patriarchal/ideological hierarchies that allow a systematic, however, logically unsound unfair, justification of domination by subjects classed into numerous higher-ranking categories over *other* subjects invariably classed into lower ranking categories e.g. man over woman, culture over nature, white over black and so on so forth.

The repletion of the novel with several traumatic events "Where did it all begin?", without any fail, alludes in a plethora of instances to the history of imperialism/exploitation in the state of Kerala. In the early sixteenth century, the Portuguese seized control of the spice trade from Arabian and thus set themselves as dominant European power till 1662. The British authority annexed the coast of Malabar in 1792 and directly accessed it, while in the princely states of Cochin and Travancore in south, it ruled indirectly. The novel suggests that with opening of Suez Canal in 1869, Kerala as well as the rest of India opened a better way for British to exploit India with the imposition of serious economic and social restructuring. In Travancore and Cochin, the British made changes in the law that gave tenants proprietorship rights but demanded tax payments in cash, thus increasing sharecropper hardships. Moreover, the British began establishing first coffee then later rubber and tea plantations on an extensive scale, initiating in the process the development of a large landless proletariat. At the same time, the British relied on collaborators within Kerala, prominently among them were the Nambudiri Brahmin class and also Syrian Christians, who benefited from close contact with British missionaries. In reference to this history, we might recall that in the novel the family's status is linked with official recognition from a church authority, not to mention Baby Kochamma's painful obsession with Father Mulligan. One extremely important field work study of Syrian Christians in the state of Kerala reports:

> British planters, towards the latter half of the 19th Century, pioneered the opening of plantations. Christians were employed in these plantations and

> probably their religious affiliations helped them in getting along with the British planters. Towards the beginning of [the twentieth] century, Christians started opening up new areas for plantations, very much modelled on the European plantations (Kurian: 41-2).

The new cash economy system which was stimulated by the establishment of financial institution within the churches and educational organizations set up by the missionaries, led to the emergence of Kerala's early banks out of investment schemes, and chit funds. Furthermore, these patriarchal structures, given that they were in place in their churches, households and governing structures, eased inheritance and property transactions with imperialist powers, whereas the Nair Hindus, who were organized in matrilineal joint households, called taravads, in which property is passed down through the mother's line, experienced significant confusion and financial loss under colonialism's cash economy. The changes that developed from relations of imperialism had a varying impact on women, though generally, as Jeffrey reporting the comments of an earlier researcher suggests: "The spread of male-dominated monogamous households constituted a 'retrograde change'" (1992: 10).

This above stated account of Kerala invariably refers to that picture of imperialism which not only transforms the economy but also casts profound consequences on social relations – especially gender and caste relations and the environment at large. It perpetuated the divisions of labor that intensified the the existing caste and gender hierarchies. It paved the way for divide and rule policy along with cash economy to inflict more exploitation of the land, in this regard nature. In this connection Gail Omvedt makes a very valid and pertinent remark irrespective of any nation but in general:

> "The accumulation of the earth's resources for the increase of capital has imposed many facets of a money economy and the logic of production for profit on regions throughout the world, but not primarily by turning people into wage laborers," but by other means, especially "force and violence against nonwage laborers" (1993: 20).

In this way, as the environmental feminist critique, we witness that *The God of Small Things* offers us a vantage point to see the so far invisible patriarchal ideological forces and its burdened legacy as the leftover of dominant hegemonic powers, strategically sustained and perpetrated after the so called end of imperialism.

This novel beautifully takes up the issue of caste in a complicated way. The notion of "untouchability" is an old age phenomenon. This word came from the Hindu notion of purity and pollution. The discourse was - "I am pure, you are polluted". A clever justification of the social difference was given with the help of the Karma theory. One is born into a "dalit" family because of one's accumulated bad deeds. On account of such birth, basic human rights were denied to the so called "lowly born". So the dalit problem is really a Human Rights problem. For human beings who are born to "dalit" parents, it is the problem of getting over the feeling of being lesser human beings, of being invisible in the history of the nation, of searching for a new identity and of redefining one's culture and roots. The dalit consciousness thus has negative and positive areas. Arundhati Roy's novel shows how terribly cruel such a system can be. But her depiction is not so simple. Here the portrayal of caste hierarchies follows the same pattern as other practices of patriarchal domination. Here the concept of ideology is in full swing. Just as ideology has the capacity to turn the things upside down to produce the web of lies as true, in the same way elite class who owns the factory and modes of production, instead of projecting the view that the wealth of a community is generated by those who labor to create it i.e. untouchable workers, the caregivers, the nurturing foundation provided by land, and factory workers – this patriarchal ideology justifies that the source of wealth belongs to those who own the enterprise. The Kochammas are considered upper class. They are factory owners, the dominating class. Mammachi and Baby Kochamma would not deign to mix with those of a lower class. Even Kochu Maria, who has been with them for years, will always be a servant of a lower class. Mammachi recalls "a time, in her girlhood, when Paravans were expected to crawl backwards with a broom, sweeping away their footprints so that Brahmins or Syrian Christians would not defile themselves by accidentally stepping into a Paravan's footprint"; "[In her day], Paravans, like other Untouchables, were not allowed to walk on public roads" (Roy:1997:71). Furthermore, when Velutha transgresses those restrictions, he is constructed as a sexual, transgender deviant, an "AC-DC," to reinforce gender and caste subordination. In the social world of the novel, elite insecurity demands the heteronormative drama of humiliation and disdain.

Velutha belongs to an untouchable class Paravan. Though the immediate cause of his death is police torture and subsequent custodial death for his alleged involvement in the abduction of children and the drowning of Sophie Moll, but in depth study narrates another treacherous story. His subsequent degradation is due to his birth – his birth as an untouchable. But significantly enough he does not have the air of being so. He has a sharp mind and he does not link himself to his caste profession. He is well expert in running the machines. In Mammachi's factory, he is in the charge of *general maintenance*. Mammachi pays him less than a regular worker and more than what is paid to a paravan. That's why upper caste workers hate him as they believe in the age old belief that Paravans were not meant to be carpenters.

Velutha commits another blunder in the eyes of those who believe in the superiority of upper caste. He dares to sin by instinctively drawn towards Ammu. They simply breach the traditional Love Laws and establish physical love. They have empathy to each other as both belong to same category marginalised and oppressed one. Baby Kochamma, the upholder of these hard and fast rules, misinforms and misreports the police. As a result Velutha is arrested and becomes the victim of inhuman suffering that ultimately results into his tragic death. Here we register a strong protest from the novelist to those people who do not allow the *others* to lead a dignified life. Dr. B.R. Ambedkar too denounces this degraded practice, "I do not believe that we can build up a free society in India so long as there is a trace of this ill-treatment and suppression of one class by another" (Ambedkar: 30).

In this way, we may safely affirm that this only masterpiece of Arundhati Roy is a brilliant critique on patriarchal/imperial proliferation of various modes of subjugation. It has the capacity to address the current burning issues which are the talk of the town. It focuses on such an issue which is not confined only to India but transcends its boundaries to embrace the whole universe. The contemporary world is on the brink of destruction due to the devastation done to Nature that comprises the forest, the environment and the man. Injustices are being perpetrated to Mother Nature and human beings alike. The exploitation is at fast and the possible elimination of social evils seems to be a beautiful dream which can never be fulfilled. Colonialism/imperialism is *back* in the garb of neoliberal globalization. The novel does not suggest any possible ending of these problems. There is no solution suggested. But it is successful in conveying its message. At least it makes us aware regarding the atrocities done to the vital aspects of our life. It advocates for the involvement of all the classes of society to come on one common front to search for new possible ways to take breath in fresh nature and environment. It warns us not to fall into the jeopardy of perpetual reification or abstraction as a commodity. It asks to retain the sanctity and identity of environment and human beings as an *individual*.

WORKS CITED

Ambedkar, B.R., *Annihilation of Caste, Dalit Classic Series-* 1, New Delhi: Blumoon Books.

Jeffrey, Robin, *Politics, Women and Well-Being: How Kerala Became 'a Model'*, London: Macmillan, 1992.

Kurian, George, *The Indian Family in Transition: A Case Study of Kerala Syrian Christians,* The Hague: Mouton, 1961.

Marx, Carl, *Capital, Volume I, The Marx-Engels Reader,* 2nd edition, Ed., Robert C. Tucker, New York: Norton, 1978, pp.294-439.

Omvedt, Gail, *Reinventing Revolution: New Social Movements and the Socialist Tradition in India,* Armonk NY: M.E. Sharpe, 1993,

Roy, Arundhati, *The God of Small Things,* New York: Random House, 1997.

□□□

3

Arundhati Roy's *The God of Small Things* : Focusing on Marginal Gender

PRASHANT SUBHASH MOTHE

Arundhati Roy's debut novel *The God of Small Things* rapidly become a world renowned literary sensation after it was published in New Delhi in 1997 and won prestigious Booker Prize Award. Arundhati Roy, the Booker Winner, demystifies gender and caste concept. She has depicted the intolerable plight of the marginalized class. Arundhati Roy herself has remarked: "The book is not about what happened but about how what happened affected people".

The God of Small Things is a protest novel which is radical, subversive, unconventional and taboo-breaking. It is in this sense that the novel would be read as a post-colonial novel because it aims at destroying the old power-structure. Roy expresses her disillusionment with the social conditions of the post-colonial world in which the untouchables of the past still face a hostile society that does not let them live as free and independent individuals.

Roy vividly portrays the acute suffering and deep frustration of the weaker sections of our society like the Paravans, the Scheduled Castes, the Scheduled Tribes, Dalits and so on. The Paravan, Velutha, whom we may call the male protagonist of the novel, is looked down upon almost at every stage in his life. As a small boy, when he visits the Ayemenem House in the company of his father to deliver the coconuts plucked from the trees in the compound, they come from the back entrance and later as a mature man, he is falsely implicated in a case of attempted rape of Ammu.

Roy powerfully portrays the miserable condition of the Paravans in *The God of Small Things.* Here discrimination expresses itself in marginalizing the 'untouchables' in their personal and public life. A complete appreciation of *The God of Small Things* requires an awareness of the caste system in Kerala. The community represented in *The God of Small Things* is Syrian Christian. The Christians of Kerala are divided into five categories: Roman Catholic, Orthodox Syrian, Nestorian, Marthoma, and Anglican. In the novel religions differences appear in the disagreements between the Roman Catholic Church and the Marthoma Church. Roy points out number of Paravans and members of other low castes converted to Christianity, they were made to have separate churches and thus continued to be treated as Untouchables. Roy aptly put in plain words as, "It was a little like having to sweep away your footprints with a broom or worse, not being allowed to leave any footprints at all" (p.57). After Independence, they were denied government benefits created for 'untouchables' because officially they were Christians and therefore Casteless. "They were not entitled to any Government benefits like job reservation or bank loans at low interest rates" (p.71).

Velutha, the Paravan, can perhaps be called the hero of the novel and he is the 'God' in *The God of Small Things.* He is a carpenter, a rebel, a trade unionist. Velutha is highly intelligent an excellent carpenter with an engineer mind, but he is also 'The God of Loss'. Roy articulates: "He left no footprints in sand, no ripples in water, no images in mirrors" (p.265). The untouchables were made to suffer humiliations at the hands of the Hindus and Christians. On the one hand we have a group of characters, Mammachi, Baby Koachamma and Kochu Maria the cook, who perpetuate the division of caste, race and gender. On the other hand, Ammu and Twins, Rahel and Estha, consciously and unconsciously resist these hierarchies. Roy throws light on, "Perhaps Ammu, Estha and Rahel were the worst transgressors. They all broke the rules...they all tampered with laws that lay down who should be loved and how. How much" (p.31).

Mammachi discovered Velutha's talent for carpentry when he was just eleven, about three years younger than Ammu. She enrolled him into the Untouchable School that was started by her father-in-law. Every afternoon after school Velutha worked with John Kelin, a carpenter in Bavaria and learnt carpentry. But his self-assurance disturbed his father, Vellya Pappen. As a result of family bickering, Velutha left home. Apart from his carpentry skills, Velutha had a way with the machines. Mammachi often said: "If only he hadn't been a Paravan, he might have been an engineer" (p.62). He mended radios, clocks, water-pumps and look after the other electrical gadgets in the house. He knew more about the machines in the factory than anyone else. He was a useful handyman in the Paradise Pickles Factory. He excels his fellow workers in the Paradise Pickles Factory, but they resent to work with him for his untouchability. Caste is the dominant factor on party lines. Even Pillai calls Velutha not by his name but by his caste, a 'Paravans' (p.278). Velutha's lack of complacency causes him many problems throughout the novel. Roy clarifies: "It was not entirely his fault that he lived in a socially where a man's death could be more profitable than his life" (p.267). At another place Comrade is seen discussing from his Touchable like job as, "But see, Comrade, any benefits that you give him, naturally others are resenting it. They see it as a partiality. After all, whatever job he does carpenter or electrician or whatever it is, for them he is just a Paravan" (p.82). Velutha is caught in between right and wrong, sanity and insanity, morality and immorality.

It is a story about the rights of the women and the untouchables verses age old restrictions imposed by the tradionalists Indian society. The higher ups in the society are able to do all kinds of damage to those who are in the lower strata of the society. Velutha certainly stands out as a very tall figure in the novel. After returning to Ayemenem, Ammu slowly got drawn to Velutha, the bare - bodied Paravan. Ammu's quest for emotional support ends in Velutha, a low caste or untouchable carpenter, whose family has been serving in Ammu's house since a long time. It was his desire to 'relive' as a touchable that triggered the tragedy. Ammu, another 'untouchable' within the 'touchable', cannot perceive happiness. Ammu, the biggest victim of the system, is an archetypal image of marginalized society. Pappachi insisted that a college education was unnecessary expense for a girl. Roy throws light on the fact that, "There was little for a young girl to do in Ayemenem other than to wait for marriage proposal" (p.38). Ammu had no choice other than accepting whatsoever her family offers her. Unfortunately her husband turns out to be a drunken man. The marriage ends in divorce. She has only marginal existence in the family structure. It is also visible at Sophie Mols funeral, "Ammu, Estha and Rahel were allowed to attend the funeral, and they were made to stand separately, not with the rest of the family. Nobody would look at them."(p.12). In his profession, he was unbeatable and even in his 'affairs' with Ammu he was unique in his own way. For Ammu and Velutha, Caste or Status do not matter. What matters most is to preserve the bond of pure love. Velutha glanced up and caught Ammu's gaze, "Centuries telescoped into one evanescent moment. In that brief moment Velutha looked up and saw things that he hadn't seen before...for the first time he realized that Rahel's mother is a woman" (p.56). Roy needs to be congratulated for exposing this foul play of post-colonial India to the entire world.

When Velutha has an affair with Ammu, he breaks an ancient taboo. He breaks the rigid social rules of the caste system. They turn deep lovers of each others, throwing away all scruples of caste, creed and community. Through an untouchable and a communist, Velutha's presence gives Ammu enough emotional and physical satisfaction and protection. Roy passionately describes their love scene as, "Her brownness against his darkness, her softness against his hardness" (p.68).

His love for Ammu and his loyalty to Ayemenem House are suspected as a betrayal. The police know that Velutha is innocent yet he is arrested on Baby Kochamma's FIR. For since the day Baby Kochamma was publically humiliated by some of them archers in Cochin, she had focused all her fury on Velutha. In her mind Velutha had grown to represent the march. Inspector Mathew tells her, "you people ...first...spoil these people, carry them about on your head like trophies, then when they misbehave you come running to us for help" (p.261). She succeeds in convincing Inspector that Velutha's attempted rape of Ammu, the children's disappearance from the house and Sophie Mol's death could not be unconnected. The high caste power is administered through the police. Velutha is tortured to death in police custody, and the high caste psyche gets a respite from low caste nuisance when, "His skull was fractured in three places -- his nose and both his cheek bones were smashed, leaving his face pulpy, undefined"(p.310).

Velutha, the 'God' in *The God of Small Things* was made to suffer humiliations at the hands of the upper-class Hindus and Christians. The right to love a man of her choice should not be scuttled in the name of religions, caste, colour and class. The traditional society was not only conservative but authoritarian for it laid down who should love whom. The ultimate outcome of the novel is the tragic death of 'untouchable' by the 'touchable boots' at the police station. God is no more control of 'small things' rather turning him to 'The God of Loss'.

In fact, this is a tale of all the untouchables in the dark alleys of History. Velutha is simply a representative of such men. The circumstances around him grow hostile and he is finally eliminated and his footprints are totally erased by the caste and gender conscious society. Roy expresses her disillusionment with the social conditions of the post-colonial world in which the untouchables of the past still face a hostile society that does not let them live as free and independent individuals. Thus, caste and gender discriminations express in marginalizing untouchables and females in their personal and public life.

WORKS CITED

De Beauvoir, Simone, *The Second Sex,* London: Jonathan Cape, 1982.

Dhawan, R.K., Ed., *Arundhati Roy: The Novelist Extraordinary,* New Delhi: Prestige Publication, 1999.

Roy, Arundhati, *The God of Small Things,* New Delhi: India Ink, 1997.

Surendran, K.V., *The God of Small Things: A Saga of Lost Dreams,* New Delhi: Atlantic Publication, 2000.

❑❑❑

4

Narrative Techniques in Arundhati Roy's *The God of Small Things*

V.S. Sankarao Rao Chinnam

"The quality of Ms. Roy's narration is so extraordinary - at once so morally strenuous and so imaginatively supple-that reader remains enthralled all the way through. A devastating first novel" (Alice Truax, 1997). Arundhati Roy's novel, *The God of Small Things,* has many outstanding characters. The setting is interesting; the voice is inimitable; the characters are multifaceted; and the plot line is puzzling. The novel has many excellent qualities provided, might have been enough to win the Booker Prize, one of the most famous literary awards; but with one more distinctive characteristic added to the mix.

There is no question that this book will long remain one of the most fascinating novels of the twentieth century...*The God of Small Things* is eminent for its comprehensive narrative technique, essentially its sophisticated narrative structure and its treatment of viewpoint. This complex fiction presents caste divisions, political categories and social status through an extremely luxuriant and sensuous language. The most important characters are true and the tale is semi-autobiographical. It is an autobiographical novel.

"From its mesmerising opening sequence, it is clear that we are in the grip of a delicious new voice... a voice of breath taking beauty. *The God of Small Things* achieves genuine, tragic resonance. It is, indeed, a masterpiece" (Christina Patterson, 1997). The novel opens with a return and a death. The novel consists a lot of layers of narratives, including two dominant narratives and numerous subordinate narratives. Ammu separated from her Bengali tea-planter husband and lingering attendances of the Meenachal River, on the backwater here Kottayam, in Karala. The central story is simple, but the plot and narrative techniques are difficult.

Alok Rai describes Roy's effort "I think of it as a sort spiral structure, a brooding around a central event whose essential contours are made known fairly curly in the novel. But at each turn of the spiral, one had been to a few more places, knows other feelings and persons and is; therefore, enmeshed in an ever denser cross-referentially, are able more contexts, more resonance, and more poignancy (19973:3). The novel opens with the funeral of Sophie Mol; the rest of the novel is voyage arbitration, on what lead to these terrible happenings.

Rahel and Estha, the story unfolds in a devastatingly captivating pace. From the funeral of an innocent child to the death of an innocent man, the man the twins loved by the day and the man their mother loved by night. *The God of Small Things* captivates the readers in a state of dazzled shock as Roy unveils, with such melodramatic prose, how the dire consequences of crossing into forbidden territory has altered the lives of everyone in its path. The heart-rending narrative goes as far as exploring the inner worlds of each character with minute detail, beautifully women around the tragedies of life. "A sad story, told every hilariously, very tenderly and very craftily" (The Pioner, 1997). The readers are easily drawn into a world of secrets, tragedy, love and madness and yet nothing prepares the readers for the calamity about to descend.

Roy's uncanny ability to draw reader's attention to her flawless portrayal of senses brings the story truly alive. "Arundhati Roy has stretched language and imagination to recreate the fun-filled, magical yet anguished world of childhood with poignant simplicity, directness and wit" (Maria Couto, 1997). Roy's humour, her fine sense of nature, her exploration of language makes the book more delight. The novel is about human nature. The book is crammed with attractive images of people, places, and situations. The narration is full of instances like this where Roy gives very beautiful description but it is lost in the dissonance of so many that sometimes the narrative jars you.

"An intricate, clever, skillfully constructed story, which overwhelms by its exuberance and verbal virtuosity" (Philip Ziegler, 1997). Accurately, in the opening of the novel lies its end. It is also a story disrespectful love between an untouchable and reputable lady. It is a tale of throbbing childhood and wrecked marriages. *The God of Small Things* is the analyses focused on the novel's use of the storytelling strategies associated with postmodernism. The credit of *The God of Small Things* is a postcolonial and feminist novel. It deals with psychoanalytical study of characters. The theme depends upon the socio-historical and political concepts in the novel.

The novel interprets its characters, their behaviour, attitudes and actions. Such a focus is essentially a politically knowledgeable choice to see this and all other fictional works of art as social-science specimen. Roy created of course by individuals addressing themselves to other individuals, but knowingly or unknowingly, consciously or unconsciously, in ways nationality or postcolonial status, class, membership within a caste system, ethnicity, and gender determine. "Roy handles the shifting surfaces of past and present with extraordinary fineness and delicacy, producing a controlled, intricate narrative structure through which the themes of love, spite, betrayal, hatred and guilt run like a spider's web. A remarkable achievement" (Supriya Chaudhuri, 1997).

The novel is a chronicle of three generations of a Syrian Christian family of Kerala. It is principally a saga novel that depicts the life, destiny and fluctuating fortunes of three generation of a Syrian Christian family in Ayemenem, a sleepy village in central Travancore. Roy's sources are varied, both individual and universal. She draws from the treasure trove of personal experience, history, and stories read and heard to invent her plots, settings, and characterizations. The novel is characterized by an unmistakable and unhesitant. This is noticeable in the basic theme the tradition ridden social background with its segregating automatic Love Laws the racial element and the sense of place. *The God of Small Things* focusing on the relationship between humans and the environment. The changes to the environment are reflected in the text through the ecological changes that Rahel notices upon her return to Ayemenem. The river is also interpreted as a barrier between classes, making the act of crossing the river an act of rebellion. The theme of death is the axis on which the novel revolves around the love laws. Only that once again they broke the love laws: that-lay down who should be loved? And how. And how much (328). Velutha's relationship with Ammu and circumstances, which ultimately lead to his tragic end, can be described as one of the themes of novel.

Thematically the book keeps into life of Keralite society and their rites and customs, tradition and patriarchal domination. The narrative directs its reader to signposts that indicate a wealth of affiliations critics frequently oppose over whether not pessimistic or optimistic about the future of society. The responses to such destructions of social systems, in light of such understandings, present-day trauma theory divulge, how, when viewed as a trauma narrative. The novel may be best read, not simply as either a pessimistic or optimistic. The description style, for instance, replicates the nature of trauma for readers to experience secondhand. Most significantly, the novel presents readers with a moral dilemma and encourages a response from readers.

In method and style, the book lulls us away from the world of simple spoken tune and cheap metaphorical creation to the world of architectural pattern and poetic mode. The story is not told sequentially, it moves back and forth in time in a kind of chronological looping method (1932:196). Roy's narrative structure makes ample use of the past and the present techniques. Roy adopts a style, which is in harmony with the new narrative strategy. The narrative strategy does not follow a traditional form. There is no proper beginning, middle and end.

Roy seems to affirm that stories do not need to conform to the traditional norm of writing. After all love happens it is never planned hence the style merely highlights this fact. It begins at a moment in time, preceded back and forth and having traveled full circles comes back to square one. The third person narration is employed throughout the novel, with all the characteristics of an omniscient author narrating the tale from shifting points of view and very often with an authorial comment or two. Roy employs a Circitous narrative events emerge elliptically and out of chronolgical sequence. There are time shifts endless fast farwords and revesals which highly enhance the effect of the narration making the novel daringly post modern.

The narrative is offered to us not Rahel but through an omniscient, omnipresent narrator. The most remarkable thing about the novel is that it has been narrated with comeliness and detached objectivity. The main thing one notices in this novel is unconventionality of the structure and chronology of the narrative, which firmly established. Roy weaves the saga of a family, of three genarations, living in the Ayemenem House. A saga, micro scoped in time, which irreversibly moves towards its dommed destiny (1997:117).

This rather age-old, universal and somewhat conventional plot line, however, becomes interesting and vital once again thanks to Roy's narrative skills and to the focus on two lovers not just from across those proverbial tracks that divide families and class, but from across caste lines. In this saga, we can discern your distinct strands of action narrated one is the tale about the doomed love between Ammu and the untouchable, Velutha. The second is the tragic drowning of the Anglo-Indian girl Sophie Mol in the Meenachal River. Interrelated with the first and the second is the third stand of action in the traumatic childhood of the twins, Estha and Rahel. These twins made the witnesses too much of the action in the first and second stories by masterly stroke of craftsmanship.

Yet a fourth story is that of the adult and divorced Rahel returning to Ayemenem. From the America, to be with her 're-returned' twin Estha and what happens to them. The first, second and third stands of action, the main action constitute the major part of the narrative, and take place in the past. The fairy tale of the grown-up twins happens in the present occupying only a little space of the narrative action. The narration of the past can be considered a macro-narrative, where as current action makes up a micro-narrative of types. In the narrative there is a brooding, introspective and circular quality. Ammu worry about madness in the family followed by her memory of path, Ammai, Thampichachan, Dr. Muthachen is all living evidences of absurd techniques. Nonsense poetry is another device.

> Hey, Mr. Monkey man
> Why's your bum so Red?
> I went for a shit to madras
> And scraped it till it Bled (211&212).

The other prominent aspect of Roy's narrative technique is the conservative use of time. "Arundhati Roy has stretched language and imagination to recreate the fun-filled, magical yet anguished world of childhood with poignat simplicity, directness and wit" (Maria

Couto, 1997). There is a constant slipping back and forth. The text plays with space and time. For example Ammu's death, which really follows quite same time after Velutha's in custody, is narrated earlier in chapter 7, whereas Velutha's death is described in chapter 19, almost towards end of the book. In the same manner, the account of Ammu's death precedes the narration of Estha being returned to his father when his uncle Chacko orders Ammu and twins out of his house following Sophie Mol's drowning. In the chapter 20 Madras Mail a study of time transfers used in chapter I would give us fairly a good plan of how they work in the rest of the book.

The text touching back and forth shatters the boundaries of past and present and cross the thresholds liberally into prospect and back from there. The process nullifies time and invests the text with a God-like power to look both ways, to the future, which is also the present, and the future (1999: 94-104). Roy freely inserts texts within texts. While transposing the text, the future time sequence is brought earlier and the past takes a place later than the future: Sorrow, however, was still two weeks away on that blue cross-stitch afternoon, as Margaret Kochamma lay yet-lagged and still asleep (266).

Roy's novel defies conservative organization and time sequence, the transposed texts, the future remembrance and the inter texts problematize the linear time chronological narrative. The back and forth movement of the text in time nullifies the time sequence. In the story telling, Roy uses many cinematic techniques, time shifts endless fast-forwards and reversals rapid editing etc. There is no time near progression of events, not in just the story of the novel but also within the individual streams of narrative.

Roy's film-scripting training enables her to structure the plot in a suspenseful juxtaposing of film like takes. History replicates itself in the integrating of Estha and Rahel, the two-egg twins, the twins were born in 1962, during the Indo-Chinese war- one of the confused phases in Indian history. The two are cujjed into history at a crucial time. The fate of the twins is inter-woven with the history of the Ayemenem house. Their birth is described thus:

> In November... after a bumpy bus
> Ride... amidst rumours of Chinese
> Occupation and Indian's impend
> Defeat, Estha and Rahel were born (40).

Roy's novel reflects the fast-changing traditions and political situation in Kerala. Comrade KNM Pillai is representative of trade union leaders and how unprincipled and hypocritical such leaders can be. She pictures the all-pervasive rebellion of Naxalism. Roy weaves into the pattern of the narrative, the reinforcement of myths that trace the fate of those who had broken taboos. She talks of two Kathakali performances that the twins watch - Karna Sapatham and Duryodhana Vadhan (1979:403). The Unspoken however splinters the outline for the sea secrets (13) in Estha's eyes the unspoken cannot be explained by the legends that articulate emotions.

Only Rahel perceive Sophie Mol's secret cart wheeling in her hitting when they lowered. Sophie Mole's tomb into the ground in the title behind the church, Rahel knew that she still wasn't dead (6 & 7). In consequence, she expires not in the river, but since Rahel notice her to be awake for her funeral (5). It is her funeral that killed her (7). When they witness the abstemious cruelty of the police officer thrashing up their communalist friend, Velutha, and get the painful lesson that blood barely shown on a Black man (316), and that it smells like old roses on a breeze (310). The ironic reference to liberty yet, goes to the intense when Estha remarks, 'India is a free country' and the authorial presentation continues.

> You could make Salk ...The orange drink lemon drink.
> Man could just walk in through the gauzedoors (197).

The novelist is ironic characterizing people who are trying to preserve the organization in order, including Inspector Thomas Mathew who efforts to instill order into a world gone wrong. According to Arundhati Roy, they are the mechanics who serviced the different parts of the same machine, that is, establishment. Humour is the leading constituent in this novel. It evokes laughter, which is an end in itself. Roy does not employ tendency comedy or utilize propensity comedy or tendency with here because she does not conceive her work as a satire.

The humour that she employs is a safe form of the comic. An important measurement to Arundhati Roy's style lies in the original use of the selectional-restriction rules violations. The exploration of the view by the narrative eye is not inert, but active and imaginative; looking at something means grasping what it looks like:

> Heaven opened and water hammered down

Reviving the reluctant old well (29).
He watched cloudy children at car windows with
Yearning marsh mallow noises (63).

The oxymorons, collocational conflicts and contradictions are for all time functional in the context. For example,

Noisy television silence (28).
Mirthless smile (239).
Beautiful ugly toads (187).
Green heat (202).
... Listening with his eyes (19).
... She could see the music as it left her violin (167).
Jungles, rivers, rice fields, communists
A lucky leaf that wasn't lucky enough (73).

The novel is a site for puns, alliteration, assonance etc., which at first offer the fake feeling of contributing nothing to the context but is in reality loaded with meaning.

Cardamom kings, coffee coconuts and rubber barons... (69).
Ballas - in - Brackets (90).
There are apparently playful expressions like
Dark of Heartness tiptoed into heart of darkness (306).

Another vital characteristic of style in Roy's novel is the lenient use of graphological sentences.

Not old

Not young

But a viable - die - able age (303).

Roy utilizes graphological style to a telling effect and often thrives in infusing breathless pace into the style. The following passage describing the man with an artificial leg on the Cochin railway platform is an exceptional example of this style. Inside it (his unstrapped artificial leg) he stored his ticket.

His towel. His stainless steel tumbler. His smells.
His secrets. His love. His madness. His hope.
His infinite joy. His real foot was bare (301).

Roy's sensitive style can be felt everywhere; style here is emphatic and brusque. In the following example her style combines perspectives, nuances and realistic detail of the surroundings in a way that is very engaging. Rahel held by Ammu's hand. A mosquito on a leash. A refugee stick insect in Bata Sandals. An Airport Fairy at a railway station. Stamping her feet on the platform, unsettling clouds of settled station dirty. Until Ammu Shook her and told to stoppit and she stopited. Around them the hostling- jostling crowd.

> Scurrying hurrying buying selling luggage trundling
> porter paying children shitting people spiting
> coming going begging bargaining reservation-
> checking (300).

The first Para here occupies graphological sentences, metaphorical expressions, and coinage (stoppit or stopited) and partial reduplicated compounds (hostling-jostling) to bring newness and originality to the expression. And the second Para reveals the brisk transaction of life that is taking place on the railway platform. Style is the soul of the novel.

The other significant trait of Roy's style in the book is her suitable and plentiful use of apt similes and exact metaphors. Metaphors and similes bring freshness they are revealing and even chocking. For example:

> ... The coconut trees were sea anemones
> Waving their tentacles.... (83).
> Automobile islands in a river of people (65).
> Clean Children, like a packet of peppermints (105).
> Chacko lay like a beached whale on the narrow hotel
> bed (119).
> ... Seeped into Kerala like tea from a tea bag (33).
> Rahel's new teeth were waiting inside her gums like
> words in a pen (37).

The novel applies the autobiographical mode of narration. It projects the writer's own life through Ammu's character. The autobiographical touches are absolutely traced in the setting of the novel be similar to Arundhati Roy's personal life in many ways. The character of Ammu in the novel symbolizes Mrs. Mary Roy, Arundhati Roy's mother. The novelist recognizes the fact that the novel proliferates in autobiographical details and she says: "It is set in the village that I grew up in...the world that I know... it is an inextricable mix of memory and imagination" (1997:6).

In this novel some characters appear to be normal, sympathetic and humane but a closer look will reveal the concealed, gloomy aspect of their mental make-up. Behind the mask, there is cunningness deception and untruth, comrade K.N.M. Pillai, Chacko Velutha etc., can be taken as example. K.N.M. Pillai does not stand completely for what Karl Marx teaches. There is an extensive gap between what Pillai advocates and what he practices. The novelist finally ridicules the emptiness of Comrade Pillai's pledged to the Communist philosophy by pointing out that Mr. Pillai's son, Lenin, now a young man, living in Delhi, is helping foreign embassies.

The young man has somewhat changed his name to P. Levin to avoid its Marxist flavour and to fit himself into the new slot easily. He is a strange case of metamorphosis of a Marxist guru's son becoming a stooge of the capitalists. In short, comrade Pillai is not what he emerges to be. Chacko, the capitalist schemes himself as comrade Chacko only to allure and take advantage of the female workers of his factory. Baby Kochamma Masquerades as a righteous person. A mask of respectability competently conceals revolting realism. She places on a puritanical veil. Previous she had her own idealistic existence when she did everything possible, including becoming a Roman Catholic nun, to seduce.

Father Mulligan. But later she adopts a 'holier-than-thou-art' attitude towards Ammu and looks for to punish her for her sins of loving a 'Paravan'. Velutha remains his accessory to the Communist party as a secret. Not a lot of citizens are familiar with the fact that he is a cord holding member of the party. On the other hand, he eagerly plays the role of an invulnerable Paravan, but does not overlook the occasion of containing an 'affair' with a lady belonging to his employer's family. His apparent humility and blamelessness is but a disguise. Further, when Rahel informs him that she had seen him the previous day participating in a Communist procession near Cochin, he vehemently rejects it.

He attempts to save his face by suggesting that is must have been his long-lost twins brother, Urumban, Pappachi is a mean domestic dictator, who brutalizes his wife, Mammachi, apparently a performance violin player of international standard. The foremost characters in the novel challenge to project them in away that is quite dissimilar from their real self. For instance, the description of the Cochin harbour terminus is an attempt to capture reality, as it would appear to a child's mind:

> Scurrying hurrying buying selling luggage
> Trundling porter paying children shitting
> People spitting coming going begging
> Bargaining reservation-checking (300).

At other instances, 'nap' becomes 'gnap' 'barn owl' becomes 'barnowl'. This purposeful linguistic experimentation is an attempt to recapture the child's world with its varied sounds and subtleties. Roy employs in the novel a wide range of literary gimmicks curious spelling, Capitalization, punctuation and spacing like

> Prer Nun Sea aushum (154).
> Mostun fortunate,
> Coca Cola Fanta ice cream rose milk (301)
> Prepare to prepare to be prepared (200).

Unusual phrases and expressions like Margaret Kochamma told her to stoppit. So he stoppitted (141). The author makes use of many linguistic and rhetorical devices, characteristics of poetry in the opening of the novel. May in Ayemenem is a hot, brooding month; the days are long and humid. The rivers shrinks and black crows gorge on bright mangoes in still, dust green trees, Red bananas ripen. Jackfruits burst. Dissolute blue bottles hum Vacuously in the fruity air. Then they stun themselves clear windowpanes and die. Fatly against baffled in the sun (1). Roy brings in local colour and environment by using Indian English, which helps her to detain the patterns of social behavior. The Indian propensity to misuse the English articles as also the absence of the required article 'a' or 'the' can be noted in the language used by K.N.M. Pillai:

> He is good worker (277)
> He is genius (274)
> One is must (310).

Fancy spelling is used as substitute for phonetic script to indicate the specific Indian English, pronunciation of people abounds in the Die-vorced (130). Ammu told her to stoppit and her stopited (300)

Wrong use of prepositions. Such as send off for send away (278) Varian Indian English pronunciation is shown in changed spellings of the words. Saar (270) Yooseless goose (312). One mint (for minuter) (134) etc. The novel uses the Indian English idioms, collocations, vocabulary items, syntax and pronunciation to a telling effect. The novel has some powerful symbols that not vague, they are beautifully intertwined with the plot. Pappachi's moth has also been skillfully used.

Whenever a dark emotion or some disaster arises in the lives of the characters, the Pappachi's moth is seen descending on the person concerned. History House represents a cruel spirit of evil which castes its malevolent influence on the lives of the novel. It has a unique quality, captures, and dreams and re-dreams them:

> The History House.
> With cool stones floors and dim walls and
> Bellowing shop-shapped shadows (53).

The sentence black crow gorge on bright mangoes is vastly symbolic. Black Crow symbolizes Velutha; Ayemenem symbolizes a state of mind and being an unlikely starting point for a love story. Velutha as the God figure is more a sign than a person, an inevitably far away from the middle class embroilments that overwhelm him. Baby Kochamma who did not even trust the twins (29) or grudged them the comfort they drew from each other (46). And rose between them like a hill (62) is the symbol of the aggressive society that rigidly differentiates between male and female gender roles.

"A novel of real ambition must invent its own language, and this one does..."(John Updike, 1997). As the narrator reveals the nuances of each character, the reader begins to see how ideology and social status conform different expressions of alienation, shame, self-loathing, violence, sexual abuse, and death. For the most part, by the end of the chapter the reader already has a good sketch of the plot as well as an overview of the themes and characters.

WORKS CITED

Abraham, Taisha, *An Interview with Arundhati Roy*, Ariel, Vol. 29, 1998, pp.89-92.

Anjali interviewed Roy, *Interview, Interview of a Week, The Indian Express*, 1997: 6.

Roy, Arundhati, *Interviewed by David Barsamian, The South Asian,* September 2001.

Roy, Arundhati, *The Greater Common Good,* Frontline 16, May 22 - June 04, 1999.

Roy, Arundhati, *Arundhati Roy to Kerala Chief Minister Antony, Frontline,* Vol.20, Issue 6, *The Hindu* 2003.

The Hindu, Arundhati Roy, And His Life Should Become Extinct Outlook, 2006.

❑❑❑

5

Socio-political Situation in Arundhati Roy's *The God of Small Things*

M. AMBIKAVATHY

The novel *The God of Small Things* by Arundhati Roy is a systematic presentation of the variegated Indian socio-cultural matrix. Often writers of English in India made deliberate efforts to depict the distress of the downtrodden classes, Gandhian ethos, contemporary social and political milieu or the private sphere of people. It is indeed very interesting to note that all the above mentioned aspects have been encompassed in Arundhati Roy's *The God of Small Things.*

The novel appears like a document on the social political and religious milieu of Kerala. The questions raised by Arundhati Roy in the novel are related to polity, society, economy, environment and status of women and projects a 1990's sensibility on the Kerala of the 1960's. There is a blend of fact and fiction in the way the novelist has dealt with reference to the communist party. Arundhati Roy's criticism of the socio-political situation moves round three nodal points; the caste question, gender issue and environmental problem.

The rigidity or caste ridden society is reflected in the situations narrated in the novel. It was a patriarchal society and education of women was not encouraged. There are strict rules regarding relationships. Marriage among homogenous groups was followed and extra activity other than house hold chores in women was not appreciated. This paper attempts, to trace the sociological profile of the society presented. Gender bias is evident in various instances such as:

> Ammu finished her schooling the same year that her father... Pappachi insisted that a college education was an unnecessary expense for a girl. So Ammu had no choice but to leave Delhi and move with them. There was very little for a young girl to do in Ayemenem other than to wait for marriage proposals while she helped her mother with her housework (38).

Thus we can understand the mentality of a society where a girl was meant to work at home and get married. In contrast another fact can also be inferred where people bent the rules to meet their needs in certain circumstances. One such instance is where we find that a girl will be educated if she doesn't get married. One instance is that a girl's father decided to educate his daughter when he knew that his daughter's behavior was against the norms of society and so none would propose to marry her:

> Reverend Ipe realized that his daughter had by now developed a 'reputation' and was unlikely to find a husband. He decided that since she couldn't have a husband there would be no harm in her having an education. So he made arrangements for her to attend a course of study at the University of Rochester in America (26).

Thus we see that Baby Kochamma was a Syrian Christian by birth but converted into Roman Catholic fold to enter a convent. When she wouldn't abide by the conditions at the convent she returned home but did not reconvert. This was the reason for a scandal. The novelist says that determination in a girl was considered worse than having a hare-lip. Because of such determination in Baby Kochamma Reverend Ipe knew that no proposal would materialize for his daughter. So to ward off scandal he sent her abroad for studies.

One surprising fact is that even though the women folk suffered from the tentacles of society steeped in it and did not appreciate any one who tried to break the manacles. This attitude is reflected in the instance below:

> Baby Kochamma disliked the twins, for she considered

> them doomed, fatherless waifs. Worse still, they were half-Hindu hybrids whom no self-respecting Syrian Christian would ever marry...Baby Kochamma resented Ammu, because she saw her quarrelling with a fate that she, Baby Kochamma herself, felt she had graciously accepted. The fate of the wretched Man-less woman (45).

Thus jealousy among women is reflected. Caste barriers were impregnable in the society during the times mentioned in the narrative. In such a society even those who managed to break free of caste barriers and tried to live life according to their choice suffered from mental recoil of the society's oppression. In the narrative the feelings if Ammu reflects this suffering.

> She had woken up at night to escape from a familiar, recurrent dream in which police men approached her with snicking scissors, wanting to hack off her hair. They did that in Kottayam to prostitutes in the land where long, oiled hair was only for the morally upright (161).

Thus the plight of a woman who has crossed the lines drawn by society is reflected in the portrayal of Ammu's suffering. Women who disobeyed were often sent out of home and soon branded immoral. The novelist uses the device of comparison and contrast between the situation of a brother and sister of the same house to denote the existence of gender bias. In the novel both Ammu and Chacko marry off their community and both get divorced while Chacko is welcomed offered pity and allowance for 'men's needs', Ammu is not welcomed and insulted even by the servant. The society's partiality is reflected in the fact where Chacko's ex-wife Margaret is considered a whore by Mammachi because she married Joe. Yet Baby Kochamma and Mammachi accepted Chacko's Marxist mind and feudal libido. Arundhati Roy is successful in portraying the social milieu of the societies through her characters.

Gender bias is well evident in the bits of conversation among characters. It is well evident that inspector Thomas Mathew purposely condemned Ammu as veshya during her visit to the police station. In the society a man who has libertine relationships is not margined out whereas moral codes are different for women. It is not only men of his status of educational background who speak ill of women but also uneducated or people of the lower economic strata tend to speak ill of women.

In the Indian society it is common for a husband to address his wife in derogatory terms. While the wife always addressed him in honorific terms. Comrade Pillai, a post graduate was not free of this habit. Whenever his wife Kalyani addressed him: "She referred to her husband as addeham which was the respectful form of 'he', whereas 'he called her ...edi Kalyani (Hey you!), bring a plate ..." (270 & 273).

Thus it is evident from the above instances that gender bias was deep rooted in all the sections of society irrespective of caste and economic distinctions.

Arundhati Roy makes a scathing attack on people belonging to upper classes; the high caste Hindus and high caste Christians. The reader's attention is drawn to the lowest castes who were forced to become bonded labourers to certain high-caste groups. They lived on the land owned by their masters and could be evicted if the master was displeased with them. They were forbidden to enter temples, not allowed to enter public markets, or bathe in temple ponds. Neither men nor women were allowed to wear shirts, blouses and were forbidden to come within prescribed physical distances of higher caste members. Though such ills have been routed out, the novel serves like a social treatise against class discrimination.

The norms have been internalized by the people and the low castes had resigned themselves to fate. The resigned attitude and gratitude with which the downtrodden served their masters is compared to a river in spate. Mammachi told her grand children about the restrictions posed on the downtrodden and it reflects the voice of the society of the sixties. She told Rahel and Estha:

> Pappachi would not allow Paravans into the house. Nobody would. They were not allowed to touch anything that the touchables touched. Caste Hindus...in her girlhood, when paravans were expected to crawl backwards with a broom, sweeping away their footprints so that Brahmins or Syrian Christians would not defile themselves by accidentally stepping into a paravans footprint.

With passage of time some of the ills began to disappear and people began to give-up certain restrictions to suit their needs. This hypocritical trend in society is reflected in the actions of Mammachi who allowed Velutha into the house to have equipments mended or to make furniture. Yet her snobbishness is reflected in the fact that: "She thought he (Velutha) ought to be greatful that he was allowed on the factory premises at all, and allowed to touch things that touchables touched. She said it was a big step for a paravan" (77).

Their snobbery was punished when her daughter took Velutha as her lover. Mammachi couldn't bear the thought that her daughter had defiled generations of breeding. She was worried that in future "people would point at them at weddings and funerals. At baptisms and birthday parties. They'd nudge and whisper" (258).

The changing trends in society are reflected in the behaviour of Velutha and Vellaya Pappen. Both were members of the downtrodden community. While the father bore everything patiently Velutha resented. On an occasion when Mammachi overcome with anger stepped forward and pushed Vellaya Pappen with all her strength: "He stumbled backwards" and fell down". He was taken completely by surprise. Part of the taboo of being an untouchable was expecting not to be touched" (256).

Thus we see that though he hadn't done anything wrong he did not get angry with Mammachi for pushing him but was shocked when she touched him. Whereas in the case of Velutha resentment is evident. Vellaya Pappen was intrigued when Velutha did not submit himself to the rules. He feared his son's education, skill and self confidence. Velutha represents the class which is yearning to be accepted while floating on the brink of society. Velutha knew that his liaison with Ammu would definitely create problems, yet when Mammachi threatened him he only replied "We'll see about that", very quietly. He was not afraid.

Classicism was strong in the minds of people and so even when the off-springs of upper class people went against the norms of society and if their actions were reported by low castes, they were rebuffed.

Comrade Pillai who was a communist was not free of class bias. His conversation with Chacko reveals his feelings. When Chacko and K.N.M. Pillai were discussing Velutha's involvement in communistic activities, he advised Chacko to send Velutha away. The low castes were also branded by their caste names by him and not by their skill.

Yet another instance of class bias is that even though the upper caste and low caste transgressed moral codes or society norms the low castes paid more for their wrongs. They were blamed more. This is evident in the case of Ammu and Velutha. Mammachi insulted Velutha but did not deride her daughter. 'Out!' she had screamed, eventually. If I find you on my property tomorrow I'll have you castrated like a pariah dog that you are I'll have you killed! (284). She calls Velutha a dog and spits on him that does not deride her daughter or call her names. Thus, we see that while Ammu went uncriticized by people, nobody had pity for Velutha.

The novel highlights hypocracy involved in politics by caricature of a local communist supporter named K.N.M. Pillai. He is often called Comrade Pillai. Through Chacko and Comrade Pillai who are champions of communism Arundhati Roy enumerates reason for the success of communistic ideals in Kerala. The questions raised by her are relevant to contemporary political polarization. In India the minorities and tribal people had allowed themselves with the communist movement enamored by the theory of class struggle but it resulted in a feeling of betrayal and led to large scale erosion from the movement. According to the author the theory of class struggle has not done anything to fight against their caste based social hierarchy in Kerala. Even famous exponents of Marxism have overlooked the caste issue which is still deep rooted in the society. Thus in the novel Comrade Pillai is a representative of such people in real life situations.

Comrade Pillai made bombastic speeches regarding Marxist theories of a classless society to workers at Paradise Pickles. But within his heart of hearts he harboured class snobbery. Once he advised Chacko to send Velutha away from the factory. He told him not to encourage Paravans in the factory, particularly one who was a member of the communist party. He told Chacko that his wife who was timid would not encourage such people into the house. He said: "See her, for example Mistress of this house. Even she will never allow Paravans and all that into her house. Even I cannot persuade her. My own wife" (278).

Further he told Chacko that the other labourers in the factory resented Velutha's presence in the factory. But he could not give a specific reason: "Nothing specifically as such, Comrade K.N.M. Pillai said. But see, Comrade, any benefits that you give him, naturally others are resenting it ... After all, ... for them he is just a Paravan" (279).

We are able to infer that even justice was denied to people of lower castes. In the arrest of Velutha the inspector, Conrade Pillai and Baby Kochamma's combined efforts are evident. The words "After all, they were not battling an epidemic. They were merely inoculating a community against an outbreak" (309) reflects the inhuman nature of the upper classes.

The hollowness of communist ideology is satirized by the novelist by pointing out that K.N.M. Pillai's son is called Lenin and he is at Delhi serving the capitalist embassies. This reveals that people don't practice what they preach.

An instance which reflects hypocracy is that ancestral homes were converted into star hotels. Following the order of the day 'The History House' was converted into a star resort. With acid sarcasm she says:

> The Hotel people liked to tell their guests that the oldest of the wooden houses, with its air-tight, paneled storeroom which could hold enough rice to feed an army for a year, had been the ancestral home of Comrade E.M.S. Namboodiripad, 'Kerala's Moa Tse-tung' they explained to the uninitiated. (126)

The phrase 'which could hold enough rice to feed an army' denotes that while he slyly held that much grain in store he kept preaching about helping the downtrodden and against capitalism. While hoarding food and accepting dowry the communist leaders made false speeches.

The novel speaks about degradation not only of environment but also of cultural arts. Arundhati Roy says globalization and the market economy and the undue importance given to promote tourism had led to deterioration of natural resources also. In the very first chapter the opening lines accentuate the badly maintained roads by the Public Works Department. Degradation of culture is presented through the plight of Kathakali dancers.

Arundhati Roy gives a vivid description of the negative aspects of the much eulogized Green Revolution with the aid of World Bank loans. Rahel a native of Ayemenem remembered the Meenachal as being warm, with green water like rippled silk. But when she returned twenty five years later the river was no more than a 'swollen drain'. It nurtured only dead fish. Though it was the monsoon season there wasn't much water because a salt water barrage had been built, in exchange for votes from the influential paddy-farmer lobby. The author's cynicism is reflected in the lines: "So now they had two harvests a year instead of one. More rice, for the price of a river".

The changing phase of Ayemenem House due to developments in the economical side is also reflected in the novel. Humorously the author says that Estha walked past baked 'Gulf monkey houses'. Her description of the Meenachal's banks can be compared to Eliot's description of the Thames in The Wasteland. Another instance which reflects decay is that because of the development of tourism, ancestral homes were converted into star hotels. "So there it was then, History and Literature enlisted by commerce. Kurtz and Karl Marx joining palms to great rich guests as they stepped off the boat" (126).

The author is a virtual champion of environmental degradation for she presents the ill effects of tourism on the natural resources like sea-water. Guests from the hotels were ferried across the backwaters from Cochin and the speed boat left film of gasoline in its wake. The author makes a wry comment that 'no swimming' signs were put up in stylish calligraphy because the sea water was toxic. There was a tall wall to put screen off the slum but "On warm days the smell of shit lifted off the river and hovered over Ayemenem like a hat". Thus we are able to discern that the government is also criticized for its laxity in preservation of existing natural resources.

Development in technology and revolutionary changes in the area of visual communications has led to the decline of traditional entertainments. There is no need for people to depend on cinema halls, theatres, roadside performances etc. to entertain themselves. This had led to changes in the attitude of people. This change is reflected in the passage quoted below:

> Baby Kochamma had installed a dish antenna...She presided over the world in her drawing room on satellite T.V. ... It happened overnight. Blondes, Wars, famines, football, sex, music, coups d'état they all arrived on the same train...now whole wars, famines, picturesque massacres and Bill Clinton could be summoned up like servants (27).

With a touch of humour the author says they all arrived on the same train. As a result of such tremendous areas for diversion people lost interest in local folk art forms. One such form is the Kathakali. The novel devotes several pages to the description of performances of few cantos from the *Mahabharata* and the plight of the performers who depend on their art for their livelihood. Since people lost interest in Kathakali the performers were forced to accept assignments at the star hotels. In the hotel truncated story performances were provided as local flavor to foreign tourists. The performers acted out episodes from epics but it was not reciprocated with comprehensive appreciation. While they performed by the pool the tourists indulged in nubile sex which was an insult to the artists. Toward off humiliation they performed in local temples and accepted the few coins or appreciation they got in return. Through the narration of cantos performed in the temple Arundhati ariy presents the cultural consciousness among people in the society. People easily accepted Draupadi's being the wife of five and Kunti becoming a mother before being married though such things were taboo. With dripping sarcasm Roy makes an appeal to the society to see the reason before blindly appreciating things of ancient origin.

This paper brings out a detailed sketch of the sociological profile of situations portrayed in the novel. *The God of Small Things* depicts the changing phase of life in relation to economic development through various events, situations and contexts with sarcasm, humour or cynicism. Impact of caste barriers is also depicted with cynicism. The narrative statements of the author and conversational excerpts of certain characters depict the society of Kerala in 1960's.

WORKS CITED

Dodiya, Jayadipsingh, Chakravarty Jaya, eds., *The Critical Studies of Arundhati Roy's The God of Small Things,* New Delhi: Atlantic Publishers.

Prasad, Amar Nath, Singh, Narendra Kumar, eds. *Indian Fiction in English, Roots and Blossoms,* New Delhi: Sarup and Sons.

Roy, Arundhati, *The God of Small Things,* New Delhi: IndiaInk, 1997.

www.novelguide.com/a/discover/nfs_000000220/nfs00000022000018.

http://www.museindia.com/showfeature13.asp?id=1207.

❑❑❑

6

Women's Woes and Wedlock in Arundhati Roy's *The God of Small Things*

Satya Prakash Prasad

The present article endeavours to study Arundhati Roy's epoch making novel, *The God of Small Things* to assess the predicament of married women in their wedlock. The proposed study is limited to the issues of women and their responses to society such as how far they resist or conform to the patriarchal hegemony in their married life.

I

Marriage is one of the deepest and most complex architectonics of human relations. Marriage is a communion, getting together of two sexes in a harmonized set-up where respect, trust and companionship are the core values. "Marriage ideally provides for love, security, companionships, social acceptability, legitimized sex, love, homogeneity of age, race and sex, stability for environment and identity for children" (Ratra, Kaur & Chhikara: 8) However, in the dominant patriarchal society like ours the institution of marriage has become an instrument of patriarchy and it is used to subjugate women.

In the patriarchal institution of marriage, women have been forced to occupy a secondary place, not imposed by their inherent deficient traits but strong cultural forces and social tradition. Simone de Beauvoir asserts: "Marriage is the destiny traditionally offered by society" (1983:445). In a traditional society where women have no freedom of their own choice, marriage proves to be another trap and they feel like caged animals. Making enormous sacrifices, a woman begins to understand gradually that marriage obstructs her growth as an individual. This has resulted in the failure of women to occupy a place of human dignity. Beauvoir observes that marriage subjugate and enslaves a woman to "aimless days indefinitely repeated, life that slips away gently toward death without questioning its purpose" (Beauvoir, 500). Women aspire for their happiness at the cost of their freedom. Beauvoir further emphasizes that such a sacrifice on the part of a woman is too high for anyone because the kind of self-contentment, serenity and security that marriage offers woman drains her soul of its capacity for greatness: "She shuts behind her the doors of her new home, when she was a girl, the whole countryside was her homeland: the forest were hers Now she is confined to a restricted space..." (502).

In India the Indian parents try to arrange the marriage of their daughters as it is taken as an obligatory responsibility on them. In such an arranged marriage a girl is given off to a groom completely unknown to her. She is taken to the marriage *pandal* like an embellished and attired goat taken to a deity for sacrifice. She marries a man to whom she has never met and her approval is taken for granted and she moves to an unfamiliar land with her groom whom she has never seen and she is denied of all her individual rights. As it is considered indecent on the part of a girl to tell her parents of her choice in marriage, so these decent girls obey their parents and silently bow down before them without questioning about their marriage or their grooms.

The patriarchal set up of our society cajoles the women to accept the deified position of their husbands:

> *Pathi swarga, pathi dhara, pathi paramaantama*
>
> *Pithri pritheema panne, printhe sarva devata* (Mazumdar, 75).

(Husband is heaven, husband is religion. The gods are pleased by pleasing the husband). The women who accept this version of marriage as their fate or destiny or consider it a religious act are the blind worshippers of their husbands and to them husband is almost like God and disobedience to husband is considered a great sin. Further, they pass on the similar ideology to their daughters, the lesson of feminine inferiority and submission. What is intriguing to note about woman in this patriarchal set- up of marriage is that she has no subjectivity; she is an absence, a dark continent and a meek victim of phallic gaze that represents an anal desire for sadistic mastery of the husband. Irigaray adds a mystic aspect claiming that since woman cannot be represented, she falls beyond the *specular* image into the realm of the mystic-beyond subject/object opposition.

Once trapped in marriage, woman has little room for escape and running away is a disgrace not only to her family but also to the whole of the society and its tradition. That's why woman never dares to come out from her marriage. Therefore, in spite of suffering she remains in marriage, and she never tries to give up her relationship with her husband. So this concept of marriage limits a woman to breeding children and looking after the home-affairs. They are expected to conform to the traditional Indian concept of womanhood [Sati,Sita & Savitri], a stereotyped woman.

II

Roy in *The God of Small Things* deals with the efficacy of marriage, compatibility of relationship within the institution of marriage and visible and invisible impacts of patriarchy that lead to subjugation of a woman in a troubled wedlock. The Novel peeps into the married life of the women characters: Mammachi, Ammu, Margaret Kochamma, Kalyani and Rahel's. As discussed earlier, Mammachi's subordinated status in her married life reinforces the acceptance of the dictates of patriarchy and epitomizes how women in our society meekly and passively comply with their husbands' domination. Mammachi is treated as an animal, devoid of any existence, enslaved, and is frequently subjected to the beatings of Pappachi. She is denied of any means whether social or economical to assert her identity. Her "concert class" talent is hooded down by frequent "vase-beatings" by her husband. After the retirement of Pappachi, she started her "enterprise", which was to give her economic freedom and recognition in society; however, this was taken in a bad taste by Pappachi:

> Pappachi, on his part, was having trouble with coping with the ignominy of retirement. He was seventeen years older than Mammachi, and realized with a shock that he was an old man when his wife was still in her prime (47).

Mammachi's success in her enterprise was perceived as an attack on the patriarchal notion of "wife", who is supposed to be perennially dependent on her husband for economic sustenance. Pappachi's resentment towards Mammchi was an outcome of his superior place granted by the institution of marriage. Mammachi had problem in her vision and any amount of cooperation from her husband in her enterprise would have scripted a success story for her, but he "would not help her with the pickle making, because he did not consider pickle making a suitable job for a high- ranking ex-Government official" (47). He took out his resentment by beating his wife with a brass flower vase every night. "[T]he beatings weren't new. What was new was only the frequency with which they took place" (47). The beatings continued till Ckhacko put an end to them by twisting Pappachi's hand round his back and warned him. Pappachi reacted at it by breaking mahogany resting chair to bits with a plumber's wrench the next morning. Like all men in Ayemenem, he did not approve of working wives. Any attempt to break the patriarchal taboo by Indian wives is taken as an attempt to shake the ideological base i.e. wives are supposed to vow down before the whims and fancy of their husbands. Pappachi, a stern patriarch sought other strategies rather, secret ways to punish Mammachi for her transgression:

> He never touched Mammachi again. But he never spoke to her either as long as he lived. When he needed anything he used Kochu Maria or Baby Kochamma as intermediaries.
>
> In the evenings, when he knew visitors are expected, he would sit on the verandah and sew buttons that weren't missing onto his shirts, to create the impression that Mammachi neglected him. To some small degree he did succeed in further corroding Aymenem's view of working wives...He would not allow Mammachi or anyone else in the family to use it (the Plymouth that Pappachi bought from England), or even sit in it. The Plymouth was Pappachi's revenge (p.48).

Mamachi's silence speaks volumes of her internalization of patriarchal values that keep on exerting pressure on womenfolk to get used to their subjugated and secondary status in a male dominated society. Ammu's observation of Mammachi's condition at Pappachi's funeral confirms the process of naturalization that Mamachi underwent throughout her married life:

> ...Mammachi was crying more because she was used to him than because she loved him. She was used to having him slouching around the pickle factory, and was used to being beaten from time to time. Ammu said that human beings were creatures of habit, and it was amazing the kind of things they could get used to. You only had to look around you, Ammu said, to see that beatings with brass vases were the least of them (50).

III

Kalyani is the character, who parallels Mammchi in her internalization of patriarchal dictates that institution of marriage exerts on women. She was married to Comrade K.N.M. Pillai, a hypocritical champion of Marxist cause. She was an unacknowledged being whose presence in her household was of no significance. It is evident when Pillai entered his house: "He had the easy authority of the house. He smiled and nodded a greeting to Chacko, but did not acknowledge the presence of his wife..." (272).

However, Comrade Pillai never misses a chance to showcase his pseudo- considerate attitude towards his wife in the presence of others. He showcases his generosity for his wife in the presence of Chacko. He says:

> Even *I* can not persuade her. My own wife. Of course inside the house she is Boss.' He turned with an affectionate, naughty smile. '*Allay edi,* Kalyani?' Kalayani looked down and smiled, coyly acknowledging her bigotory (278.).

It is very apparent that Kalayani does not have any say in her wedded life and her voice/consent is appropriated and taken for granted. The Malyalam word "edi" which is used by Pillai to address Kalyani can be approximately translated as, "hey you!" not an honorific word for addressing anyone. On the other hand she refers to her husband as "addeham", which is the respectful form of "he" (270). Kalyani's silence suggests her tacit acceptance of her subordinated and inferior status. She is a stereotyped woman who confirms the dictum of *Patidevta,* the deification of husband. "Comrade

Pillai took off his shirt, rolled it into a ball and wiped his armpits with it. When he finished, Kalyani took it from him and held it as though it was a gift. A bouquet of flowers" (272).

IV

Ammu, the daughter of the sour tempered Imperial Entomologist, Pappachi and his much-battered wife Mammachi. She is the product of a disturbed household. She was denied of college education. She did not have any option as in Aymenem "there was very little for a young girl to do other than to wait for marriage proposals while she helped her mother with the housework. "Since her father did not have enough money to raise a suitable dowry, no proposal came Ammu's way" (38). She was desperate to escape from the marooned life of Aymenem and "the clutches of her ill-tempered father and bitter, long-suffering mother" (39). In Calcutta at someone else's wedding reception, Ammu met her future husband. He was working as an assistant manager in a tea estate in Assam. He proposed to her to which Ammu readily gave her consent. Ammu's acceptance to his proposal was a way out to unfetter herself from the traditional predicament of a married woman that she had been witness to, especially in the bouts of her father's violent treatment to Mammachi. In fact she had learnt to live with that "cold calculating cruelty": "Ammu didn't pretend to be in love with him. She just weighed the odds and accepted. She thought that *anything*, anyone at all, would be better than returning to Ayemenem..." (39).

Her nod resulted in immediate solemnization of her wedding. A wedding that was an "elaborate" typical "Calcutta wedding with all paraphernalia but love. Ammu broke the patriarchal dictates of Rev. John Ipe's family and thus stereotyped image of women by indulging in intercommunity marriage. Her marriage led her away from her parents and Aymenem into a new territory of independence. Ammu cherished her new status of a liberated woman: "She wore backless blouses with her saris and carried silver lamé purse on a chain. She smoked long cigarettes in a silver cigarette holder and learned how to blow perfect smoke rings" (40).

Her joy ride soon turned into a nightmare when "her husband turned out to be not just a heavy drinker but a full blown alcoholic with all of an alcoholic's deviousness and tragic charm...he lied so outrageously [even] when he didn't need to" (40). Her predicament is not as different from Mammachi as a married wife. Like Mammachi she is also subjected to domestic violence at the hands of her husband. Her husband treated her as a commodity to be bartered for his job security. In Indian society woman is largely seen as an object, only the owner/proprietor changes with the gradual change in her stations. At first father takes her as a burden to be disposed of to anybody who appears to be affordable so far as amount of dowry is concerned, then her husband and finally after him it is her son who assumes the charge to implicate her under the patriarchal dominance.

Ammu's husband went to the extreme of putting forth before her the indecent proposal that Mr. Hollick offered him:

> Mr. Hollick proposed that Baba [Ammu's husband] go away for a while. For a holiday. To a clinic perhaps, for treatment, for as long it took him to get better. And for the period of time he was away, Mr Hollick suggested that *Ammu be sent to his bungalow to be 'looked after'* (Italics mine, 42)

A wife is beaten when she says something and she is also beaten when she does not say anything. A wife does not have any say in a patriarchal set up of marriage. Ammu's silence at her husband's abominable proposal to sleep with his boss in order to evade the lingering threat of loosing his job was taken as a potential resistance to Baba's traditionally superior male status that the institution of marriage accords. Infuriated at her silence he took resort to physical violence and abuse to salvage his male ego: "he lunged at her, grabbed he hair, punched her and then passed out from the effort" (p.42). Unlike Mammachi, Ammu was not the one who would easily be cowed down. She was a rebel "with a reckless edge of a suicide bomber". She vehemently retaliated at the violence of her husband in an equal measure: "Ammu took down the heaviest book she could find in the book -shelf - *The Reader's Digest World Atlas-* and hit him with it as hard as she could. On his head. His legs. His back and shoulders" (42).

Her life started rotting as "drunken violence" and "post-drunken badgering" by her husband had become a part of her daily routine. When it crossed the limit of tolerance and it started including her children, she took a bold step to divorce/leave her husband and returned to Aymenem, "to everything that she had fled from only a few years ago". Her bitter experience as a married wife led her to despise the institution of marriage itself. She became fully aware of the subverting nature of marriage in which a woman's voice is muffled and her space is encroached upon. In fact she does not have any "Locusts Stand I".

> When she looked at herself in her wedding photographs, Ammu felt the woman that looked back at her was someone else. A foolish jewelled bride. Her silk sunset-coloured sari shot with gold. Rings on every finger. White dots of sandalwood paste over her arched eyebrows. Looking at herself like this, Ammu's soft mouth would twist into a small, bitter smile at the memory - not of the wedding itself so much as the fact that *she had permitted herself to be so painstakingly decorated before led to the gallows.* It seemed so absurd. So futile. Like polishing firewood. (Italics mine 42-43).

It is noteworthy to point that Ammu's perception of inevitiblity of marriage did not change to a great degree despite the physical violence and mental tortures she witnessed in Mammachi's married life and suffered in hers own. For a woman, marriage appears to be a necessary evil in the lack of economic sustainability. "Ammu knew that weddings were not something that can not be avoided altogether. At least not practically speaking" (44).

Her perception regarding marriage is essentially because of the fact of her subject formation under the persistence influence of dominant patriarchy which makes a woman envision marriage as a way out from the stale and stolid life. An escape. However, she had the courage to break off with it, knowing fully well the treatment that she was to receive. Her opting for an inter-community marriage, though unsuccessful can be read as an assertive action against the framers of the "Love Laws" and her bold decision to divorce her alcoholic, violent and uncaring husband justly associates her with the movement of women's emancipation and empowerment.

V

Margaret Kochmma, "the bushy eyebrowed waitress" (241) belonged to a well to do English family. Her father owned a bakery and her mother was a Milliner's assistant. In her youthful assertion of independence she moved out of her parents' home and aspired to put herself through a teacher training course and looked for a job at oxford. She shared a small flat in oxford with another waitress. But even at oxford, Margaret clung to family values she had rebelled against and continued to lead the small, tight life that she imagined she had escaped. She met Chacko at a café and mutual attraction sown the seeds of love between them. Despite her father's dislike of Indians whom he considered to be sly and dishonest, she married to Chacko without her family's consent. Her father did not even attend the wedding. Thus, she did break the "Love Laws" by placing her fancies prior to any code of law that forbade her from realizing them. She found in him "a tortured Marxist at war with an impossible, incurable Romantic- who forgot the candles, who broke the wine glass, who lost the ring. Who love to her with a passion that took her breath away" (245). Her marriage with Chacko was mere "a tentative acceptance of herself" as she had always thought of "herself as a somewhat uninteresting, thick waisted, thick ankled girl. Not bad looking. Not special" (245). Being married to chacko made her feel "as though her soul escaped from the narrow confines of her island country into the vast, extravagant spaces of his". The joy ride of her marriage came to a halt just in a year when she realized the pressures of living together with a job-less husband who did nothing except adding to her woes. Chacko's scholarship was stopped and Margret Kochamma was the one who had to take care of both household work and to arrange money as "there was the full rent of the flat to be paid". The pressing situation of her household gave Margaret Kochamma a crystal clear vision of her unwise decision of marrying Chacko:

> A year into the marriage, and then the charm of Chacko's studently sloth wore off for Margaret Kochamma. It no longer amused her that while she went to work, the flat remained in the same filthy mess that she had left it in. that it was impossible for him even to consider making the bed, or washing clothes or dishes. That he didn't apologize for the cigarette burns in the new sofa. That he seemed incapable of buttoning up his shirt, knotting his tie *and* tying his shoe laces before presenting himself for a job interview (247).

Marriage is of course not all about indulging in sexual adventures day in day out. The efficacy of marriage lays in the sense of mutual responsibilities on the part of the both husband and wife. Margaret showed a great deal of concern towards Chacko's penury by supporting him economically to the best possible way she could. But Chacko instead of making things good for the household, he aggravated the condition by fanning his patriarchal lineage that he received from Pappachi. He could have managed the petty household job when Margaret used to be away for her job, but he opted against it. He certainly despised doing the odd household jobs considering these to be women specific ones and doing them would alter his traditionally defined role of a husband. Margaret Kochamma realized it after the birth of Sophie Mol that for well being of herself and her newly born daughter, "she *had* to leave Chacko. She finally divorced him and married Joe who proved to be a better husband and caring father so long as he lived. For Margaret, Joe was everything that Chacko wasn't-- "Steady, Solvent, Thin": "Margaret Kochamma was happy with Joe. Happier perhaps she would have been had she not had those wild precarious years with Chacko. She thought of Chacko fondly, but without regret" (249).

VI

After the death of Ammu, Rahel "grew up without a brief. Without anybody to arrange a marriage for her. Without anybody who would pay her dowry and therefore without obligatory husband looming on her horizon" (17). She took refuge in the urban world, Delhi, away from the shadowy world of Aymenem, willfully ignorant of "love- laws". There she met Larry McCaslin, who "held her as though she was a gift. Given to him in love. Something still and small. Unbearably precious" (19). Being isolated from the gentry because of "her waywardness and almost fierce lack of ambition", she "drifted into marriage like a passenger drifts towards an unoccupied chair in an airport lounge" (18). Her marriage was a means to escape from the horrors that she had experienced in her childhood. Apparently, she thought it to be a respite to piece herself together. But, contrary to her assumptions, Larry could not understand the support that she was in need. He was rather offended by her indifference and exasperated at her look. "But when they made love he was offended by her eyes. They behaved as though they belonged to someone else...He was exasperated because he didn't know what that look *meant*" (19).

Roy in the form of Larry McCaslin, typifies the dominant patriarchal notion, which assigns women to be life less objects, potentially capable of owned and subjugated under the whims and fancy of husbands. Coloured with this notion Larry never tried to provide a much needed emotional support that could have alleviated Rahel's wounded self. His frustration of not being able to completely own Rahel, eventually, resulted in their divorce. For Larry, Rahel was only a "gift" not at all an individual in flesh and blood.

VII

Arundhati Roy delineates two groups of women characters in her novel as far as their approach towards their marriage is concerned. One group which includes the characters like Mammachi, Kalayani and the women in Aymenem, who tacitly accept the traditional notion of marriage and willfully accept their fate. Their sufferings in their wedlock are mainly because of their lack of will to assert their individuality. The other group which includes the characters like Ammu, Margaret Kochamma and Rahel. They also suffer, but they are not passive sufferers. They resist to the subverting effects of marriage by asserting their rights of equality before the apparently dumb society in a hope to find their muffled voices heard. Arundhati Roy voices the optimism through the apprehension expressed by the twin: "They knew that things could change in a day" (339).

Indeed there is a silver lining of hope amidst the dark cloud of patriarchy and women must find a room of their own.

WORKS CITED

1. De Beauvoir, Simone, *The Second Sex*, Trans. and Edit. H.M. Parshley, New York: Vintage Books, 1974.

2. Mazumadar, Shudha, *A Letter of Life*, New Delhi: Manohar Book Service, 1977.

3. Katra, Amiteshwar, Praveen Kaur and Sudha Chhikara, *Marriage and Family in Diverse and Changing Scenario*, New Delhi: Deep and Deep Publication Pvt. Ltd, 2006.

4. Roy, Arundhati, *The God of Small Things*, New Delhi: Pengiun Books India, 2002.

7

A Study of Child Abuse in Arundhati Roy's *The God of Small Things*

ANJU BALA AGRAWAL

In *The God of Small Things* (1997) Roy creates a microcosm that encompasses wife battering, infidelity, molestation, emotional insecurity, pride and death within one family. Through this microcosm, Roy explores the often chaotic social and political history of India. The characters' unquenched desires, unfulfilled assurances, broken marriages, shattered faiths, unreasonable hate and planned revenge-all these are the crux of the novel. These complex and complicated problems bring them nothing but frustration which culminates in perpetual suffering. The Booker citation declared that Roy, in her novel "funnels the history of South India through the eyes of a seven year old twin". Besides all these aspects, one important aspect that Roy has raised is 'Child Abuse'. The novel is a glaring example of child abuse in various forms. It also portrays psychological study especially of child psychology.

Set in Kerala, India, during the late 1960s when Communism rattled the age-old caste system, the story begins with the funeral of young Sophie Mol, the cousin of the novel's protagonists, Rahel and her fraternal twin brother, Estha. In a circuitous and suspenseful narrative, Roy reveals the family tensions that led to the twins' behaviour on the fateful night that Sophie drowned. Beneath the drama of a family tragedy lies a background of local politics, social taboos and the tide of history all of which come together in a slip of fate, after which a family is irreparably shattered. Roy captures the children's candid observations but clouded understanding of adults' complex emotional lives. Rahel notices that "at times like these, only the Small Things are ever said. The Big Things lurk unsaid inside". Plangent with a sad wisdom, the children's view is never oversimplified, and the adult characters reveal their frailties and in one case, a repulsively evil power in subtle and complex ways. This "piercing study of childhood innocence lost" mirrors the growing pains of modern India. Twin sister and brother Rahel and Estha are at the center of a family in crisis and at the heart of this "moving and compactly written book". Rahel and Estha are fraternal twins whose emotional connection to one another is stronger than that of most siblings: "Esthappan and Rahel thought of themselves together as ME, and separately, individually, as We or US. As though they were a rare breed of Siamese twins, physically separate, but with joint identities"[1].

Not only, these two children, but their mother Ammu is also prey of child abuse. Before discussing the issue of child abuse in *The God of Small Things,* let us know what child abuse is.

Child abuse is the physical or psychological/emotional mistreatment of children. In the United States, the Centres for Disease Control and Prevention (CDC) define child maltreatment "as any act or series of acts of commission or omission by a parent or other caregiver that results in harm, potential for harm, or threat of harm to a child".[2] Most child abuse occurs in a child's home, with a smaller amount occurring in the organizations, schools or communities the child interacts with. There are four major categories of child abuse: neglect, physical abuse, psychological/emotional abuse, and sexual abuse.

Though the story is told by Rahel, Ammu is main character of novel. It is Ammu's life along with her relatives that is woven in the thread of the story. Neglect is where the responsible adult fails to provide adequately for various needs, including physical, emotional, educational, or medical need. As regards to neglect, for the first time, we find in Ammu's life. She does not find love that is the right of a child whether male or female. Ammu's childhood is itself a tragic tale. In Roy's terminology, she is like a Mombatti (candle) in a big house unable to face the surge of wind. As a little girl, Ammu had to endure some unbearable nightmarish experiences. Parents who physically abuse their spouses are more likely than others to physically abuse their children. However, it is impossible to know whether marital strife is a cause of child abuse, or if both the marital strife and the abuse are caused by tendencies in the abuser. She saw with open eyes cruelty of her father, Pappachi, who used to beat her and her mother Mammachi with a brass vase. Once it so happened that her father tore apart the shoes that she had brought for herself. She was also deprived of higher education because according to Pappachi "a college education was an unnecessary expense for a girl"(38). Whereas Chacko, the brother of Ammu was sent to Britain for higher studies. Roy depicts the cruelty and schizophrenia of Pappachi: "Not content with having beated his wife and daughter, he tore down curtains, Kicked furniture and smashed the table lamp" (181).

Thus, Child abuse is a part of Ammu's life. Not only neglect, she has to suffer physical abuse like beating first at her home by her father and later at her husband's home. "He flogged her with his ivory-handled riding crop"(181). It had stopped the normal development of her personality. She had learnt to live with this cold and calculating cruelty. It was this cruel behaviour of her father that when Ammu gets a chance to go to Calcutta to her aunt, she falls in love with a man and within five days, he proposes her and she gets ready to marry as she does not want to return Ayemenem. It was her ill luck that here, too, she does not get a good treatment. Her husband is a drunkard. He wants to send her to his English manager Mr. Hollick to save himself. When he sees her silent at this issue, as it is clear from her silence that she'll not go to Mr. Hollick, he is infuriated. "Suddenly he lunged at her, grabbed her hair, punched her ..."(42). Violence was not limited to Ammu but these "bouts of violence began to include the children". She wants to save her children from any kind of abuse. It is partly herself and partly because of children that she leaves her husband's home. She is not welcomed at Ayemenem.

The novel is written from the point of view of the twins, Estha and Rahel. Rahel and Estha, the two central characters in the novel are born in a tea-estate in Assam. But they are dislodged from their home when Ammu divorces their father. They reach Ayemenem but here too they are uprooted. Estha is sent back to his father but is forced to return to Ayemenem when his father migrates to Australia. So, whether it was in Assam or Calcutta or Ayemenem, Estha had not struck roots anywhere. He is like "Karna, the abandoned child (p. 231)." A very significant act revealing the alienation of Estha can be traced in the chapter 'Wisdom Exercise Notebooks' where "Estha had rubbed out his surname with spit and taken half the paper with it. Over the whole mess he had written in pencil unknown. Esthappen unknown (156-57)." Thus Ms. Roy does a marvellous joy of conjuring the anomalous world of childhood, its sense of privilege and frustration, its fragility, innocence and unsentimental wisdom. She shows us uncanny spiritual connection of the twins with each other and their longing for their mercurial mother's approval. Even at the age of seven, Estha is the reserve one, dignified in his Elvis pompadour and pointy beige shoes. Rahel is the curious one, wayward, ardent and solitary in her pride. They are considered socially segregated and isolated both on the religious and the ethnic grounds as they have a mixed parentage. Their father was Hindu and their mother was a Syrian Christian. Besides it their father was a Bengali and mother was a Keralite. Being the children of a divorced woman, they are neglected and abused. They are not liked by any member of the family. The maternal uncle Chacko tells Ammu that children are not his responsibilities. At another occasion, he tells the children that Ammu has no right in his family. Their childhood household hums with hidden antagonisms and pains that only family members can give one another.

The family's tragedy revolves around the visit of Chacko's ex-wife, widowed by her second husband, and his daughter, Sophie Mol. It is within the context of their visit that Estha will experience the one horrible thing that should never happen to a child, during their visit that Ammu will come to love by night the man the children love by day, and during their visit that Sophie Mol will die. Her death, and the fate of the twins' beloved Untouchable Velutha, will forever alter the course of the lives of all the members of the family, sending them each off on spinning trajectories of regret and pain. The story reveals itself not in traditional narrative order, but in jumps through time, wending its way through Rahel's memories and attempts at understanding the hand fate dealt her family.

Rahel is a child of broken home and a daughter of a divorcee mother staying in her ancestral home. She did not get love and affection from her elders that a child so badly needs. Her emotional needs remain unfulfilled. Right from her birth, she had been a sufferer. As a child she had seen the suffering of her mother and the insult and ignominies that were inflicted on her and the tortures she had been subjected to. Of course her mother had all the concern for her, but in a hostile atmosphere she was utterly helpless. When Ammu died at the age of thirty one, Rahel was nearly eleven. After the death of Ammu, she was more neglected than ever. She had lost the last moorings that she had and began to drift from school to school, spent eight years in a college of Architecture in Delhi without a degree. In Delhi, she met Larry McCaslin, who happened to be in Delhi collecting material for her doctoral thesis. He met Rahel and found in her 'a jazz tune'. He followed her into a bookshop where neither of them looked at books and Rahel "finally drifted into a marriage like a passenger drifts towards an unoccupied chair in an airport lounge" (180). Rahel realized within the short time of their marriage that something was lacking in their love relationship. They could not understand each other and decided to divorce. Her marriage does not last long. Having separated from her husband, she does various jobs in America. When she gets a letter from Baby Kochamma announcing Estha's return to Ayemenem, she leaves her job and returns to Ayemenem.

Estha is also forlorn and desolate character. He suffers more than his sister. It is because he is submissive and aggressive like Rahel. He also leads an unhappy life. He is a neglected figure like his mother and sister at the Ayemenem House. At the funeral of Sophie Mol, all the three, the mother and the twins are made to stand separately. Baby Kochamma also dislikes them. In fact it is she that's why children suffer endlessly. The maid servant Kochu Maria also reminds Estha of his position in the house. She says to him that she would complain to Mammachi: "Tell your mother to take you to your father's house. There you can break as many beds as you like. These are not your beds. This is not your house" (83).

Out of all the possible forms of abuse, emotional abuse is the hardest to define. It could include name-calling, ridicule, degradation, destruction of personal belongings, torture or destruction of a pet, excessive criticism, inappropriate or excessive demands, withholding communication, and routine labelling or humiliation. Victims of emotional abuse may react by distancing themselves from the abuser, internalizing the abusive words, or fighting back by insulting the abuser. Emotional abuse can result in abnormal or disrupted attachment disorder, a tendency for victims to blame themselves (self-blame) for the abuse, learned helplessness, and overly passive behaviour.

How Estha and Rahel become the prey of emotional abuse that shatters their lives. Baby Kochamma carry Rahel and Estha to the Kottayam police station and persuades Estha to identify Velutha as the man responsible for kidnapping and murder. The accusation was false and ill-founded yet Estha had to concede to the proposal of Baby Kochamma he thought that this was the only way to save his mother. Baby Kochamma said to him: "Do you want to save Ammu or shall we send her to jail?"(318). Estha suffers such type of humiliation. He has to make a statement against the man whom he loves as a father. The death of Sophie Mol was an accident but it is thought of a murder. Estha's torture is more mental than physical. Even after a false statement before the police, he could save his mother and himself from going to jail, but their sufferings didn't end. Now their position deteriorated so much that Ammu decided to do some job so that she could live separately with her children and till then Estha is sent to his father much against his wishes.

It is a heartbreaking moment when Estha is put on the train by Ammu. Though it is not easy for Ammu, she has to send him only for some time. To quote: "As soon as I get a job. As soon as I can go away from here and get a job" (324) in a mood of panic Estha says: "But that will be never!" (325) Ammu shows before him a picture of future life when they three will have everything of their own. (But alas this never happens because of premature death of Ammu.) They hold hands through the window; as the train begins to move. Estha voices his familiar complaint when in need of his mother: "Ammu! Feeling vomity!' (326) as the train moves Estha's voice lifts into a wail. Not only Estha, but Rahel is also sad at the separation as her condition at the station platform indicates: "Rahel doubled over and screamed and screamed" (326). This is an example of emotional abuse. Twins are generally more attached to each other than other siblings. Separating them has a deep emotional effect on them. Rahel and Estha's separation also affected them though in a different way. Anyhow he finished his school education without participating in group activities. His college education was retarded and he found himself engaged in a domestic work like sweeping, cooking and shopping. He led an isolated and solitary life. By and by he stopped talking. After twenty three year, he was sent to Ayemenem. Till then he had lost his speech. The loss of speech is attributed to his ill treatment by Baby Kochamma, Kochu Maria, inspector Mathew and the soft drink man. He did not protest against his tormentors and so he could not open his mouth. Besides his sense of shame and sin born out of the evil treatment of his mother is also responsible for his going into silence.

> That such an innocent child was subjected to the worst cruelty to the adults and his childhood was destroyed and his life ruined for no fault of his own, constitutes a major tragedy in the novel. Such won to destruction of childhood is staggering to our imagination and pathetic to our heart[3].

More than other members of family, Ammu unconsciously becomes the cause of emotional abuse of her children and to some extent responsible for shattering their lives completely. For Rahel and Estha, Ammu is both 'Maa' and 'Baba'. They can't tolerate Ammu's abuse. When Ammu's illicit love affair with Velutha is disclosed and she is locked up, children ask her the cause of her lockup. In an emotional outbursts, she rebukes:

> 'Because of you!' Ammu screamed. 'if it wasn't for you I wouldn't be here! None of this would have happened! I wouldn't be here! I would have been free! I should have dumped you in an orphanage the day you were born! You're the millstones round my neck!' (253).

This abuse had hurt Estha so much that he decided to leave the house and go to the house which he had made at the back verandah of the History House. He had furnished this house with a mat and all his toys. Unable to understand Ammu's problem and deeply hurt by this treatment, he decided to leave the house that very night though it was dark and raining. He thought that Ammu didn't want them any more. This decision of leaving the house left indelible mark. As the boat drowned by which they were crossing the river, drowned. They were saved but Sophie Drowned and therefore dead. Later, Margaret, mother of Sophie slapped Estha as she thought Estha responsible for her daughter's death. This led Estha's banishment.

Not only, physical and emotional abuse, but sexual abuse has also been described by Roy. Child sexual abuse (CSA) is a form of child abuse in which an adult or older adolescent abuses a child for sexual stimulation. The effects of child sexual abuse include depression, post-traumatic stress disorder, anxiety, propensity to re-victimization in adulthood, and physical injury to the child, among other problems. Child sexual abuse is also strongly connected to the development of Complex post-traumatic stress disorder and borderline personality disorder. Roy has described the incident of Child abuse in detail and it's after effects. Estha as a child Goes to see a movie. He is happy. During the movie, he begins to sing a song so other audiences feel disturbed. Ammu asked Estha to shut up. He remains shut up for a moment. But then, he again desires to sing so as ask Ammu to go out. Ammu, embarrassed by her disturbance let him go outside. Estha alone exits and sits in a sofa in the Abhilash Talkies Princess Circle Lobby and sings a song in nun's voice:

> But how do you make her stay
> And listen to all you say?
> How do you keep a wave upon the sand?
> Oh, how do you solve a problem like Maree ... yah?
> How do you hold a
> Moonbeam
> In your hand? (101)

An Orangedrink Lemondrink man, who was sleeping on the counter, wakes up and threatens Estha to make him awake. Then he persuades Estha to drink Lemon, and involves him in sex act. Estha, a small child, does not understand the meaning of this activity, but he is so much frightened, that he becomes the prey of fever. As he is unable to say anything, Ammu doesn't understand anything. Even at night, he is unable to sleep. His trauma is thus described: "Estha alone walked weavily to the bath-rooms. He vomited a clear, bitter lemony, sparkling fizzy liquid. The acrid after-taste of a littleman's first encounter with fear" (119).

Persons like Estha - made to pass through travails and trauma-lose all strength and will-power. They drift aimlessly falling victim to the sinister forces let loose all rungs of society. Lapses of Estha and Rahel can't be called to be product of their will as society has not allowed them to form a will or personality. If they are amoral their society is more so. So Rahel and Estha are tragic figures like Oedipus, the hero of Sophocles' great tragedy *Oedipus the King*. Like him they are the victims of society that has betrayed them. Destitute families mutilate their own children to make them more profitable beggars. Greater crimes under cover go undetected. Yet society gets more and more morality conscious.

Thus, the novel is an extensive study of child abuse. The writer has described child abuse and its related factors in the lives of its protagonists. Society should understand how different factors destroy the lives of innocent children so much that they can't pass a normal life. The novel is autobiographical to a great extent as it is a document of the author's personal life. Ammu, in the novel, represents Arundhati's mother Mrs. Mary Roy. The author who herself passed an insecure and isolated childhood, confesses in one of her interviews that a child's vision for the adult world in the novel is the outcome of her own life, lived as an unprotected child. Though much has been drawn from Roy's personal life but it never becomes sentimental or personal in the ordinary sense of the word. She herself comments: "The texture is autobiographical, the incidents are not. The novel, an experience of thirty seen years of Roy's life, is a portrayal of the maturing of Estha and Rahel"[4]

REFERENCES

1. Roy, Arundhati, *The God of Small Things*, New Delhi: Penguin Books, 1997, p.2. (All the references to the text are from this edition and have been indicated by page numbers in parentheses.)
2. Leeb, A.B., R.T. Paulozzi, L.J. Melanson, C. Simon, T.R. Arias, *Child Maltreatment Surveillance: Uniform Definitions for Public Health and Recommended Data Elements*, 1 January 2008. Centres for Disease Control and Prevention. www.cdc.gov/ncipc/dvp/CMP/CMP-Surveillance.htm.
3. Roy, Amitabh, *The God of Small Things: A Novel of Social Commitment*, New Delhi: Atlantic Publishers and Distributors, 2005, pp.95-6.
4. Purie, Arun, *India Today*, Vol. xxii No.31, October 1997.

❑❑❑

8

Shashi Deshpande's *That Long Silence* : Sexual Contentment Vs. Emotional Bond in Marriage

ANIL VERMA

"Though it was *That Long Silence* (1988) that won the award, Shashi Deshpande herself calls it an uncomfortable work, something that I do not like to go back to because there is so much anger and confusion in it" (Ravindran Shashi). These are the remarks of Shashi Deshpande an Indian writer in English, for her own creation, the novel named *That Long Silence* (1988), which won her the Sahitya Academi Award in 1990.

This Karnataka born and a Bombay educated writer has degrees of Economics and Law as well as a course done in Journalism at Bhartiya Vidya Bhavan, Mumbai, and gained experience for a couple of months as a journalist for the magazine *Onlooker* (SAWNET: Bookshelf: Shashi Deshpande). She has written four children's book, a number of short stories and nine novels and so many perspective essays. She has also received Padma Shri Award in 2009 for *That Long Silence.*

Deshpande as a writer is always concerned with the problems faced by a woman in a patriarchal society. Like most of her novels, this very novel also deals with the life of an ordinary, well educated woman. As a matter of fact, the novel has touched, like most of Indian pieces of fiction, so many aspects of our society like, male domination, desire of male child in the family, husband's maltreatment towards their wives, poverty, description of the life style of lower strata of our society and condition of its woman. Besides these social aspects, it deals with the personal problems like identity crisis and insanity. So, the novel contains a variety of themes in its complex storyline, but the major concern of the novel appears to be the theme of marriage.

Marriage, an eight letter word is familiar to everyone but everyone does not know, what it means exactly. The institution has its own place and importance in every society and culture, but of course, the values and experiences differ from culture to culture and person to person. In western cultures, marriage becomes a matter of personal choice. You are free to choose your life partner. Even after marriage there are no restrictions, both husband and wife are free to do whatever they want to. They live with each other, but they are not bound to be in the relationship if they don't feel comfortable with each other. If they feel that they do not love each other and cannot live with each other, then they are free to step out of the marriage without any restrictions.

They are free to choose their different paths once again. In the western societies marriage is an affair of two individuals and these individuals have full liberty to take their decision without any third party's consent. But the same thing is not possible in patriarchal societies like India at all. On the contrary in India, marriage, besides being the bonding of two individuals, becomes a matter of social respectability and family honour. In India traditionally and culturally, most of the marriages are arrange marriages, not based on the love for each other but on the needs, of human life, related to marital bliss. Most of the times, the two individuals who are going to get married, have no role to play in the whole affair of choosing a life partner. Even worse, many times two individuals are there in bed on their wedding night to have sex without a single word's interaction, before. Once you are married to someone, you are bound to live with that person throughout your life. Even if you do not feel compatibility or any type of emotional attachment with the other, he/she have to remain in the relationship, because of social respectability and family honor, as a divorce is considered highly disgraceful for a person, and for his/her whole family. And if unfortunately a woman gets divorce, the society makes the situation much more difficult for her with its rigid convictions and conservative behaviour. Though in the modern age, people have got liberal outlook towards life, but still, people in

India, like to follow the traditional way to be in marital relationship and inculcate the same tradition and values in their sons and daughters.

Similarly, every person has his point of view, perceptions and experience about marriage. To the opinion of some, it is a highly sacred relationship between husband and wife, a lifelong companionship, which ends only after one's death, and for some people, it's a compromise, made out to meet the need of a companion to lead this harsh long life. In India family is supposed to take all these decisions on your behalf. Now the things have changed a little otherwise earlier almost all the couples did not know anything about each other before their first sexual encounter. In some of the cases their interaction starts after several sexual encounters. Family lays the parameters for the suitability of a boy or a girl. It is not only about the two individuals only a number of other persons are involved in the decision making and many times their opinion is of highest value, and has to be accepted religiously. And there are a number of things to be considered before final consent. Finally in the western world only two individuals are the decision makers and in India the whole society is responsible. For some others, it is a speculation, a gamble, inevitable, in which your whole life is at stake, and you do not know, what is going to be there for you once this happens in your life. For some, it is love, passion, caring and sharing, but for some it's a burden, a string around their neck which cannot be removed. On the whole, if there is love and mutual understanding, marriage is a real heaven, but lack of these traits, make marriage a burning hell.

There are two stems of nuptial relationships, physical relationship and emotional relationship. The absence of any of these traits means, there is something wrong, something ominous, and something disastrous. In a love marriage, husband and wife are already in love and are sexually attracted to each other. Of course they also have a great emotional attachment, because of which, they decide to live with each other. In an arranged marriage, the situation is quite different. The parents of the couple arrange the marriage for them. The husband and wife do not love each other they just get ready to marry each other out of filial responsibility. After marriage they try to understand each other and love grows out of this. This love leads to emotional attachment and this emotional attachment leads to physical attachment. In patriarchal societies like India most of the times the marital relationship starts with the fulfillment of carnal desires and then it goes on to emotional attachment. Sometime, it is physical relationship and then love happens which leads to emotional attachment. For the girl most often it's a very horrifying experience initially, because after marriage she has to obey her husband no matter what he asks her to do. One can only speculate that only in rarest of rare case a male will seek the consent of a female otherwise it is always a forced activity. Most of the times, there is no love, no emotional attachment, but only physical need. Such a relationship leads to unfortunate disaster. Now the question arises, what is more important in a marriage, sexual contentment or emotional bonding? Can there be only physical contentment without emotional attachment or can there be a marriage with strong emotional support and attachment but no carnal bliss. The novel *That Long Silence* has this very question as its theme. The novel deals with Jaya, her martial life and her role as a wife. In Indian context, a wife acts as a subordinate to her husband. All essential decisions of their future are taken by the husband. A wife has to change herself according to her husband and in- laws. It is a sort of compromise for an Indian bride. It often happens that a wife's interests are not supported by her husband. It certainly affects the marital relationship. This is the thing, which happens to Jaya. "A husband is like a shelter tree... without the tree, you're dangerously unprotected and vulnerable, and so you have to keep the tree alive and flourishing, even if you have to water it with deceit and lies" (Deshpande, 32).

In India marriage especially for a girl means security. In the process of the selection of a boy the most important thing is status of the boy, financial condition, connection, properties and future prospects etc. One reason for this is security of the girl, second, a girl in patriarchal society never say no to any decision taken by her family for her, in case she expresses her will it becomes a big issue. Parents in search of these things are not worried about the age of the male. Sometimes the difference is far too big to be accommodated and then it also leads to the dissatisfaction in physical desires. Through this only one purpose gets served and, on top of that it is taken by the ones who are not a part of the marriage and basic essentials of a successful marriage are kept at stake. Though the marriage will last forever but there is nothing because of which we can call it a successful marriage.

This is the advice, which Jaya gets from Vanita Mami, after her marriage. An advice, almost every Indian girl gets from her parents before marriage. But for a girl like Jaya, it is something odd, and loathsome. She is a girl with quite modern taste and highly short temper. Her father treats her unlike an Indian father treats her daughter.

You are not like the others, Jaya 'Appa had said to me, pulling me ruthlessly out of the safe circle in which the other girl had stood, girl who had performed Pujas and come to school with turmeric dyed threads round their wrists and necks, girl who, it had seemed; asked for nothing more than destiny of being wives and mothers. While I, Appa had said, and I had agree, would get the chat field prize, or the Ellise prize, go to oxford after my graduation...'You' are going to be different from the others Jaya...Appa had assured me (Deshpande, 136).

Most of the times for a father a girl child is most lovable and they pay a lot of attention for their needs and welfare, because of this they always treat them better than boys or equal to boys. This is not at all a bad thing infect the whole struggle is for this only, but the negative side of this is that when the same girl faces situations like where her marriage is to be fixed, and even more after she gets married she finds all the values she held dear for such a long time all false and unrealistic. Her education and knowledge, everything loses its meaning. The only things she is expected to learn is a set of skills developed by the society for a girl or a female, to believe in that and to follow it religiously.

Whenever Jaya has a fit of fury, her father says: "I am sure you can do better, you can't stop at that" (Deshpande, 82). This makes her calm down. After Appa she no longer gets that treatment, a treatment fascinating and beautiful in itself. When it comes to her marriage, she gets a proposal from Mohan, an Engineer with a good job and good family. At that time she herself does not know what she wants in her future husband. She feels that all girls are looking for something, but they are not willing to tell, because either they don't have a name for it or they can't speak it.

If we had been forced to name it, the thing we were trailing, I suppose we would have called it love, something we saw in movies between Raj Kapoor's and Nargis, Carry Grant and Deborah Kerr. It mean a handsome young man saying 'I love you'... we tried this grab of love on all the young men we came across, wondering each time - will this fit? And then, as we grew into young women, we realized it was not love, but marriage was that destiny waiting for us...It has been our parents who had taken charge of these vague desires of ours and translated them into hard facts...Doctor, Engineer, Government official, college lecturers... for me the refrain had stopped at engineer (Deshpande, 91).

As a girl grows into an adult physically and emotionally, she develops a kind of image in her mind as what her life partner will be like, in physical appearance, emotionally and overall. But finally when it is the time of real decision making she has no place in it. Because it is the family which will decide what is required in a boy. Everything that a girl thinks before becomes an unfulfilled dream like what it was before.

Jaya hates Mohan, when she comes to know that he has said that he wants an educated and cultured wife. She says: "Cultured! Damn, damn... I can't possibly marry a man who uses that word. Call it of... (Deshpande: 92) "An educated, cultured wife '... Did all men go about with precize ideas little that" (Deshpande, pp. 90-91).

We are living the twenty first century but still the psyche of the males is dominated by the patriarchal thinking. They are looking for a cultured and educated wife. So the next question is what is the meaning of this word cultured? The answer obviously is, a girl who does not ask questions nor does express herself, a girl who is passive and is ready to take everything as an order which comes from her husband's side. Because sometimes it may happen that a girl who is educated is aware of her rights and may ask questions on certain things and these qualities are not supposed to be good for a wife in a patriarchal society. The more a girl is submissive the more she is fit to be a wife.

But Jaya's brother wants to get rid of his responsibility of an unmarried sister, so he manipulated the things and makes her realize that Mohan is not asking for dowry, so her kakas and brother will not have to arrange money for her. So it is Mohan who, desires to marry her and she simply accepts without protest. There is a long list of challenges for a girl in India and one of them is dowry at the time of her marriage. This is one of the biggest reasons for female foeticide. Most of the times a girl surrenders to the decision of her parents because it depends on the financial position of a family. Finally it becomes a liability on a daughter's part.

Love means caring and sharing, when you love somebody you support him/her and encourage his/her interests. This very mutual encouragement and support brings forth emotional attachment. But if there is no support, care and encouragement, love never happens nor does not emotional attachment. Jaya got her name from her father. He named her Jaya – for "victory" (Deshpande, 15). But after her marriage she gets a new name from her husband Suhasini. A name gives identity to an individual and she loses her identity soon after her marriage. As a wife she cannot even complaint about it. "If I disowned the name, he would never fail to say reproachfully, 'I choose that name for you'" (Deshpande, 15).

This is also one of the practices in Indian society to change the name of a girl after marriage. Taking this otherwise it's a practice to symbolize the male superiority over female. Every human being is given a name right after birth. What is the significance of a name? It is the identity of a human being of which one feels proud, and what if all of a sudden somebody comes to you and tell that this name does not suit you/I do not like this and I'll call you by another name. The name I am going to give is the most fitting. It's not about the good/bad name but it's about power, possession and making the other to follow, and to tell that it's my right and privilege to take decision and your duty is to follow that with a smiling face. No one has a right to change his/her partner's name neither a husband nor a wife. It's sheer attack on someone's identity, used as a medium to dominate the other. In such situation love can never bloom.

Anger is an emotion like love, hate, laughter and weeping. Which needs outlet like every other emotion we cannot expect a person to be totally devoid of anger whether it's a man or a woman but for Mohan "Anger made a woman 'unwomanly' (Deshpande, 83).

When once in a fit of fury Jaya accused him of something, he is shocked that he does not talk to her for many days". "How could you? I never thought my wife could say such things to me. You are my wife... He had kept repeating" (Deshpande, 82). "My mother never raised her voice against my father however badly he behaved to her" (Deshpande, 83).

After this event, Jaya changes herself completely. She learns to get control over her anger and accommodates herself to the traditional role of a woman and wife, to care for her husband, children and for her house. To cook food, wash utensils and left over on the table. She get so accustomed to this new job as a wife that her husband does not think that she needs any other job and does not allow her to do any job as he thinks he is earning enough and there is no need for her to help him in supporting the family. Jaya is a writer she writes stories and tries to get those published also. Mohan initially takes pride in introducing her wife as a writer to his friends. But when he gets the approval for her stories to be published, he feels upset and scolds her. When one of her story gets prize and is considered for publication soon, he feels more disturbed. He thinks what his friends and people will think when they will come to know that Jaya has written a story of her own marital relationship with Mohan. After this Jaya stops writing, sacrificing the most wonderful talent of her personality, just because her husband does not like it. Marriage should be based on equal rights. There should be no restriction on one's job or hobby, just because the other does not like it. We cannot expect any possibility of love happening in such a situation. It is a compromise a very dreadful compromise made in order to maintain that hollow relationship, in which, the wife has started to care about her husband and has changed herself according to her husband and in-laws expectations. But, the husband is still imposing his liking on her, without even thinking about the affect which was of course not good, on his wife due to his dominating and careless attitude towards his wife's interests. After that, something new happens in their married life.

Their marriage is now ornamented with *Silence*, a deep long silence, which has engulfed the every possibility of love and emotional attachment between them. There remains only silence and sex. "...Silence was the only weapon. Silence and Surrender" (Deshpande, 36). Sex is a biological need. Every normal human being has this physical urge. Is it valid to call this love? Is it the true definition of love? Jaya is also looking for these answers. She does not have any emotional of love like feeling for her husband. But she craves for his touch even in her silence, when she does not express her feeling about him, the activity exist without any feeling of comfort.

First there's love, then there's sex- that was how I had always imagined it to be. But after living with Mohan I realized that it could saw easily to be the other way round. "Love...Yes, what else could I call it but love when I thought of how I had longed for his physical presence,... what else could I name it when I thought of the agony it had been to be without him, when his desires, his approval, his love, had seemed to be the most important thing in my life...."(Deshpande, 95).

For a female, physical pleasure becomes a name of love. She has to look beautiful for him and to read all those woman magazines giving tactics to maintain love in your marriage. How a woman should behave in bed so that her husband does not take it otherwise. "Don't let yourself go. How to keep your husband in love? Keep romance alive in a marriage...It was ridiculous, he would have slept with me faithfully twice a week whether I creamed my face or not, whether I brushed my hair a hundred times or not, whether I wanted him or not..." (Deshpande, 96).

She does everything to please her husband, even cuts her long hair as her husband wants her to have a hair cut 'like Mehra's wife'. At the same time she has having a sense of guilt about her feelings that she just can't do without her husband. She justifies her feelings by saying that: "Love is a myth, without which sex with the same person for a life time would be undurable" (Deshpande, 97).

She is living in the illusionary world of love. But somewhere she also knows: "... it is the act of sex that really affirms your aloneness" (Deshpande, 98) and after one night of usual silent sex she realizes that they have just touched each other's bodies, but their hearts are still untouched by the feeling of love. "... It had come to me in one awful moment- that I was alone: The contact, the coming together, had been not only momentry, but wholly illusory as well. We had never come together only our bodies had done that. I had begun to cry then, despairingly, silently, scared..." (Deshpande, 98). After the realization her marriage and wifehood become a burden for her. "Two bullocks yoked together...it is more comfortable to move in the same direction. To go in different directions would be painful and what animal would voluntarily choose pain?" (Deshpande, 12).

This becomes her definition of marriage. She feels as if they are not human beings but, animals and animals do not know what is emotion, feeling and bonding, they know only force, physical force. Her husband's presence in the flat at Dadar becomes a burden for her. And one day all limits are crossed. Mohan accuses her of being careless about his worries and tension about his job, which he possibly will lose now. He says that all this, he has done is because of her and the children. As a wife she has not lived up to his expectations. Her general knowledge is also very poor. She also accuses him of not allowing her to write stories, though she has written them in secrecy. She also accuses him of not allowing her to take up some job. Mohan's anger was on it's peak and he says that jaya has been always complaining "each relation evolves its own vocabulary. Our had been that of love, which I had thought would come to us naturally and inevitably, had passed us by,..."(Deshpande, 116).

There remains a vocabulary of silence or anger. Jaya even on such a grave moment's laugh at the reminiscences of some childhood experience, which offends Mohan and he leaves home. In his absence Jaya leads a life of mental agony as if she is on the verge of losing her mental balance. She waits for Mohan to come back and sometimes also thinks him to dead and herself as a widow. She also thinks about her difficult relationship with her son and daughter. In that state of mind she feels that one of her relative Kusum, the insane Kusum was in much more better position than her's, at least she decided by her own, when to live and when to die. She feels:

> Deception, lies, evasions-was this all we had been able to offer each other in our years together? The relationship of man to woman is the most natural of one person to another Karl Marx- yes, Karl Marx it was who'd said that natural? When we are forever resenting, our need of each other? How wrong you were about this Mr Marx (Deshpande, 132).

She realizes that she has failed in this relationship her marriage has made her a coward, who likes to stay at home, safe and secure. Ultimately she recites lord Krishna's words do as you desire we should do only what we desire. When she comes to know that Mohan is coming back and she will be again with her husband and children. She decides to have a say in her life, to do what she desire. Then again this thought "why am I making myself the heroine of this story? Why do I presume that the understanding is mine alone?"(Deshpande, 193). There could be a possibility of change in Mohan. And if not so, there is always hope.

So a relationship, a marital relationship must have emotional bonding as the basic stem of love and also physical contentment only physical contentment, but cannot lead to a healthy marital relationship. There should be mutual understanding and respect for each other's interest's and desires. Only then you can call a relationship a perfect marriage.

Shashi Despande has tried to show the Indian marriage in its most happening form. But there is need to change this deep rooted thought that only wife cares for her husband and husband only imposes his own likings on her. When husband and wife would come at the same level of understanding, love and respect marriage would be a heaven and then it will really not matter, whether the marriage is an arranged marriage or a love marriage, love will be there forever. Shashi Deshpande as an Indian writer has portrayed all these issues and emotions very efficiently and dexterously in the work *That Long Silence*.

REFERENCES

Deshpande, Shashi, *That Long Silence*, New Delhi: Penguin Books, 1988.

http:/lifehistoric.blogspot.com/2009_06_olarchive.html.

http://www.litencye.com/php/speople.php?rec-true UID-1242.

http://en.wikipedia.org/wiki/shashi_deshpande.

http://biographyjrank.org/pages/4267/Deshpande_Shashi.html.

Shashi Deshpande's *That Long Silence and Small Remedies*, October 9, 2207. nandantk.blogspot.com/2007/10/shashi_deshpande_that_long_silence.

❑❑❑

9

Anita Desai's *Fire on the Mountain* : A Study in Images and Symbols

ARVIND M. NAWALE

The definitions of imagery and symbol have been given in different ways by different scholars and critics time to time. M.H. Abrams defines it as:

> Imagery (that is images taken collectively) is used to signify all the objects and qualities of sense perception referred to in a poem or other work of literature, whether by literal description, by allusion, or in the analogues (the vehicle) used in it sillies and metaphors (1985:76).

According to C. Day Lewis, it means:

> A picture made out of words and An epithet, a metaphor, a simile may create an image; or an image may be presented to us in a phrase or a passage or the face of it purely descriptive, but conveying to our imagination something more than the accurate reflection of an external reality (Lewis: 1955:4).

Broadly speaking, imagery is used for assigning some resemblance, correlation or congruity. By its character, any image is "mere vivid than any statement" (Kenner: 1975:28). In simple words, an image is one that represents actions, approach, feelings and state of mind of particular character or situation referred with.

Unlike an image, a 'symbol' is anything that signifies something else. According to M.H. Abrams:

> A symbol, in the broadest sense of the term is anything which signifies something else; ...As commonly used in discussing literature, however, symbol is applied only to a word or set of words that signifies an object or event which itself signifies else; that is, the words refer to something which suggests a range of reference beyond itself (1985:168).

Occasionally, if an image recurs as a leitmotif in any work, it becomes a symbol. In the words of Welleck and Warren: "an image is—if it persistently recurs both as presentation and representation it becomes a symbol" (1949:189). Ezra Pound and T.S. Eliot have shown their keenness for this literary device by using highly suggestive images and symbols which have added a typical depth and complexity to their poetry.

Here in this paper I want to dwell on the imagery and symbols of Anita Desai, one of the major Indian English novelists, as employed by her in her novel *Fire on the Mountain* (1977) I do not want to suggest here that Anita Desai is as much obsessed to the imagery as Ezra Pound and T.S. Eliot like imagists were. But it is also true that imagery and symbols are not utterly absent in her novels. She rather uses images and symbols cautiously and insidiously. As a result, her images and symbols remain strictly functional than decorative.

In Anita Desai's novels, the use of an image or symbol can be understood solely as it functions within the novel as a whole. In capturing the intensity of the feelings of the female protagonists and to describe their inner world, the device of imagery and symbols seems to play a significant role in her *Fire on the Mountain.*

An examination of the use of symbolism and imagery in the novel *Fire on the Mountain* proves the novelist's depth, insight and skill beyond doubt. Images of viciousness, aloneness, annihilation and obliteration are consistently used in order to reflect the alienation of the characters in the novel. An impression of introverted introspection is twisted with the help of several images. For example, when she receives a call from Ila Das, Nanda Kual watches the white hen: "still starting at the hen which was greedily gulping down bits of worm, she thought of her husband's face and the way he would plait his fingers across his stomach" (22).

This image of hen pecking at a worm is suggestive of Nanda Kaul's present interior disorder. Her earlier period suffering at the hands of the disloyal partner and her present alertness about the ruthless realities of life are linked by this image.

Another important image used repeatedly is that of the pine tree which stands scalded and alone: "She was grey, tall and thin she fancied she could merge with the pine tree and be mistaken for one. To be a tree, no more and no less, was prepared to undertake" (04). Nanda's this identification with the pine trees suggests her desire for extraction from life. The same case is with the image of the burnt pine tree. Raka, when she looks at the forlorn hills and burnt pine trees, she reminds the vainness of her survival:

> This hill, with its one destroyed house and one unbuilt one, on the ridge under the fire-singed pines, appealed to Raka. There was something about it-illegitimate, uncompromising and lawless. The sense of devastation and failure drew her, inspired her (90).

Alongwith this, the images of insects like lizards, birds like eagles and parrots come about at regular intervals to highlight thematic and symbolic appeal.

Unlike images, there are a number of symbols that intensify the philosophic implications of the novel. For example Carignano, Nanda Kaul's residence, is symbolic of the isolation and bleakness of Nanda Kual's life. Like Maya's dark house in *Cry, the Peacock*, Sita's house in *Where Shall We Go This Summer?*, Carigno in this novel stands symbolically for emptiness of Nanda Kaul's life."What pleased and satisfied her so, here at Carignano, was its barrenness" (04). This stands symbolically for not only of Nanda Kual's lonely and barren life but also of Raka's.

The eagle symbol is also frequently used in the novel. The sight of the eagle flying high, makes Nanda long to be able to soar like the bird: "She was higher than the eagles, higher than Kasauli and Sanwar and all the other hills" (61). Thus Nanda Kaul's wish and Raka's attempt merge in the eagle-symbol, which denoted their angst and quest for values.

Raka symbolically stands for those children who undergo

persistent torment for no fault of their own and are rendered voiceless depression at the hands of the coldhearted and wallowing parents. Raka is a symbol of ruined childhood. In fact, animal imagery is profusely used to describe her in the novel. To her great-grandmother Nanda Kaul, she appears like "one of those dark crickets that leap up in fright but do not sing or a mosquito, minute and fine, or their precarious legs" (39). Raka's "extravagantly large and somewhat bulging eyes (39) make Nanda Kaul feel "more than ever her resemblance to an insect". Besides, she has "large and protruding ears" (40).

The forest fire scene has symbolic overtone. The title of the novel, Fire on the Mountain is highly symbolical. The mountain symbolizes Nanda Kaul and the fire is symbolic of Raka's wild nature. Nanda is the dry, hard-bitten by time and age. Raka is still, hasty and aggressive like forest fire. Raka's setting the mountain on fire suggests her denial of the society and symbolizes the eradication of human weakness through fire.

As in other novels, in *Fire on the Mountain,* too, Anita Desai uses books and poetry. By introducing one stanza from Hopkin's poem, Anita Desai highlights the character of Nanda Kaul who quotes it and the poem symbolizes her desire to be away from the monotonous of life. The same symbolic effect is achieved by introducing an allusion to a passage from *The Pillow Book* of Sei Shonagon which begins with a title *When a Woman lives Alone*. It symbolically stands for the lonely and desolate life of Nanda Kaul.

The characters of Nanda Kaul, Raka and Ila Das are studies of women as symbols. Nanda Kaul symbolizes angst of alienation. Raka symbolises the individual's search for meaning in pointless life. Ila Das stands for the conflict between the individual and the forces of determinism. The attitudes of these three female protagonists of the novel symbolically represent T.S. Eliot's three conditions which he expressed in his *Four Quartets*. If Nanda Kaul, symbolically stands for detachment, Ila Das stands for attachment to self and Raka for indifference. These three characters are also the symbolic manifestations of Desai's alter ego that gives expression to her outlook on life.

The critic S. Indira points out that the significance of use of imagery and symbols in *Fire on the Mountain* in comprehensive manner. To quote her:

> It is the charming mosaic of imagery woven so skillfully by the novelist that makes the Novel a work of art ... Imagery alone makes it possible and, in the process, the novel gains a richer texture and greater depth ...The significant house imagery, the images of plants, colour, atmosphere and moon -- all contribute to the textual density and symbolic centrality of the novel (Indira 1994: 96).

WORKS CITED

Abram, M.H., *A Glossary of Literary Terms,* Delhi: Macmillan India Ltd., 1985.

Desai, Anita, *Fire on the Mountain,* London: Penguin Book, 1977.

Indira, S., *Anita Desai as an Artist,* New Delhi: Creative Book, 1994. .

Kenner, Hugh, *The Image: What the Words Actually Name,* In Martin and Furbauk, 1975.

Lewis, C. Day, *The Poetic Image,* Cambridge: Cambridge University Press, 1955.

Martin, G. and Furbauk, P.N., Editors, *Twentieth Century Poetry,* The Open University Press, 1975.

Welleck, Rene and Warren, Austin, *Theory of Literature,* London: Penguin, 1949.

❏❏❏

10

Multi-cultural Dimension of Contemporary Society : Explorations in the Dynamic Works of Anita Desai

ASHOK KUMAR

Anita Desai is one of the most distinguished Indian novelists, short story writers, screenwriters, and children's writers. She is best known for her studies of Indian life and especially noted for her sensitive portrayal of the confidential verve of her female characters. A number of of Desai's novels explore tensions between family members and the alienation of middle-class women. In her later novels Desai has dealt with such themes as German anti-Semitism, the demise of traditions, and Western stereotypical views of India. She has written exclusively in English since she debuted in the mid-1960s. Throughout her novels and short stories, Desai focuses on the personal struggles of Anglicized, middle-class women in contemporary India as they attempt to overcome the societal limitations imposed by a tradition-bound patriarchal culture. Set amid the cultural and social changes that have swept India since its independence from Britain in 1947, most of Desai's narratives validate the importance of familial bonds and explore the tensions that exist between different generations. In her later works, Desai has addressed such themes as German anti-Semitism, the dissolution of traditional Indian values, and Western stereotypes of India. As a contemporary Indian female author, Desai has been identified with a new literary tradition of Indian writing in English, which is stylistically different and less conservative than colonial Indian literature and concerns such issues as hybridity, shifting identity, and "imaginary homelands," a phrase coined by Indian novelist Salman Rushdie.

Desai was born as Anita Mazumdar to a German mother, Toni Nime, and a Bengali businessman, D.N. Mazumdar in Mussoorie, India. She grew up speaking German at home and Bengali, Urdu, Hindi and English outside the house. She first learned to read and write in English at school and as a result it became her "literary language". Despite German being her first language she did not visit Germany until later in life as an adult. She was a student at Queen Mary's Higher Secondary School in Delhi and received her B.A. in English literature in 1957 from the Miranda House of the University of Delhi. The following year she married Ashvin Desai, a businessman. They have four children, including Booker Prize-winning novelist Kiran Desai. Her children were taken to Thul (near Alibagh) for weekends, where Desai set her novel *The Village by the Sea.* Desai has published novels, collections of stories, and books for young readers. In all these works, Desai has set about interpreting her country for outsiders. Her fictions are largely a domestic one. She is interested primarily in the lives of women in India since Independence, the lives of women in the modern Indian nation state, rather than the history or politics of the subcontinent on a more extensive scale. Desai's work represents a unique blending of the Indian and the western. Her novels catch the bewilderment of the individual psyche confronted with the overbearing socio-cultural environment and the ever-beckoning modern promise of self-gratification and self-fulfillment. In the face of this dual onslaught, her protagonists, male or female Maya, Sita, Monisha and Amla; Sarah, Nanda and Raka; Bim and Tara; Devan, Baumgartner are seen poised rentalizingly at different junctures of the philosophic spectrum.

Anita Desai is persistently concerned with the crisis of interface between man and woman, between the individuals and the social world. Her most important apprehension is to portray the psychic states of her protagonists at some crucial juncture of their lives. Consequently, the most intermittent themes in her novels are "The hazards and complexities of man-woman relationships, the founding of individuality and the establishing of individualism of her characters" (Narsimhan, 1976: 23). She is a contemporary indo-English writer, extensively acclaimed, not only in India but also in the world of fiction writing. She appears on the literary horizon after independence, focusing on the contemporary issues. Desai has added a new dimension to the contemporary Indian English fiction. She has secured a unique and significant place due to her innovative thematic concerns and deals in her fiction with feminine sensibility.

The distinctiveness of Anita Desai's fiction lies in her treatment of feminine receptivity. In India where women have redesigned role, which does not allow any room for individualism, identity and assertion, Anita Desai talks of women who question the age old traditions and want to seek individual growth. They try to reassess the known in a new context and find a meaning in life. Desai suggests that a balance between the conventional, pre-set role of women and the contemporary issues has to be struck. Her female protagonists try to discover and rediscover meaningfulness in life through the known, the established. These characters are not normal but different from others. They do not find a proper channel of communication and thus become alienated and start brooding about their lives. All their wanderings and reflections finally bring them into new vistas of understanding, which they had formerly ignored or rejected.

Desai has initiated her vocation as a novelist in 1963 with the publication of *Cry, the Peacock,* which was subsequently followed by *Voices in the City* (1965) and *Bye-Bye, Blackbird* (1968). In the late 1970s, Desai published the critically acclaimed novel *Fire on the Mountain* (1977), which won the National Academy of Letters Award, and *Games at Twilight and Other Stories* (1978), her first short story collection. During the 1980s, Desai enhanced her reputation with the novels *Clear Light of Day* (1980) and *In Custody* (1984), both of which were short-listed for the Booker Prize, England's highest literary award. Desai later adapted *In Custody* as a screenplay, which Ismail Merchant and James Ivory produced as a motion picture in 1993. In 1982 Desai published the children's work *Village by the Sea: An Indian Family Story,* which won the Guardian Award for Children's Fiction. Desai has published the novels *Journey to Ithaca* (1995) and *Fasting, Feasting* (1999), which brought her a third nomination for the Booker Prize, and *Diamond Dust: Stories* (2000), her second short story collection.

Cry, the Peacock, was published in Britain by Peter Owen, a publisher specializing in literature of the British Commonwealth and continental Europe. Desai's works engage the complexities of modern Indian culture from a feminine perspective while highlighting the female Indian predicament of maintaining self-identity as an individual woman. This chronicles the morbid dread, descent into madness, and suicide of Maya, a young Delhi housewife who is trapped in a loveless, arranged marriage to the much older Gautama, a misogynistic lawyer. The novel foreshadows several of the major recurring themes in Desai's works – the problems of independence and communication, the influence of the West, and the tensions between religious and domestic interaction. This is mainly concerned with the theme of disharmony between husband and wife relationship. Desai looks in to the reasons for marital discord and illustrates how such discord affects the family. Sometimes, the inability of an individual to be responsive to the behavior patterns of her partner leads to strain and tension in the relationship, while sometimes it is on account of varied levels of sensitivity that strained relationships occur. In this novel Maya and Gautama have strained relationships because of their incompatible temperature. Maya is dreamy, sensitive and emotional, while Gautama realistic, insensitive and rational. Maya is poetic and high-strung Gautama detached, philosophical and remote. Maya has tenderness, softness and warmth, Gautama is hard and cold.

Voices in the City (1965), is a sequence of events about three siblings, Amla, Nirode, and Monisha, and their different ways of life in Calcutta. Amla sees the city as a monster, Nirode sacrifices everything for her career, and Monisha cannot bear her stifling existence in the household of a wealthy old Calcutta family. Set in the late 1950s, *Voices in the City* illustrates Indian society still in transition more than a decade after India's independence from British rule. The novel is broken into four sections – the first three are named after a trio of young adult siblings from a Himalayan village who, separately and for different reasons, have moved to Calcutta. As the narrative follows each sibling individually, Desai illuminates the myriad ways that their respective social class defines their self-identities. In this novel, Anita Desai's concern is primarily with human relationships and how in the absence of meaningful relationships the individual suffer. She probes the psychic compulsion that may affect an individual in forging long term and significant relationships and how an individual is affected if he is unable to forge such relationships.

Bye-Bye, Blackbird, – her first novelistic foray into a country beyond India – Desai portrays the intense *xenophobia* and prejudice that manifested in England during the influx of commonwealth immigration in the 1950s and 1960s. The novel opens with Dev, a young man from Calcutta, arriving in England to attend the London School of Economics. He eventually moves in with two old friends, Adit and Sarah, an Indian-English interracial couple. As Dev becomes enamored with the English way of life, Adit becomes more and more nostalgic for his family's home in India. *Bye-Bye, Blackbird,* which moves out of India to look at wider postcolonial issues of displacement, is the most accomplished of Desai's early novels. Ostensibly a typical third-world immigrant novel focusing on the lives of Dev and Ajit, two Indians in Britain, and the racial discrimination with which they have to contend, it is ultimately more about the alienation Ajit's wife, Sarah, suffers in her own country following her marriage to an Indian and her changed position in relation to the (British) nation state.

The same as in *Cry, the Peacock, Where Shall We Go This Summer?* (1975) centres around a distracted wife looking to flee her marriage. The plot follows Sita, a housewife in her early forties, as she arrives on the rustic island of Manori after a twenty-year absence. She has brought along two of her four children, having abandoned the others with her businessman-husband in their home in Bombay. In the third trimester of yet another pregnancy and convinced that the world is hopelessly marred by cruelty and violence, Sita has returned to the island because she believes that it possesses magical powers which can safely terminate her pregnancy.

Nanda Kaul in *Fire on the Mountain* withdraws into a private world of self-willed isolation. Desai has commented on her work: "My novels are no reflection of Indian society, politics or character. They are my private attempt to seize upon the raw material of life". *Fire on the Mountain* brings a definite sense of politics to her hitherto essentially family-focused dramas. It is another female-centred narrative that portrays the lives of three women – the elderly Nanda Kaul, her great-granddaughter Raka, and Nanda Kaul's lifelong friend Ila Das – who one by one retreat to Carignano, a small villa in the Himalayan hill station of Kasauli, to escape the brutal patriarchal worlds in which they have each lived. Criticism of *Fire on the Mountain* has tended to focus on Desai's detailed study of her three female characters – particularly her presentation of Nanda Kaul – without paying sufficient attention to her attack on patriarchal oppression, which, Desai forcefully suggests in this novel, not only limits the opportunities given to women in India, but mentally and physically damages them.

In *Fire on the Mountain,* Desai explores the feminine sensibility and a woman's intrinsic aspiration to know herself in terms of not only her relationship with her family but also in terms of her individual identity and its relationship with the world at large. In the novel, Nanda Kaul and her husband Prof. Kaul do not have a warm relationship. He has cared little for his wife and family. He carried a lifelong affair with another woman. Nanda could not belong to the family and her position is no better than a house keeper. Her husband is responsible for this. He is such a coward that he could not marry a Christian lady because he could not dare break social conventions. Outwardly, the Kaul's are an ideal couple for university community but from inside their relationship is all-barren. Novel shows Desai's tragic vision of life, in which the innocents suffer. They pay a heavy price for their sincerity and innocence, as ordained by an unkind fate.

In *Clear Light of Day,* although the fires of Partition riots burn in the background, Desai's interest is again firmly focused on the difficulties facing a woman who attempts to assert her identity within the family framework, on the relationships Bim, the central female character, has with the various members of her family. It is about the fragmentation of a family played out against the backdrop of a fracturing nation. Set against the historical backdrop of Delhi before the Partition of 1947, *Clear Light of Day* recounts the saga of the Das family, a Hindu clan from Old Delhi. The main characters are three of the four Das siblings: Bim, who is unmarried and teaches history at a women's college; her younger sister, Tara, who lives in America with her diplomat husband, Bakul, and their two teenage daughters; and their elder brother, Raja, who has given up his aspiration to become a poet and lives as a rich, fat businessman in Hyderabad with his Muslim-heiress wife, Benazir, and their five children. The story begins with Tara's visit to the now run-down family homestead in a suburb of Old Delhi, where Bim continues to live and to take care of their autistic younger brother, Baba. Tara has come to India to attend the wedding of Raja's eldest daughter, an event that Bim is boycotting, having long been estranged from her once beloved brother.

> No one said Bim, slowly and precisely, 'comprehends
> better than children do. No one feels the atmosphere

> more keenly – or catches the nuances, all the insinuations in the air – or notes those details that escape elders because their senses have atrophied, or calcified (*Clear Light of Day*, 1980).

Thus, the serenity and aggravation of the central female character in *Clear Light of Day* (1980), Bim Das, an apparently independent woman who is hostage of her past memories, are conveyed by zooming in on several details of the house where she lives, signifying decay and dullness. Bim's sister Tara, who is visiting her in the crumbling family mansion in Delhi during the momentous days of Partition, observes that 'the dullness and the boredom of her childhood, her youth, were stored here in the room under the worn dusty red rugs, in the bloated brassware, amongst the dried grasses in the swollen vases, behind the yellowed photographs in the oval frames – everything, everything that she had so hated as a child and that was still preserved here as if this were the storeroom of some dull, uninviting provincial museum'.

In *Clear Light of Day,* Desai treats other form of man-woman relationship. Bim carries a childhood image of her brother Raja – romantic, poetic, dreamy – whereas Raja is rational, pragmatic and materialistic. She gets angry about Raja as she feels that he does not reciprocate towards her feeling normally because during childhood they had close emotional relationship which she feels as an adult Raja is shunning. Bim is Raja's admirer and she encourages him in every act and ambition. They want to be the heroin and the hero when they grow up and go away into the big world away from their old parental home. In this way, they have greater mental and temperamental affinity with each other than with the other brother and sister. Both of them are bold, independent and possess a fiery impetuous spirit. When raja is sick, Bim takes care of him with love and devotion thinking that he would take her father's place the day he recovers. However, to her utter dismay, when Raja gets well, he decides to go away to a distant place.

Desai's characters in many novels are members of the Anglicized Indian bourgeoisie, whose marital problems are in the forefront. Her characters often adopt escapist ways to cope with the boring everyday life or world outside comfortable living. The generational confrontation in *Clear Light of Day* is echoed in most of Desai's other works from the early *Fire on the Mountain* (1977), which considers the relationship between a recluse grandmother and her granddaughter, to the later novels *Journey to Ithaca* (1995) and *Fasting, Feasting* (1999). In the former, the spiritual pilgrimage to India of a young and wealthy European couple, Matteo and Sophie, is a later version of that of their ageing guru, the Mother, while the latter depicts the struggles of Uma, Aruna and Arun to strike a balance between their parents' expectations and their own personal realization. Typical of Desai's other fiction is also the use of the house as a place of confinement for women. Like Bim, Nanda Kaul in *Fire on the Mountain*, Lotte in *Baumgartner's Bombay* and Uma, her mother and Mrs. Patton in *Fasting, Feasting* rarely walk through the streets of their cities and towns. In her article 'A Secret Connivance', Desai describes in similar terms the fate of Indian women who 'have had to confine themselves to the domestic scene - few women have had any experience of the world outside their homes and families'.

The Village by the Sea is the story of a family overwhelmed by misfortune in the traditional fishing village of Thul, on the west coast of India near Bombay. With the mother ill and bedridden and the father an unemployed, abusive alcoholic, the brunt of the family responsibilities devolve upon the elder children, the adolescents Lila and Hari, both of whom have stopped attending school in order to fulfill these duties and care for their two younger siblings.

In Custody (1984) is Desai's paradoxical story about literary traditions and academic illusions. The central characters are Nur, an Urhi poet, who has fallen on hard times, and Deven, a professor of Hindi, who realizes that the beloved poet is not the magical genius he has imagined. *In Custody,* in many respects a delightful and sad comedy in a Narayanish sort of vein, marks a broadening of Desai's oeuvre. The novel plots the disillusionment of Deven, a young Hindi lecturer at a college in the small town of Mirpore, and the various calamities that befall him after he is persuaded to go to Delhi to interview his hero, India's greatest living Urdu poet, Nur – only to find himself being dragged deeper and deeper into Nur's unsavory world. For all its comedy, there is certain despair in this novel, which presents the decline of Muslim Urdu culture in the North of India in the years following Independence and Partition. *In Custody,* focuses on theme of marital discord and relationship problem. In this novel, Deven and Sarla lead an unhappy marital life. They are quite different from each other in their temperaments. Deven is a Hindi lecturer in a college and Sarla has no interest in literature. She is ignorant that she concludes her husband's frequent visits to Delhi for meeting his girl friend. Sarla is a picture of an abandoned wife. *In Custody* revolves around Deven Sharma, a middle-aged man who once dreamt of becoming a poet but who was forced to take a job teaching Hindi in order to support his wife and child. A sharply incisive social comedy, *In Custody* dramatizes the tensions between worldly and spiritual concerns through Deven's almost-obsessive attempts to interview Nur, the greatest living Urdu poet.

Based on Desai's own Eurasian heritage but narrated from a male perspective, *Baumgartner's Bombay* concerns themes of alterity and hybridity. The novel – Desai's first to feature a non-Indian protagonist – recounts the tragic life and violent death of Hugo Baumgartner, a Jew who has immigrated to India in the late 1930s from Nazi Germany. The story opens with Hugo's murder and the ensuing chapters alternate between scenes of his last hours and flashbacks that take us chronologically through his life.

> Even though his cigarette stank – it was a local one, wrapped in a *tendu* leaf, fierce enough to make his head swim – he could smell the distinctive Indian odor -- of dung, both of cattle and men, of smoke from the village hearts, of cattle food and cattle urine, of dust, of pungent food cooking, of old ragged clothes washed without soap and put out to dry, the aroma of poverty (*Baumgartner's Bombay*, 1988).

Hugo Baumgartner, is a Jew who fled from Nazi Germany to India, only to find that he cannot be fully accepted by Indian society either: he is first interned in a camp for Germans during the second world war, and then remains a stranger, in post-independence India. In the end, his escape to India is pointless as he is killed by a German drifter whom he is trying to set free from drug addiction. The novel is a powerful literary embodiment of Desai's claim that East and West are parallel, not contrasting, worlds. Despair of a different hue characterizes *Baumgartner's Bombay.* Here, through a series of flashbacks, Desai looks at the life of a now-elderly German Jew who fled to India fifty years earlier in the 1930s to escape the Nazis, and who stayed on after Independence only to be murdered in Bombay by a German youth he tried to help. It is another brilliant portrait of alienation.

In *Journey to Ithaca* (1995) Desai scrutinized the temperament of pilgrimage to India through three characters, Mateo and Sophie, young Europeans, and Mother, a charismatic and mysterious woman, whose story is an earlier version of their own. Desai's perspective on India is more European than in her earlier works. The first half of Desai's next novel *Journey to Ithaca* focuses on Matteo, an idealistic Italian, and his temperamental girlfriend, Sophie, a hard-bitten realist German. The countercultural pair marries in 1975 and immediately set off for India, chiefly in pursuit of Matteo's dream of enlightenment, which has been inspired by his reading of Hermann Hesse's *Journey to the East.* They in the end arrive at an ashram in northern India that is led by a charismatic, elderly woman who calls herself the "Mother". Although Sophie remains unimpressed by the "Mother," Matteo is enthralled by what he finds to be the spiritually edifying environment, and they remain for several years, during which time they have two children. Most of the novel's second half consists of Sophie's retracing of the "Mother's" life, which is presented in the form of flashbacks to the early 1920s.

The various strands that can be traced through Desai's previous nine novels are brought together in near perfect synthesis in *Fasting, Feasting.* In keeping with her earlier novels, there is a return to a focus on the family, and in particular the lot of women trapped in traditional family structures in a rapidly changing postcolonial world. This is an almost plotless novel that looks at the lives of two daughters and the son of a traditional Indian family in the modern world. *Fasting, Feasting* contrasted American and Indian culture, and male and female roles. Arun studies in Massachusetts, his sister Uma lives in India in a small provincial city. Uma lives with her parent whom she calls MamaPapa. "It was hard to believe they had ever had separate existence, that they had been separate entities and not MamaPapa in one breath... MamaPapa themselves rarely spoke of a time when they were not one. The few anecdotes they related separately acquired great significance because of their rarity, their singularity". Uma's attempts to leave home and marry create a disaster. *Fasting, Feasting* recounts the disastrous attempts of an Indian daughter to leave her parents' home and achieve independence without marriage. Her parents, referred to as the indivisible unit MamaPapa, barely notice their daughter's aspirations as they lavish all of their attention on their only son.

Fasting, Feasting might have as its epigraph the author's affirmation 'that different lives are parallel lives', as constant correspondences are drawn between an Indian and an American middle-class family. Uma's traditional Indian parents, desperately trying to arrange a good marriage for Uma with disastrous consequences, suffer from the same lack of communication with their children as the Pattons, the American suburban family where Uma's brother Arun is staying while on vacation from his American University. Whether Desai's characters live on the banks of the Ganges or amidst the excesses of Massachusetts, they cannot find meaningful personal relationships other than with their own solitude.

The short story collection *Diamond Dust* features a selection of tales set in North America and India – although Indian characters and concerns figure in all of them – illuminating Desai's thematic preoccupation with the psychological effects of multiculturalism.

Desai's *The Zigzag Way* (2004), is set in 20th century Mexico. In this novel Desai has departed from her familiar territories and set the story of identity and self-discovery in Mexico.

Thus, Desai has intellectual thoroughness and stunning portrayals of world community, particularly her insistence on the multicultural dimension of contemporary Indian society. Although some critics say that Desai's fiction depends too heavily on the mundane and trivial, others have defended her attention to detail, arguing that this feature breathes life into her fiction and contributes to its often humorous tone. Critics have equally extolled Desai's short stories, tracing the thematic similarities between her short fiction and novels. However, several reviewers have asserted that Desai's later stories set outside of India are inherently stronger, faulting Desai's skewed perspective on more recent developments in Indian society and noting her inappropriate use of Indian idiom. Postcolonial literary scholars have focused on Desai's use of Indian settings in the majority of her works, contending that colonial appropriation of Indian cultural values remains an obstacle for postcolonial writers. Others have explored the effects of English culture on the subjectivities of Desai's urban Indian middle-class characters, suggesting that the unspoken gendered and imperialist premises of colonial culture inhibit the potential growth and artistic expression of the formerly colonized. Feminist critics have assessed the psychological development of Desai's female characters in terms of the patriarchal Indian family structure while evaluating Desai's representation of the Indian feminine within the context of other Indian literature written by women.

Despite the fact that most of these columnists have esteemed the complexity of the family relationships depicted in Desai's novels, several have objected to their resolutions as either too simplistic or perpetuating patriarchal values. Consequently, Anita Desai presents to reader her outlook with reference to complexity of human relationships as a big contemporary problem and human condition. So, she analyses this problem due to shows changing human relationships in her novels. She is a contemporary writer because she considers new themes and knows how should to deal with them. Anita Desai takes up considerable contemporary issues as the subject matter of her fiction while remaining rooted in the tradition at the same time. She explores the anguish of individuals living in modern society. Desai deals with complexity of human relationships as one of her major theme, which is a universal issue, as it attracts worldwide readers to her novels. She strives to show this predicament without any interferes. Desai is undoubtedly one of the major Indian English writers of her generation. If her reputation is established on her early portraits of domestic disharmony in traditional Indian families and the suffering of women in a largely patriarchal world, her later novels demonstrate that she writes equally well about the world of men, about Indians abroad, and about Westerners in India. Above all, she demonstrates again and again how gender issues are central to politics and the nation as well as in the family. Consequently, Desai has academic severity and brilliant portrayals of world society, predominantly her assertion on the multicultural dimension of contemporary society.

WORKS CITED

Abrams, M.H. and Stephen Greenblatt, *Anita Desai, The Norton Anthology of English Literature,* Vol. 2C, 7th Edition, New York: W.W. Norton, 2000, pp.2768-2785.

Alter, Stephen and Wimal Dissanayake, *A Devoted Son by Anita Desai, The Penguin Book of Modern Indian Short Stories,* New Delhi, Middlesex, New York: Penguin Books, 1991, pp.92-101.

Bande, Usha, *The Novels of Anita Desai: A Study in Character and Conflict,* New Delhi: Prestige, 1988.

Belliappa, Meena, *Anita Desai: A Study of Her Fiction,* Calcutta: Writers Workshop, 1971.

Choudhury, Bidulata, *Women and Society in the Novels of Anita Desai,* New Delhi: Creative Books, 1995.

Desai, Anita, *Interview by Yashodhara Dalmia, The Times of India,* 29 April, 1979.

Dhawan, R.K., *The Fiction of Anita Desai,* New Delhi: Bahri, 1989.

Fawzia, Afzal-Khan, *Cultural Imperialism and the Indo-English Novel: Genre and Ideology in R.K. Narayan, Anita Desai, Kamala Markandaya, and Salman Rushdie,* University Park: Pennsylvania State University Press, 1993.

Goel, Kunj Bala, *Language and Theme in Anita Desai's Fiction,* Jaipur: Classic, 1989.

Gopal, N.R., *A Critical Study of the Novels of Anita Desai,* New Delhi: Atlantic Publishers & Distributors, 1995.

Indira, S., *Anita Desai as an Artist: A Study in Image and Symbol,* New Delhi: Creative Books, 1994.

Jain, Jasbir, *Stairs to the Attic: The Novels of Anita Desai,* Jaipur: Printwell, 1987.

Jena, Seema, *Voice and Vision of Anita Desai,* New Delhi: Ashish, 1989.

Kanwar, Asha, *Virginia Woolf and Anita Desai: A Comparative Study,* New Delhi: Prestige, 1989.

Kumar, Suresh A.V., *Six Indian Novelists: Mulk Raj Anand, Raja Rao, R.K. Narayan, Balachandran Rajan, Kamala Markandaya, Anita Desai,* New Delhi: Creative Books, 1996.

Mukherjee, Meenakshi, *The Twice-Born Fiction,* New Delhi: Arnold-Heinemann, 1972.

Narsimhan, Raji, *Sensibility Under Stress,* New Delhi: Prakshan, 1976.

Pathania, Usha, *Human Bonds and Bondages: The Fiction of Anita Desai and Kamala Markandaya,* Delhi: Kanishka, 1992.

Prasad, Madhusudan, *Anita Desai the Novelist,* Allahabad: New Horizon, 1981.

Rao, B.R., *The Novels of Mrs. Anita Desai,* New Delhi: Kalyani, 1977.

Selvadurai, Shyam, ed., *Anita Desai: Winterscape, Story-Wallah: A Celebration of South Asian Fiction.* New York: Houghton Mifflin, 2005:69-90.

Sharma, Kajali, *Symbolism in Anita Desai's Novels,* New Delhi: Abhinav, 1991.

Shrivastava, Sharad, *The New Woman in Indian English Fiction: A Study of Kamala Markandaya, Anita Desai, Namita Gokhale & Shobha De,* New Delhi: Creative Books, 1996.

Singh, R.S., *Indian Novel in English,* New Delhi: Arnold Heinemann, 1971.

Solanki, Mrinalini, *Anita Desai's Fiction: Patterns of Survival Strategies,* Delhi: Kanishka, 1992.

Srivastava, R.K., *Perspective on Anita Desai,* Ghaziabad: Vimal Prakashan, 1984.

Sunaina Singh, *The Novels of Margaret Atwood and Anita Desai: A Comparative Study in Feminist Perspectives,* New Delhi: Creative Books, 1994.

Tripathi, J.P., *The Mind and Art of Anita Desai,* Bareilly: Prakash Book, 1986.

❑❑❑

11

Anita Desai's Novels as Women's Fiction

P. ROOPANA

Among the Indian English women novelists, Anita Desai occupies a unique place and has caught the imagination of readers in a fascinating way. This Indian novelist and short story writer is eminent for her sensitive portrayal of the inner life of her female characters. She explores the tension between the family members and the middle class women's lack of correlation in several of her novels. Though the other Indian-English women novelists like Kamala Markandaya, Ruth Prawar Jhabwala, Nayantara Sehgal, Shashi Deshpande, Shoba De, Arundhati Roy, Kiran Desai, etc., have explored the Indian women in all their multiplicity, Anita Desai's focus has been unambiguously different. As a matter of fact, she has far deeply plumbed the psyche of the Indian women and has provided a fictional justification of her statement that literature should deal with the most "enduring matters". She illustrates her insights into the feminine behaviour in the Indian context by externalizing the interior cobwebs and the darkest labyrinths of her female characters.

Kamala Markandaya's female protoganists, pitted against poverty and starvation, fight out a gallant battle and finally establish themselves in tune with the Indian women's identity. The image of the Indian woman, loving and caring, is juxtaposed with the western woman, subjective and possessive, in her novel *Possession.* Ruth Prawar

Jhabwala also assumes the same pattern as she exposes her heroine to the social prejudices, gender bias and her familial compulsions. Bharati Mukherjee's main concern is the search for identity for the expatriates who suffer existential angst of belonging nowhere after their estrangement from historical and cultural roots. Shashi Deshpande probes into the depressive influence of locale in vitiating human relationship to the extent of absurdity. Entrapped in the narrow confines of traditional society, a woman even in a metropolitan city finds no escape but to adopt a stoic attitude and thereby transcend the feelings of happiness and sorrow in order to preserve her intact. Shoba De in her inimitably whacky and satirical way lambastes the male world for its pretentiousness and sex-obsession. Mostly it is only after the initial surrender to the materialistic Pomp and show and outer manifestations of life that the women of her novels revolt against the male supremacy, carving out for themselves an independence and autonomy. In *The God of Small Things* Arundhati Roy presents a small world with ordinary human beings, in easily recognized and comprehended situations, a world where one is ensnared in the social taboos and meaningless traditions. And the latest to join this band of writers is Kiran Desai who with her debut novel *Hullabaloo in the Guava Orchard* reveals promise and brilliance that belongs to an artist with a cultural inheritance. Though she is the daughter of Anita Desai she has not chosen her mother's favourite domain -- the labyrinths of the feminine as a subject in *Inheritance of Loss*. It is a psychological study concerning the issues of love, destiny and conflict expressed through the interior as well as exterior action. The central character's reticence and inaction is symptomatic of his frightening loneliness, bitterness and protest. He is too timid to discover any authenticity and meaning for insipid existence.

From *Cry, the Peacock* to *The Zigzag Way* has been a long and consistent journey, for Desai, into the complex yet vivid world of feminine needs, compulsions, obligations, responsibilities and above all individuality. The most recurring and predominant theme in the novels of Anita Desai is the complexity of human relationships, particularly the man-woman relationships. Her women characters possess refined sensibilities with the complexion of aesthetes. Her male characters, on the other hand, are rational, pragmatic and logical. This temperamental incompatibility triggers a sense of frustration and alienation among her women characters. Emotionally starved and unfulfilled women revolt against the male dominance and demand their rightful place. They declaim against their dream-like, monotonous and insipid existence. This confrontation with reality and circumstances lands them in a quagmire of crisis.

In order to highlight her female characters, Desai always introduces a contrasting male character. Anita Desai uses the technique of contrasting and juxtaposing not only while portraying characters, but also when she depicts settings and situations; her tendency to juxtapose could thus be seen even in her descriptions of the different stages of the same character.

Maya in *Cry, the Peacock* and Monisha in *Voices in the City*, both female protagonists experience almost identical circumstances. The peculiar familial situations in which they have to live, impact an experience stifling for both of them. Their whole existence sways aimlessly amidst the turbulence of their psychic storms. The life's rosary is snapped, beads fall and scatter, rolling off in a thousand directions, both making it impossible to reassemble or rearrange. Overwhelmed by the life-denying impulse and caught in the vortex of a sinking whirlpool, they take their last decisive step to commit suicide.

Maya, the main protagonist in *Cry, the Peacock* is a dreamy, imaginative, temperamental and hyper-sensitive woman. She hails from a rich and aristocratic family in Lucknow. Her father is a leading lawyer, living an exemplary life of the Apollonian commandment of order and discipline. Both Maya and Arjuna, her brother, are blessed with the plentitude of a wealthy family. The family dynamics, however, do not prefigure the stereotyped roles for both of them while Maya exults in the lambency of her relationship with the father, Arjuna revolts against his aura. Maya is married to Gautama, a younger protégé of her father. Maya's visit during her early childhood to an albino astrologer and his prediction haunts her throughout her life. She fails miserably in adjusting with her husband and all her efforts to negotiate with the peculiarly odd circumstances of her life prove futile. The novel ends with the fall of Gautama from the parapet and the neurotic Maya's return to her father's place.

Maya's quest for love and psychic relatedness is possible only through the masculine principle and only then she could be the embodiment of the feminine effulgence. In fact, in her relationship with her husband she did not merely aspire for physical and mundane love but also wanted to achieve an ideal man-and-wife relationship.

Maya's deprivation of the prospect of motherhood further complicates and aggravates her difficulties and problems. The feminine in Maya feels frustrated and depressed because even after four years of marriage she has not become a mother. The absence of a resonant relationship with her husband could possibly be compensated in some measures if a child was born. Being childless, her fondness for her pet-Toto becomes intense and exaggerated.

Like the heroine of *Cry, the Peacock*, Monisha in *Voices in the City* too is a typical child of Anita Desai's imagination. If Maya's problems arise due to her heightened eros, Monisha's troubles lie in her passivity; lie in her under-utilized or un-utilized eros. In both the cases the conflicts and crisis begin with marriage. The author records Monisha's psychic turmoil through Monisha's own diary. Like Maya, Monisha also has to wrestle with a partner into the materialistic pursuits. Monisha fails to strike a healthy equation with her husband because of his absolute surrender to the joint family structure. She clamours for fulfillment of her risen sensibility and seeks authenticity and affirmation in her relationship with her husband Jiban. And ironically she finds herself planted in a stifling, tradition-bogged atmosphere of the joint family where her need for intellectual fulfillment is denied.

Monisha is, no doubt, endowed with an intellectuality which becomes the distancing factor between her eros and her husband, his family. Yet she is a woman who can perceive things intellectually yet emotionally so that she could comprehend the great canyon between birth and death.

Anita Desai endows her characters with a subtle sensibility which makes them distinctive and a class apart. No woman with a peculiar sensitivity and the will to meaning can entertain a feeling of superiority to those who are incapable of appreciating the finer strands of emotionality. Monisha's withdrawal from active participation in her house and her confinement to her room studying Kafka or Dostoyevsky fills her mind with a notion of superiority.

Both Maya and Monisha succumb to the endogenous depression emerging from their respective life-situations. They protest against the male dominance but are deeply entrenched in a man-dominated society. A woman cannot afford to express her rage and resentment due to her dependence on men. Under such conditions, women inevitably turn their aggression against themselves. They transform the cultural devaluation into feelings of worthlessness and inferiority. Desai has beautifully expressed their hostility and aggression against the male world which ultimately results in their anger converting into self-deprecation.

Bye-Bye, Blackbird, which moves out of India to look at wider postcolonial issues of displacement, is the most accomplished of Desai's early novels. Ostensibly a typical third-world immigrant novel focusing on the lives of Dev and Ajit, two Indians in Britain, and the racial discrimination with which they have to contend, it is ultimately more about the alienation Ajit's wife, Sarah, suffers in her own country following her marriage to an Indian and her changed position in relation to the (British) nation state

Where Shall We Go This Summer? tells the story of an oppressed mind. Like all her earlier novels this particular novel also illustrates the tension between family members and, more specifically, the loneliness, isolation and alienation of the middle-class women. Sita, the female protagonist, is again the central character of this novel. Sita is pregnant with her fifth child takes refuge from her marriage at the utopian land of a magic island. Sita desperately takes refuge from the mundane realities of her marriage in the island, which happens to be the homestead of her deceased father. It is when Sita feels that she is again pregnant for the fifth time then the irritations and grittiness of life becomes somewhat heavy to bear for her. She makes an attempt to shut down emotionally and isolate herself from the daily chores. It is then she feels the dire need to fade far away and dissolve to the utopian land, which is the island where her dead father lived. The catastrophe of the story lies where Sita is seen perturbed with the very idea of bringing another child, as it is indeed something more than what she can handle. She physically escapes to the island and hopes to remain pregnant forever with the baby. A neat summation and a tidy approach make *Where Shall We Go This Summer?* a heart-rending story of a dejected female. The story ends leaving the feeling of an intense pain of a young middle class wife who so passionately desires to bid goodbye to the hypocrisy and boredom of her daily existence.

Desai's exquisitely crafted fifth novel *Fire on the Mountain*, brings a definite sense of politics to her hitherto essentially family-focused dramas. It is another female-centered narrative that portrays the lives of three women – the elderly Nanda Kaul, her great-granddaughter Raka, and Nanda Kaul's lifelong friend Ila Das – who one by one retreat to Carignano, a small villa in the Himalayan hill station of Kasauli, to escape the brutal patriarchal worlds in which they have each lived. This novel deals with the existential angst experienced by the female protagonist Nanda Kaul, an old lady living in isolation. It also projects the inner turmoil of a small girl, Raka, who is haunted by a sense of futility. Thirdly, it presents the plight of a helpless woman, Ila Das who is in conflict with forces that are too powerful to be encountered, resulting in her tragic death. Thus solitude, alienation, futility of human existence and struggle for survival form the major themes of the novel.

Fire on the Mountain falls into three sections, each further divided into several short chapters of unequal length. The first section titled "Nanda Kaul at Carignano" runs into ten chapters. This section deals with Nanda Kaul, the main protagonist's lonely life in Kasauli. "Raka comes to Carignano" forms the second section and it contains twenty one chapters. It portrays Nanda Kaul's change of attitude towards Raka, her great granddaughter. The final section "Ila Das leaves Carignano" is divided into thirteen chapters. This section presents the tragic end of Ila Das, Nanda Kaul's childhood friend. In all, the book runs to 145 pages. The structural unity, as suggested by the section captions is offered by Carignano, Nanda Kaul and Raka, running counter to one another complemented by that of Ila Das also provide unity of structure. Like the other works of Anita Desai, the present novel contains revolves round the existential angst experienced by the women protagonists.

In *Clear Light of Day*, although the fires of Partition riots burn in the background, Desai's interest is again firmly focused on the difficulties facing a woman who attempts to assert her identity within the family framework, on the relationships Bim, the central female character, has with the various members of her family. It is about the fragmentation of a family played out against the backdrop of a fracturing nation. Unlike Maya in *Cry, the Peacock*, who is unable to shake off the fears and obsessions, Bim doesn't leave her house, she doesn't seek any escape. She rejects all modes of escape, both physical and emotional and continues to stay amidst the drabness of Delhi, in the cemetery like silence of the family house.

In the same way, in *In Custody,* Desai's presentation of man-woman relationships in a patriarchal society reveals her concern and understanding of different forms of woman's experiences through an effective interplay of motive and the medium. The women in the book seem vicious, specially the enraged young wife of Deven's hero, the poet Nur. Just as the male characters are entrapped in an unsuccessful world, the female characters feel frustrated within a patriarchal society that reduces them to clinging to these men who fail to provide them what they want. Deven's wife Sarla hates him and feels disgusted at his failures. All her dreams of a luxurious life are dashed to the ground because of his meager income. But the way she registers her protest is nothing more than a symbolic dissatisfaction with her lot. It may be because of the centuries of serfdom that runs through their blood that these women fail to rebel openly.

Sarla never lifted her voice in his presence-countless generations of Hindu womanhood behind her stood in her way, preventing her from displaying open rebellion. Deven knew she would scream and abuse only when she was safely out of the way, preferably in the kitchen, her own domain. Her method of defense was to go into the bed room and snivel, refusing to speak at all, inciting their child to wail in sympathy. Desai is an advocate of the legitimate rights and freedom of such unfortunate women.

A novella for young people, *The Village by the Sea* tells the story of a family beset by misfortune in the traditional fishing village of Thul, on the west coast of India near Bombay. With the mother ill and bedridden and the father unemployed and abusive alcoholic, the brunt of the family responsibilities devolve upon the elder children, the adolescents Lila and Hari, both of whom have stopped attending school in order to fulfill these duties and care for their two younger siblings.

Journey to Ithaca, the novel opens with Matteo & Sophie, husband & wife: husband, an Italian and wife a German. Like all the other couples in Desai's novels, they are also not happy with their married life. But, here, the problem is not alone of temperamental incompatibility; rather it is something deeper than that. Matteo is an ascetic, a mystic and Sophie is a practical woman. It is the search of the Eternal Truth which makes Matteo alien to Sophie. They have two children but Matteo does not feel any attachment to them. They live their grandparents in Italy. Matteo has been feeling the qualms of a disquiet soul since his childhood. He was a failure at school; in the studies and in games too. He was kept at home under the guidance of a tutor who had given him. Herman Hesse's book *The Journey to the East*. This book, alone revealed him meaning of the meaningless life. It whetted Matteo's quest for God. All the efforts of his parents, to involve Matteo in business proved futile. He set out for India after his marriage. From one temple to the other, from one guru to the other, till in the presence of the Mother, he realized the Supreme Bliss. He dedicates his whole life to understand the mysteries of life and, in the end, we see Matteo as an ascetic, weeping at the tomb of the Mother.

The various strands that can be traced through her previous nine novels are brought together in near perfect synthesis in *Fasting, Feasting*. In keeping with her earlier novels, there is a return to a focus on the family, and in particular the lot of women trapped in traditional family structures in a rapidly changing postcolonial world. At the same time Desai extends her interest in the West in this cleverly structured novel. *Fasting, Feasting* is an almost plotless novel that looks at the lives of two daughters and the son of a traditional Indian family in the modern world. The novel opens with Uma, the eldest daughter now in her forties, still at home and firmly under the authority of her parents. Through a series of flashbacks, the first part of the novel looks at how Uma came to be in this position. It is a view of a traditional Hindu family, including arranged marriages. The second part of the book shifts abruptly to the United States. If in the first part India is presented for Western eyes, in the second part the tables are effectively turned and America is viewed through Indian eyes when Arun, in the U.S. on a college scholarship, finds himself living with the Patton family during summer vacation. It is a carefully balanced novel of contrasts: between East and West; lack and excess; lack of ambition (for Uma and Melanie) and too much ambition (for Arun and Rod). It further explores the gendered condition of the nation state, both in Indian and the U.S.

Her latest novel *The Zigzag Way* is about a story of Eric, an American graduate student from Boston who loses interest in his exercise of turning his thesis on immigration patterns in 19th century Boston into a book on immigration in general. Losing the details in generalities bore him. Following his girlfriend Em to Mexico City, his travel ends in a ghost town that was formerly a mining town on the Day of the Dead. This final section is a departure from Desai's usual writing, which usually stays grounded in realism, not magic.

The novel's title, which describes the way Indian miners used to climb the tunnel to confront the air currents that entered the pits from outside and made respiration harder, also describes the way Eric's own path leads him in his discovery of his ancestry and ancestors.

Women play strong characters in the novel, as they seem to do in many of Desai's work. Emily comes across rather cold and she seems to have been intentionally drawn pale, white, blond, a WASP from Philadelphia, as a counterpoint to Eric and his family, Maine coast fisher folk. Eric too seems rather like a ghost, wondering and wandering, pondering the question of why he and his father are drawn to strong women. I am not sure if he finds his answer but he asks some interesting questions.

Of the two women characters, Dona Vera and Betty, Vera is by far the more colorful. Unfortunately we meet her first when she is drawn with a heavy hand, a stock figure. A plot devise to revive Eric's memory of his childhood when he hears her lecture, she is also the vehicle to provide a narrative of the Huichol Indians and pre-Columbian Mexico. No matter, she is a splendid device. As the plot develops we see several facets to her life and personality develops. Several threads of narratives, the Christian conversion and the survival of the Indian gods and goddesses that the conversions have not managed to erase the anti-Semitism and the twists it took in pre-war Europe in Vienna, and Vera's very personal torments all weave in, making her quite a complex and layered character. She also has a secret that she keeps from the scholars who come to her hacienda for their research on the Huichol.

Betty is another vehicle, this time to portray the lives of the Cornish women who arrived here as the wives of the miners in the early 19th century. Desai has skillfully brought her to life in these pages with the way she loads her narrative with particular details carefully chosen to reveal character, history, and action as the Mexican revolution stirred by Pancho Villa and Zapatta gets underway. It is to her graveside that Eric comes to discover the meaning of his own journey.

It is a thoughtful book and a window to a slice of Mexican history and the Cornish immigration and their history of silver mining, all of it told in Desai's style with economy and grace. Most of the female characters in Desai's novels appear to make a genuine attempt to establish a warm, intimate relationship and restructure and rearrange their psychic existence. They strip themselves of the pretence which beguiled them into an evasion of the recurring sense of personal in adequacy. They find their retirement to the realms of illusion absurd and irrelevant and they appear to enter into a feasible equation with life. Her fiction has covered themes such as women's oppression and quest for fulfilling identity, family relationship and contrasts the crumbling of traditions, and anti-Semitisms. Desai uses her fiction as a site for studying the role of women in society and there by indirectly offer a critique of the existential social set up that marginalizes women. Therefore her novels can be called women's fiction.

WORKS CITED

Gopal, N.R., *A Critical Study of the Novels of Anita Desai,* New Delhi: Atlantic Publishers and Distributors, 1999.

Juneja, Renu, *Identity and Feminity in Anita Desai's Fiction, Journal of South Asian Literature* 22.2, 1987, pp.77-86.

Parmar, Virender, *Women in the Novels of Anita Desai,* Misc, 2000.

Ramamurthi, K.S., *The Indian Women Novelist in English, Littcrit 4.1,* 1978, pp.33-42

Upadhayay, Purvi N., *Narrative Technique in Bye-Bye, Blackbird, Critical Essays on Anita Desai's Fiction,* ed., Jaydipsinh Dodiya, New Delhi: IVY Publishing House, 2000, pp.107-122.

❑❑❑

12

Women in Anita Desai's Novels : An Appraisal of the Three Novels *Cry, the Peacock, Voices in the City* and *Fire on the Mountain*

MAITHRY SHINDE

Indian women writers are one of those shimmering stars whose writings have created a niche in the world of literature. As writers they have voiced their stance as effective contributors to the society through their works. In theme they have explored the atrocities and maladies to which the dominion stratum has been giving a deaf ear. As torch-bearers they have represented against the female sufferings, social and political prejudices resisting further maims. However, their themes eventually grew beyond voicing against suppression, addressing several issues of the society while celebrating their feminine demeanor that happens to trigger their confidence. Beyond feminism and discrimination, romance, spirituality and patriotism have also been used as motifs in their plethora of offshoots. It is through the writings of such veterans like Kamala Markandaya, Bharati Mukherjee, Anita Desai, Kiran Desai, Kamala Das, Arundhati Roy, Shashi Deshpande and Shobha De, that the effervescence of humanity, love, compassion and endurance have spread far and wide and across the globe.

Anita Desai a very promising Indian novelist in her works attempted to unveil the tapestry of the Indian subjugated women who were voiceless and unarticulated for many a centuries. Throughout her novels and short-stories she has depicted the struggles of the anglicized, middle-class women of contemporary India. Her novels present women, especially from the middle-class portray their psyche, their sufferings, emotions and desires. It is through her novels that one can say, light on the status of the woman is depicted. Feminism and man-woman relationship are the usual motifs that Desai promulgates on. Her protagonists are but a depiction of the 'Real Women' who have had varied experiences because of the culture and the traditions that have bided them. One can observe that her works feature women belonging to various strata of the society, in other words, her characters are not always the straight jacketed sufferers who have been victims of the patriarchal culture. Her women have grown from time to time and from novel to novel. They are all unique acquainting themselves to the audience, that they are still reflections of the society. The women portrayed in her novels have evolved from self-alienation to self-identification and self-assertion. The character's self annihilation is transported to emerge as self identified women, as the novelist's understanding of the world becomes more profound and matured. Desai's technique of treating each character in a unique way has made her writings page-turn novels. Although marital incompatibility is the backdrop of most of her novels, Desai's technique of treating each women in her novels emerge as exquisite pieces of that serendipitous bent of creativity. Each woman is a creation that has evolved from the womb of the writer's pen.

Desai's first novel *Cry, the Peacock* [1963] explores the psyche of Maya the protagonist and also the strained man and woman relationship. Maya, the wife lives in the dream world of having her husband Gautama around her, caressing, loving and embracing, if not at all times, at least at moments when she needs an emotional companion. Gautama is simple, practical and realistic in his approach. It isn't that the couple does not love each other, expression of love is varied. Maya wishes to have those cozy and fragile moments with Gautama that her physical and mental body yearns for. Gautama's manifestation of love towards Maya restricts with fulfilling his responsibilities towards her and providing her with all the material comforts that Maya is used to at her father's house. His profession as a lawyer makes him pre-occupied with his ablutions, and not understanding the mental and physical needs of his wife become a major setback in his relationship. The two are bound together but the relationship appears to be just a formality or for that matter a monotonous responsibility. Maya suffers immensely when her expectation each time is killed by Gautama's pragmatic approach towards situations and life. Her emotions are lacerated when she expects that congenial support from him when the pet dog Toto dies. Gautama expresses sympathy by arranging for the burial and consoling her in his own practical manner. She and her emotions are not understood she feels and treats him disdainful. Each time she feels ignored and alienated, each time her frustration and mental demands grow. Her inefficiency in coming to terms with practicalities and maintain a sunny disposition according to the vicissitudes of life is seen. "Telling me to go to sleep while he worked at his papers, he did not give any thought to me to either the soft, willing body or the lonely wanting mind" [9].

Their temperamental polarities give space for dissatisfaction and detachment. The mnemonic words of the astrologer that proclaim death to either of the couple in the fourth year of their marriage percolates her delirium. She evolves as a psychotic unable to find a rhyme or reason to have thoughts that could be constructive for herself or the family. Her perpetual thoughts about not being wanted ruffle her psyche while deadly thoughts seek refuge in her mind to lead her to something obnoxious. The solitary mind, Gautama's lovelessness, her motherlessness, the astrologers words haunt her to get into a vortex of death and annihilation. Search for oneself, search for companionship have superseded and destruction and damnation have become her ultimate resort. She nurses lethal desires as her mind is ruled by satanic thoughts, she exterminates Gautama and commits suicide in the end. Anita Desai's first protagonist is treated by her as a very defiant character making her become a slave to destruction-an outcome of isolation and alienation.

Anita Desai's novel *Fire on the Mountain* [1977] paints the three protagonists Nanda Kaul, Raka and Ila Das each with a different colour. The intricacies of relationship, the palpations of kinship are well depicted in this novel. After all the responsibilities she had doled out during her lifetime as the wife of a Vice-Chancellor, Nanda Kaul out of vengeance, wishes to lead a solitary life in her house at Carignano of Kasauli hills, void of responsibilities. One can see that Anita Desai has breached the paradigm of identifying woman as sacrifice incarnate in this novel. To speak of a woman who wishes to live those last days of her life just for herself and in serenity is unusual and Nanda Kaul is quite contended for having made such an attempt. She feels that she has lived enough for others, discharged her duties, her physical and mental being have been devoured thoroughly, she herself wants to be discharged. Her great granddaughter Raka's, visit does not overwhelm her, in fact it distracts her immensely. "It seemed hard, it seemed unfair, when all she wanted was the sound of the cicadas and the pines, the sight of this gorge plunging, blood-red, down to the silver plain [p.19].

Raka is no more than an irksome spot on the landscape of Kasauli, an intruder, and she moaned the thought of taking her responsibility. Raka's restlessness, her secret wanderings make Nanda Kaul reproachful. Soon Nanda Kaul changes her views of Raka as she sees herself in Raka, a person who longs for loneliness. Their clamoring for loneliness has different perspectives. If Nanda Kaul wanted seclusion because of her overwhelming past responsibilities, Raka was a recluse by nature, there was no scope for her to bind herself with anyone. She is the daughter of an ill-matched couple who reminiscences of the dreadful days and nights that have made her child-stoic. Although not blatantly expressed, she represents those countless children who bear the repercussions of self-indulgent parents. Raka develops a fanatical curiosity in the forest fire, a condition subjective to her inner conflict. Later by the end of the novel she sets the forest on fire, a demonstration of riot and anguish against the oddities of life to wipe out the old and futile and make room for the new and significant.

Ila Das another character is introduced as Nanda Kaul's friend. She has good relationship with the family also because of Mr. Kaul the Vice Chancellor who recommends a job for Ila as a lecturer in Punjab University. After the retirement of Mr. Kaul, Ila's stay under the new Vice Challenging becomes detrimental, hence she leaves the job and comes to Kasauli to work in the Social Welfare Department. This fetched her just a pittance, but still she never asks Nanda Kaul to allow her to stay with her, nor does she beg the grain seller for some extra grains. Desai introduces Ila as a good Samaritan, as a propagandist against atrocities, against the social evils, against child marriages in the surrounding village. "Well, so I go along my way, trying to do my duty, going from house to house and especially wherever I hear there's a child marriage in the offing, and threaten them and tell how them they can go to prison for committing a social offence" [129].

This invites fury of Mr. Preet Singh along with the other villagers. She emerges to obliterate the child marriages of which Preet Singh's seven years daughter's wedding is one. Ila is supported by a meager pay but wages a lone battle against the dictates of the society with strong conviction. Preet Singh vows to revenge her and while Ila is on her way home from Carignano after having met Nanda Kaul, he waylays her, molests and murders her.

Thus the three characters in Anita Desai's *Fire on the Mountain* are characters living in isolation. They carry with them the loneliness, but each character's contended portrayal gives scope for the reader to understand that woman and atrocities are complementary. Desai delves deep into the inner psyche of these characters very subtly thereby projecting the contended, the innocent and the victimized women. There is never a word of oppression or dissatisfaction uttered in the novel by the writer, still Anita Desai's technique of conjuring up with the characters is remarkable. Old wounds are uncovered in the intense heat of summer and tragedy becomes inevitable.

In *Voices in the City* Anita Desai's lucid and powerful expression makes it a reflection of the corrosive effects of city life upon an Indian family. It is the story of an Indian family where the siblings Nirode and his two sisters Monisha and Amla are caught in the labyrinth of social changes. Nirode is portrayed a dissatisfied young man whose aspirations do not see the day light because of his standoffish nature. As an employee being servile towards the bosses irritates him and hence plans to bring out his own journal as he does not believe in collaboration. There are instances when Amla the youngest sister gets to know of his unsuccessful pursuits, when time and place have given him nights of insomnia and despair. The novel unfolds to showcase that the city has involved these strange people plunge into exotic lost events.

> She began to get over the shock of seeing Nirode less than half the size he had been at their last meeting, four years ago, at the nervous and ceaseless movements of his skeletal hands, burnt at the finger tips to an iodine tinge by nicotine, at the unkempt and unclean mass of his long hair, his clothes, too big for him and worn thin, hanging loosely as shrouds upon his bony frame [153].

The other protagonist of the novel is the timid Monisha. She has faced immense ignominious situations in the hub of the joint family and can be called the subjugated one making her live a secluded life. She has been caught in the muddle of domestic chores of the family, her childless state, the oppression and humiliation meted out to her by the in-laws family. They all sum up to take a toll on her. Her better half Jiban proves to be a bitter half who has added to her distressed state. He is unconcerned about her well-being. Anita Desai portrays Monisha as one of those countless voiceless victims who endure the atrocities caused to them without even a whimper. Jiban is like many other men who take pride in the patriarchal culture and suppression despite knowing the fact that the wife is the major contributor within the family, contributions that are beyond materialistic ones, virtuous contributions of love, sympathy, compassion and endurance are all synonymous to her. Each time she has been run over and each time her instincts are rutted. Monisha does not live her life in reveries, expecting Jiban to love or caress her, in spite of her rudimentary needs not being taken care of. She is exploited every moment after her wedding and lives a life of alienation. She retreats from life by setting ablaze while finding no other resort for her distressed mind and body. Self annihilation seems a better option rather than self assertion. Unlike her sister Amla who chooses to learn from the lessons of life, Monisha has a myopic attitude towards life. She gives enough room for her convicts not to mend their ways and continue with their ruthless satanic deeds. Her inner trepidation goes unheard as she submits herself to self destruction.

Amla the youngest of the siblings is portrayed as a vivacious character who is all enthused like a zealot to climb up the world of advertisements in the new city of Calcutta. She is utterly disturbed at the sight of Nirode and Monisha who appear devoured by the nuances brought to their life. She gets to imbibe that their lives are in doldrums when she says: "this city of yours, it conspires against all who wish to enjoy it, doesn't it?"[153] Like a flower that blossoms amidst the slush, Amla is the consummate one who is not affected by the nitty-gritties of the life in Calcutta. As a commercial artist she moves to Calcutta after completing her studies in Bombay. She is a poised person who does not get worked up by the transition that happens despite her relocation. "I've come here to work,' she said, made defensive by that laughter. I've played enough in Bombay. And

I've heaps of ideas-I wonder if I'll get the chance to use them, as a commercial artist'" [154].

She has come with an indomitable spirit to pursue her career, but the real life, in the vicissitudes of the city, show her disgust and detachment. She is unable to maintain a sunny disposition for some time when she falls into the courtship of Dharma who is a sequel of her disturbed mind. She estranges herself from the tumult that she gets into and stands against the oddities of the city life. Unlike her sister Monisha she does not give room for despair and passivism and gets along with the regular pattern of life. Her exuberance and talent does deserve her ebullient life, but Anita Desai portrays her as a person who comes to terms with the sundry overturns of life. Desai has painted this character with a paint that has filled her with the best of colours filled with life, colours that are not fictitious but the colours that are and ought to be seen in every woman. Amla hasn't turned a neurotic like Maya from Desai's previous novel or timid like her sister Monisha. She is a person who deserves an appraisal for her sturdiness, for her rationality. Her extroversion makes her look for the possible good things that can happen to her.

WORKS CITED

1. Desai, Anita, *Voices in the City*, New Delhi: Orient Paperbacks, 2001
2. Desai, Anita, *Fire on the Mountain*, London: William Heinman Ltd., 1977.
3. Bande, Usha, *Amla Dharma Love: An Enigma in Voices in the City, Indian Women Novelists Set I, Vol III*, Ed., R.K. Dhawan, New Delhi: Prestige Books, 1991.
4. Agarwal, Krishna Avtar, *Post-Colonial Indian English Literature*, Jaipur: Book Enclave, 2007.
5. Desai, Anita, *Cry, the Peacock*, London: Paten Owen, 1963.

❑❑❑

13

Theme of Loneliness in Kiran Desai's *Inheritance of Loss*

SAROJINI SUDHA

Kiran Desai is the third Indian to win the Man Booker Prize in 2006. Her *Inheritance of Loss* is set in the Darjeeling Hills at the time when the Gorkhas initiated a Movement for a separate Gorkha land. The novel revolves around the lives of an embittered, retired Judge Jemu bhai Patel and his orphaned granddaughter Sai. Born in Gujarat in a peasant family Jemu acquired a heavy dowry and a girl of fourteen as his wife which made him possible to go to England and qualify for an ICS. Jemu Patel had a disappointing family life, losing his wife and daughter and having only the false pride and dignity. He returned to his house, an old mansion built by a Scot man, Cho Oyu to spend the rest of his days alone.

Desai deals with various themes such as colonialism, global conflicts, regional insurgencies, capitalism, economic disparity, exile etc.There is loss upbraided as the title suggests but the loss leads the characters to loneliness which ultimately becomes a sort of psychological disorder, that the character's identity is exposed. Her characters suffer from such loneliness or isolation. It is natural to be lonely but it becomes an imparity when the loss is profound and uncommunicative. Loneliness leads to frustration and self-hatred that draws them away from society, an introvertal situation, when instigated becomes madness. This condition can be expressed in various ways, as the case may be, by the different characters in the novel. The theme of loneliness or isolation is utilized to shape certain characters like J.P. Patel, Sai, cook, Biju etc to provide a particular vision on the crucial aspects of their identities. The writer applies such ideas of loneliness to express the social and inner isolation suffered by the characters. The realities in which these people live become harsh and intolerable for them that they are disappointed and dissatisfied in their lives that they isolate themselves from society.

Jemu bhai Patel suffers loneliness due to his racial self hatred. This is evident from the very beginning itself when he reached England for his studies. "He worked twelve hours at a stretch, late into the night, and in thus withdrawing, he failed to make a courageous gesture outward at a crucial moment and found, instead, that his pusillanimity and his loneliness had found fertile soil"(39).

This solitude later grew into loneliness and later a habit which crushed his identity itself. He was left aloof and ladies moved over when he sat next to them in the bus for the simple reason that "he stinks of curry" (39). He hated the oriental in him and he became a stranger to himself that he was obsessed with the awful quest for pale skin and European civilization. To the end of his life he suffered from inferiority complex.

The anglophile in him aggravated that he hated his wife, family, community and anyone for not being British. After serving the British as an ICS officer he returned to settle in Kalimpong in a crumbling old relic of a mansion from the colonial era. The tight calendar schedule of his life went on without obstruction and he enjoyed the life of authority. The arrival of Sai in the Cho Oyu household made the judge diffident and at a loss to provide the love and warmth she needed as he was hiding from his own life and lived a life of pretence. In spite of this her arrival made him remember his past and the terrible things he did to his wife and parents. There was regret in him when he thought about his unhappy father. His loving father walked away from him when Jemu blamed him for the unhappy familial life: "It was a mistake to send you away. You have become like a stranger to us" (306).

He wondered if he had killed his wife for the sake of false ideals. At one particular moment he even loved her. But he had robbed her dignity, shamed her family and his own just because they became unsuitable to his living and his position. The judge had a lasting love for his dog, Mutt. He could not bear to loose her too because in his lonely life Mutt was the silent companion who understood him better. Even Sai considered her grandfather an animal and dog human:

> Grandfather, more lizard than human,
>
> Dog more human than dog (32).

The dog always accompanied him – a quaint sort of a dog which "gazed at him like an adoring spouse" (34) when the dog was robbed the judge had gone to every door step in search of her and finally to the police station where they ridiculed him as they were engaged in more serious matters than searching a dog. The desperate Jemu went down his knees and prayed to God to return Mutt.

The final loss creates a madness in him that made him slap his cook black and blue. He knew that he could not endure the loneliness in the big house without his dog which was his shadow, his wife, his daughter, his friend, and himself. The only communication he had with his inner self is with the dog which understood the silence of the master. Without Mutt the judge is alone.

Sai, Desai's heroine is sixteen year old and lonely. She lost her parents in an accident that killed her space astronaut father and mother in Russia. She was left in a convent in Dehra Dun. Funds paying for her schooling and boarding at the convent school ran out and the nuns returned her to her sole known relative her maternal grand father J.P. Patel. Sai settled into the Cho Oyu house where there was no love and warmth but decay and deficit. She felt orphaned even when her parents where alive and so it made no difference when they were killed and she alone. "I am an orphan, Sai whispered to herself, resting in the infirmary. My parents are dead. I am an orphan" (27).

Life at Cho Oyu was not as she had expected. The morose grandfather was not a good companion that she took the company of the cook who was much friendlier. Later she formed a friendship with the middle aged sisters Lola and Noni who tutored her and kept her happy. Young and lonely Sai met the person who experienced the same loneliness and fell in love with him -- he is Gyan, a young Nepali student who was hired to teach her Mathematics. There is of course a powerful feeling of love or rather a companionship which saves her from despair and dispels her isolation. Bt Gyan is lost to her when he is absorbed into the 1986 Gorkha insurgency. She is thrown to desperation and longing.

"Sai thought of how it had been unclear to her what exactly she longed for in the early days at Cho Oyu, that only the longing itself found its echo in her aching soul". (223) The Movement of the Gorkhas had led the country surging with riots and Sai even blamed Gyan for whatever happened around. "Marooned during Curfew, sick about Gyan and sick with the desire to be desired, she still hoped for his return. She was bereft of her former skill at solitude" (250).

But Gyan did not come and she went in search of him only to be ashamed for him. They had a hot talk and Sai blamed him for the robbery of the gun at Cho Oyu. Furious Gyan pushed her into the bush and bet her with the stick. She was angry and insulted at her loss of Gyan. It was then that Mutt was robbed which created a confusion and misery and she felt grateful when she went searching Mutt in the large landscape around the house because, "Sadness was so claustrophobic" (309).

The sadness led to loneliness and then to madness during which she decided to leave Cho Oyu. Even towards the end she hoped for Gyan when she saw a figure move towards the house. "Gyan? She thought with the burst of hope. A message: I will love you after all" (324).

She no longer wants to be alienated from people especially Gyan but she is alone. Another person who lives a lonely life in the Cho Oyu house is the cook. He comes from the uneducated poor lot of the society who do not even deserve a name. His life there at the old house is to take care of the judge and his dog. He is the only person who established communication with the outside world from the house, but he is bound to be lonely who had lost his wife and also sent his son Biju off to work on a cruise ship which deposited him in New York. Living alone in a little hut, "It pained Sai's heart to see how little he had" (13).

He is an innocent country man who kept telling about his son in America, to everyone he meets, made him drive away his loneliness and he had a feeling that his son is nearby whenever he spoke about him. He was also fond of Mutt and when he was stolen he took the blame that it was his fault that Mutt was lost. In his desperation he drank a lot and confessed to the judge and took the punishment from him who bet him mercilessly. When Sai rushed to defend him the cook said: "Let him kill me. What is my life? It is nothing. Better that it is gone. It is useless to everyone. It is useless to you and to me. May be that will give you satisfaction it will give me satisfaction. Go on" (320).

This confession and this opening up dispel his loneliness unlike the silent judge or Sai and he is fortunate enough that his son Biju returns to him. Biju his son was unfortunate that he hopped from one bad job to another always in despair for acquiring the green card which he never could. Living in rat infested apartments, Biju's life is a juggling act and not at all far from the poverty, his father believed he had escaped. He bears the weight of terrible loneliness and did not know how to re-live alienation because, "He had been abandoned among foreigners "(99).

Biju home sick and missing his father, he returned to kallimpong when there was a violent insurgency. Without a green card and uncertain of his future he arrives home dressed in nothing but a woman's nightie. Gyan, the hired tutor was not a suitable person for Sai to fall in love. She realized that he was not as she had thought about him. "The house did not match Gyan's talk, his English, his looks, his clothes or his schooling. It did not match his future" (256). Sai at his door step felt distaste for him, then for herself. "How had she been linked to this enterprise, without her knowledge or consent?"(256). His love for her was only due to the isolation he felt. Later he joined the Gorkha Movement not as much for the course but as an outlet to vent his own rage and alienation.

Finally there was Noni - Nonita who lived with her sister Lola - Lalita in Mon Ami cottage. Lola lost her husband in a heart attack and her spinster sister Noni moved in with her. Living on a little pension the two sisters keep company with each other and to escape loneliness Noni taught Sai and thus the three lonely souls together forced isolation out. The other minor characters who share the sense of loss include Father Booty -- a Swiss priest, who runs an unlicensed Dairy and Uncle Potty. Everyone is in someway alienated by their environment and experiences clinging on to aspects of the colonial past and while not belonging to the old ways and not fitting in with the new. Loneliness becomes a complex psychological disorder that isolates the persons from social affairs and interactions as in the case of judge, to some extend Sai.

The identity of the person is created through the social, cultural interactions with people but loneliness or isolation deprives him/her of acquiring the completeness of identity. The problematic of identity is taken by Cornel West who theorizes the formation of Post modern cultural subjects as "Fragmented subjects pulling from past and present innovatively producing a heterogeneous product" (241).

Due to the identity crisis or non identity no one is happy in the novel. Everyone is missing something fundamentally in their lives and suffer some far of "separateness or loneness" that leaves them dissatisfied. The book has a growing sense of despair and decay but Kiran Desai ends the novel with the kind of golden luminous light that imparts and reveals truth and hope.

WORKS CITED

Desai, Kiran, *The Inheritance of Loss,* New Delhi: Penguin Books, 2006. (All the quotations are culled out from this edition).

West, Cornel, *Reader's Guide to Contemporary Literary Theory,* New Delhi: Pearson Education Ltd., 2007.

❑❑❑

14

Kiran Desai's *The Inheritance of Loss* : A Post-modern Perspective

SMITA A. MUJUMDAR

The term 'Post-modernism' means different things to different people. There are different versions of post-modernism. The word originally used in architecture by Toynbee. Soon it is known as cultural situation, a critical practice and an economic condition. Post-modernism is not synonymy for 'contemporary' even though it is certainly present in the contemporary context. In fact, the term post-modernism has been in vogue. It is a critical tag for a host of contemporary writings. The notable elements of post-modernism or post-modernist body of literature can be stated as:

1. Playfulness which results in cheating the reader in an unexpected resolution in the end.
2. Fragmentary nature of the work shattering the fictional illusion.
3. Form of personal idiosyncratic even weird vision of life. It provokes teases, confuses, amuses and bewilders the reader in a playful, formal manner. It jolts the reader into fresh awareness of the things, free from the pre-ideas. Post-modern view defamilarizes the world.

"Post-modernism as literary phenomenon owes its existence to the culminative impact of a number of pursuits and disciplines:

anthropology psychology, linguistic philosophy, literary theory etc. It is to be seen as a new kind of polymath having emerged in the eventful post World War II years" (Bhatnagar: 1999:3).

It is specific literary movement in culture and criticism. It is marked by radical indeterminacy. In Donne's words, it is - "The new philosophy, calls all in doubt. It is all in pieces, all coherence gone, All just supply and relation..." (Donne: 1611:23).

'Post-modernism' is a process of dislocating and disturbing a social order and social stability. The initial era of this century (21st century) is an era of deconstruction of construction of post-modernism. (Deshpande: 2007:21) Post-modernism is in fact, an international modern phenomenon not only in the field of literature but also in the areas of painting, dancing, music, film industry, medias like TV, journalism and economics of 'nations'. Post-modernism is very akin to the trends of globalization and multiculturalism. They have created a popular culture with features like rebarbarization and revalgarisation. It is complete liquidation of the ways of thinking. The new trends of post-modernism are: "breaking the frame, revising history, revisiting tradition, techno culture, hybridism, fact meets fiction, popular culture and high culture collide. Post-modernism then contains both destructive and a reconstructive tendency includes selflessness. Post-modernism with all its facets is reflected in literature.

Post-modernist literature is a one written after World War II and 1960's, initially it has sprung up in the states of America and Europe. The practitioners of post-modern movement have broken the modern tradition of liberalism and humanism by a variety of means. Post-modernism points to the collapse of western - liberal humanism. It is a reaction in this sense, to modernism. In some aspects it differs from modernism.

"Modernism cultivated austerity, post-modernism is interested in pleasure. Modernism tried to capture reality through individual consciousness which was equivalent to life, for post-modernism 'realism' is just an incoherent and deluding notion". (ebid: P.18).

To speak about post-modern English fiction, it differs from modern fiction. Post modernism inherits the fragmentary self. Postmodern novel is divided into non-fiction writing, problematic novel, tabulations, pop-fiction or science fiction etc. This kind of fiction is a most reactionary movement. It is so because post-war people faced a distorted decadent traditional humanism. Like Restoration literature, post-modern literature is characterized by licentiousness, down-gradation of art, liberty in any matter and and destruction of boundary line between art and non-art.

Post-modernistic literature has become global due to mass media. It got global range and affected the worldwide scenario. Eminent writers across the countries have written their fiction in the stream of post-modernistic thought and style.

Post-modern fiction is described as apocalyptic that is a literature that registers the dissolution of narrative, self and represented world. There is too much interpolation of verse in the form of songs, inter-textually preference or the colloquial to the formal language and inclusion of a large body of scientific information. People (characters) in it are neither liberal nor human, they are in fact, discouraged from being characters.

The sense of fragmentation in relations, in culture, in family and in nation is indicated through the strategies of techniques used in writings; in the use of montage and collage, in mixing of genres in an unexpected manner. Since postmodern culture is mass-culture, all canons are discredited, the traditional values are flouted, and culture is decanonized. Art is trivialized and carnivalzed. It reflects the comic or absurdist ethos of post-modernism. They mixed genres and media, modes of aesthetic thinking and conceptual art, film and literature, advent - grade and mass-culture, the tragic and comic, the sublime and ludicrous, interior monologue and magic realism.

All kinds of stuff are lumped together, into a form which reflects new aesthetics corresponding to the post-modern situation. Contradiction, permutation, discontinuity, randomness and short circuit are the six narrative strategies noted by David Lodge which are generally used by post - modern fiction writer. The plots in postmodern fiction are complex, incomprehensive. Unknowability is one of the major aspects of post-modernism. The themes in the post-modern fiction are globalization, multiculturalism, Diaspora, nostalgia, economic inequality, fundamentalism, terrorism and violence. Sense of loss, alienation, dislocation, disintegration, cultural displacement is the marked features of Post-modernism.

The post-modern novels illuminate the consequences of colonialism and imperialism of global conflicts and global changes due to economic policies dominated by America. The global and local conflicts of religion, race, nationalism, regionalisms have been in the thematic areas of these post-modern novels. The crushed values and shattered relations, cut off lives and loss of self, loss of identity and rootlessness, spiritual vacuum and quest for self, such are the concerns of post-modern writers. The rise of techno culture and media culture has connected the developing countries to the developed nations increasing the commercial economical purpose in every walk of life: Global economic changes affected life drastically e.g. moll-culture destroyed small shopkeeper's business. The policies of government, consumering and industrialization led Indian farmers to suicidal deaths. The rise of gatekeeper journalism, cultural imperialism interference of politics in every walk of life, corruption, bad effects of sex-dominated media (TV) cyber-crimes all these are results of globalization. It is now happening in contemporary period. And post modern writers have featured them in their writings. The development of science and scientific discoveries encourage them to write science fictions and there is a good number of science fiction.

Indian writers are not far away from these post-modernist movements and on-coming trends of post-modern world. The effect of post modernism or globalization over India like developing country is a mixed one. It is beneficial to limited group economically though it looses culturally and at the personal level of human relations. A large part of India remained untouched by the benefits of global revolution. In spite of global revolutionary economical changes the level of inequality between developed and developing countries are not reduced and there is no equal distribution of gains of globalization.

Today in India globalization appears to be Westernization or Americanization because of its unchallenged presence in the areas of economic activities and technological advancement, communication and warfare. It is and it can not be discarded. It is inevitable.

We now largely tend to associate globalization to post-modernity. Globalization is intrinsic feature of multinational stage of capitalism. The present role of India is not leading but of consumering in the process of globalization.

> It is not new to India. Its effect on India is notable. As third world society India is already divided society, 'Unity' and 'nation' (nationality) is lost. It is

> essential to resist globalization. In the process of globalization it aggravates uneven development existing between developed and developing nations. Though the world has become richer, it presents misery, made it a world of extraordinary deprivation and staggering inequality (*The Indian Journal of English Studies* - vol. X LIV 2001, P. 52).

It has been ever happening phenomenon in India in different periods and globalization - attacks on India are not new. But present phase is subtler than the previous encounters. It is most sophisticated and subtle for invisible institutions or interest groups from abroad and native come together and reap the consequent benefits leaving the nation subjected to fragmentation, division and loss. But Dr. Abdul Kalam has expressed hopefully that India will succeed in receiving globalization critically, judiciously and truly ensure fair and equal sharing of benefits of the process. He says in his *Vision India 2020,* "India has to excel in three domains of 'Shastra', 'Shastra' and 'Arthashastra". Only by doing so, will it succeed in eradicating inequality at eco-socio-political, at national, making its voice heard at international fora (*Ibid*: P.35).

Taking note of these all pervasive changes, in a brief survey of Indian fiction in English we can notice that the recent trends in global fiction nationalized as postmodernism have been successfully used by some recent Indian English writers writing in English.

In recent years, in the history of Indian English fiction Sulman Rushdie's novel *Midnight's Children* (1980) was the first Indian manifestation of the international trend of Post-modernist novel writing. With this novel there has begun a new era in the history of Indian English fiction. His novel was the major text to represent the spirit of the 'new novel' in regard to its form and content.

This new novel in India has embodied a new sensibility which is radically different from the Indian English novel of the earlier period of Raja Rao, Mulk Raj Anand, R.K. Narayan and even from the other generation of Anita Desai, Sahagal, Jhabwala and many other modern Indian writers of post-independence era. The Indian ethos influenced by freedom-movement or post-independent characteristic of socio-political and psychological novel is radically changed in new era of Post-modernism.

With *Midnight's Children,* other succeeding novels in India project a new perception and a new vision of Indian social, cultural scene with new approach. It is unmistakably Post-colonial and Post-modern in its spirit and identity. They have a strong post-modernist new on the planes of form and content that represents a breakthrough. Here came in swarming a host of new signatories intensifying the spirit generated by Rashdie's novel *Midnight's Children.*

Amitav Ghosh, Upmanyu Chattergee, Shashi Tharoor, Allan Sealy, Shobha De, Shashi Deshpande, Arundhati Roy, Kiran Desai, Vikram Seth, Sunetra Gupta, Manju Kapoor like post modern writers of 21st century have created a new novel with new perception about Indian life and Indian sensibility with their own experience and observation of the world wide trends in the wake of globalization.

> Their works have given a radical orientation to Indian English fiction. Indian English fiction is now on equal terms with its American and European counterparts. Moreover, their voices have been authentic, natural honest and full of confidence. Indian intelligentsia found their true aesthetic articulations in these work (Tripathy: 2008:33).

These writers are involved in the epistemological process to know, understand and communicate the Indian World of realities in the post-colonial period. They are highly innovative in their use of fair and aesthetic representation. They have subverted modernist modes, broke up narrative continuity, and violated usual syntax and coherence of narrative language. They used completely new modes of narration at graphic and colloquial levels. They have changed traditional ways of presenting characters emphasizing dehumanization of their characters.

The new writers represent contemporary Indian reality ontologically in its general or specific sense used by Mchale, the writer of 'Post-modernist fiction'. In true sense of the word:

> Indian English novel today is characterized by the elements of Post-modernistic fiction by presenting literary anomalies through colloguing of literary germs, resisting traditional literary modes of judgment. It has created an elastic frame which expands obediently to contain every kind of subversion (Connor: 1989: 126).

They also tend to subvert the foundation of our accepted modes of thought and experience in philosophical context. They too reveal the 'meaningless term, the underlying 'abyss' and 'voids' or nothingness of life. Thus we find in new Post-modernist Indian English novel, the incarnation of modernism and postmodernism. The Indian Post-modernists are in search of new areas of faith as a substitute for the debunked value system. In their fictional attempts of using new techniques they seem to belong to the contemporary mainstream of novel writing.

The novels like – *The circle of Reason (1980), English August (1988), The Great Indian Novel (1989), Bombay Duck (1990), Trying to Grow (1990), Memoirs of Rain, The Glassblower's Breath (1993), The Inheritance of Loss* (2006) and such many are closely related to the post-modern novels in America. They display all elements of Post-modernism with culturally fragmented and disintegrated form of life in the ethos of modern era.

The emergence of the new generation of Indian writing in English has been enthusiastically received recognition by the forgiveness even with awards of international status. Arundhati Roy, Kiran Desai, Arvinda Adiga have been awarded with Prestigious Booker Prize and many others may be in the nomination for it in future.

In the light of this successful and significant contribution of Indian English fiction to Post-modern movement in world literature, it would be better to concentrate and focus our attention on recently published and well acclaimed novel of Kiran Desai, *The Inheritance of Loss* in Post-modern perspective.

The attempt is made here after examining the concept of Post-modernism to trace out its elements in Kiran Desai's novel *The Inheritance of Loss* focusing the trend of globalization and multiculturalism which is at its thematic centre. In every respect The Inheritance of Loss is proved to be a novel of Post-modernist movement in its form, content, narrative strategy, language use, style and view point etc. However, the paper restricts to the thematic aspect of the novel in post-modern perspective.

In this novel Kiran Desai narrates the story of unsuccessful and tragic love affair of her female protagonist, Sai and her maths-tutor Gyan, but more than this, with touch of humour and irony Kiran

Desai explores into inexplicable and mysterious world where beauty and truth lie within reach but invisible. It is novel not only of love affair of Sai, the young girl. Sai is the observer and witness of such many things happening in India in modern-postmodern and recent years of globalization. The author tries to explore and put before us almost every contemporary international issue: globalization, economic inequality, fundamentalism, terrorism migration and such like post-modern problems. Yet it has a moral vigour. It is the story of how peace of mind and of peaceful place is disturbed by violent advent of global as well as local incidents.It narrates thus disturbed peaceful life of the old retired judge Jemabhai Patel who is living at the foot of mount Kanchenjunga in his home Cho Oyu, which at present shows little sign of its former glory. He lives in isolation, cut off from the present society and all hubbubs of modern life. He is cynic, eccentric, loves peace and loneliness. But all the tranquility and peace of his life is completely shattered by the unexpected intrusion of his granddaughter Sai. Sai comes to her grandfather after the accidental death of her parents. Her grandfather has to accept her unwillingly. Her arrival disturbs his isolation, he wanted to forget his past and it comes before him in the form of Sai. Sai is symbol of western culture rather of hybrid culture. Her western style, behavior and western medium culture causes tremendous sensation and psychological upheavals in the life of the judge. She manages well but he is disturbed. This is not only disturbance in his life but is at domestic or personal level. Also his life is disturbed by the intrusion of the revolutionaries of the separatist 'Gurakha movement' which was then in force.

The novel presents a live and sensational picture of the multi-problematic lives of the Indians who suffer a lot many globalized effects. This is the story of Indians who are flowing with a strange force in the unavoidable flow of modernization. It shows how post war conditions and problems of the western world have been spread all over the eastern world under the guise of globalization. The novel describes a world where people forgetting their culture of heritage, are biased about caste, creed and religion. It depicts a world of agonies, pains despair, disharmony and inhumanity. These all are gifts of globalization. The world came close by technical development and scientific progress but the humans are separated, the unity and integration is lost–It is fatal loss and 'loss' has become our 'inheritance'.

The title suggests such sense of despair and desperation due to this all-pervading loss. Unexpectedly Sai returns to her own land, her grandfather's land whose life she shatters, her falling in love of native of gurkhaland -- a Nepali is again shattering issue to both to herself and to her lover. Her parent's marriage had also been disapproved and she losses their company and love before she understands it well. She is not loved by her cynic and whimsical grandfather she seeks for true love and fails everywhere. Sai is true representative of Indian circumstances which has become hollow, yet searching for love and unity, harmony and integrity.

The problems and violence aroused due to demand of separate states have created havoc and humans are thoroughly separated from their own land and their own 'self'. Judge is such self-separated fellow, lives in loneliness. He is portrayed as an eccentric or sarcastic who ignores his family and friends and finds comfort in the company of his pet dog Matt. Sai's arrival forced him to recall his past, his wife & family whom he always looked down or insulted for the sake of his own false ideals.

Gyan, tutor and lover of Sai is such contradictory character who is a misguided Nepali youth. He is torn apart because of his love for Sai on the one hand and his hatred for everything that Sai represents in Indian Society. He is involved in both Sai and in the 'Gorkha separatist movement'. The circumstances pulled him into the movement and he cannot go back or accept Sai's love. It is the time of unrest when the whole of Kalimporg burns under the fire of separation - the GNLF fighting for the separatist state, the police hiding their own identity rather than protecting others, the common man in a state of fear and shock and death unexpectedly crawling over shadowing the grand and saintly Kanchenjunga.

With the story of Sai and her grandfather the parallel runs the plot of the pathetic tale of Biju, the son of cook in the house of the judge. He is working as a cook in America. He belongs to the shadow class of immigrants. His story brings in the theme of migration and human exploitation - His despair and pathetic predicament is pointed out with the modern problem of migration. He lives and works in America as illegal servant in Harish Harry's Gandhi cafe. Harish Harry exploits him cruelly and pays him low wages without providing any facilities. Such many immigrants are living in America and their parents and relatives in India are proud of them for their being in foreign countries.

Moreover, these youngsters are forced by themselves and their parents to go abroad (America) to earn money and not to think to return. Their parents do not understand their immigrant - class problem and the boys cannot speak openly about their desperation or exploitation. They have lost all glamour and hopes about their future and also lost their identity. They do not belong to either country, Biju is thus representative of this class-fellows. His father has told him not to return to India and he continues to live hard life in America like rich country. This is also effect of modernity and craze for modernity and craze for new cultural identity.

Biju notices the absurdity of America and suffers cruelty in the behaviour of the Americans and his master. But he is like slave; he becomes more conscious about his own wretched and helpless condition. He knows about himself that he is like an insect in the 'basmat rice sack' in his hotel. It is too absurd and ridiculous that his father thinks it is thing to pride when Biju is made waiter there and is called upon to prepare 'Angreji Khana'. He thought it is his promotion from Indian food maker to Angreji Khana maker.

Biju however, feels sense of exile without having any kind of social standing. The story of Biju in America and the judge in India is really the story of 'immigrated' exiled' and 'lost' Indians in their own country and abroad (in the stay abroad). The globalization brought the countries together economically yet the disparity between the developed and developing countries - has not gone. It has widened the gap at the cost of cultural loss. They have created master-servant issues in new ways. Russian communism failed in modern era but this new Americanism started affecting the eastern countries, eastern cultural life and relations of people in the third world. The dominance of American and slavish mentality of Asiatic is at the stake. Consequently, the conflict started to throw away this American dominance at global level and the wars in resistance of American dominance disturbed the whole peace and life of the world. It uprooted the values of life and its deceptive face created an attractive glamour, for third world countries.

The Inheritance of Loss pictures this entire post-modern scenario with multiple themes related to the post-modernistic trends. The novel moves between first and third worlds emphasizing the agonies of exile and ambiguities of post-colonialism. It deals with mixing up different cultures and its impact on Indian society which gives way to cosmopolitan culture. The author talks about the suffocating predicament of the low Indians working abroad. The inequality issue is not abolished in spite of changed Indian economical policy and entry of foreign rich and affluent civilization. Mobility and migration are the markers of our times and they feature commonly with the post-colonial subjects. Kiran Desai depicts this feature through characterization of Biju. The theme of nostalgia is in the story of Biju, his desperate efforts for survival in foreign country and his father's false notions about foreign status are ironically stated in the novel. Kiran Desai has presented miserable life of such many illegal immigrants living in America craving to return but can not return to their own country. Their pathetic condition becomes more and more intensive. This problem of illegal immigrants is a current issue which is discussed forcibly and effectively by Kiran Desai in this novel. Along with Biju are shown the nationals of Pakistan, Africa, Zanzibar, Malasia etc. These are the laborers that undertake ill-paid jobs in the hope of bright future, but receive only humiliation and exploitation. They are after green- card to live as legal citizens of America. They do not get it and remain illegal immigrants working like donkeys for their selfish master, living in the dirty places, hiding their identity.

The novel throws light on this current problem breaking through the traditional methods of expressions. In its honest efforts Desai tries to awaken a human consciousness to the hard truth of our existence, full of compassion for the people living in rich, modern techno-cultural ethos. Its characters represent the reality and actual reaction. Kiran Desai uncovers the invisible reality as she describes the lives of the people fated to experience the modern life as a continuous affront to their notion of order, dignity and justice. Her artistic power in expressing it is marvelous. She makes experiments with language. Here is used colloquial language of immigrants and Indians as they use it in its hybrid form which is called as 'khichadi' type English, suggesting that hybridity lies not only in culture but in language also. Such type English is a common feature of immigrants and Diasporas writers. It is specially used in the dialogic space of the text relating to lower and middle class characters of Indian society.

The Inheritance of Loss strikes many readers by many ways. It offers an overwhelming bitter view, "People in the west are scarcely aware of this overwhelming feeling of humiliation that is experienced by most of the world's population" (Orphan Pamal: 2008:9/11). The novel is a more remarkable for its attempt to portray realistic yet pathetic predicament of suffering lot a third world population than for its other Post-modernistic features regarding form and style etc.

All post-colonial apprehensions are reflected in this novel. It depicts post-colonial effects. The term 'Post-colonialism' seeks to emancipate the oppressed depressed, the deprived and the down trodden all over the world. The oppression could be political economic, social or gender based. There are two forms of colonization: one is the physical conquest of territories, the other is the colonization of minds, selves and cultures. The first mode is violent, transparent in its self interest and greed. The second is that of the rationalistic modernists and the liberals who claim to have the responsibility of civilizing the universal world.

Colonialism has faced to a certain extent ambiguity, nostalgia, inferiority complex among the certain classes of Indian society, which too and nakedly depicted in this novel with great caution and craftsmanship. Gyan, a Nepali boy suffering from inferiority complex, hates everything that is English, yet loves Sai, English mannered girl. He is highly prejudiced, bias-minded. Also we see colonial cultural enslavement in the character of Jemubhai Patel. He wants to adopt everything that is English and hates all that is Indian including his mother and wife. Thus the novel emphasizes the agonies of exile inferiority and ambiguities of Post-colonialism.

The novel deals with mixing up of different cultures and its impact on Indian society. The characters are racing between colonial and post-colonial India suffering the same feelings of loss, of nostalgia, of dislocation and displacement, exiled in every sense. They are mentally slaves to Post-colonization and strangers to their own homeland. It is most satiric narration of a disintegrated culture and pathetic predicament of Indians in Post-colonial and postmodern period. The novel concludes that in the modern situation the man with his biased, confused and racial attitude has lost the power of visibility and he walks with faltered steps towards the direction of unfair world. Unknowingly they enter the uncomfortable situation and unwisely they bring misfortunes to all. Imagination has taken new directions where people crave not for beauty and poetry but for separation and subjugation. The thirst for blood rises continuously and the quench is never satisfied. Humanity is in crisis, globalization is at stake and beauty is in chain. So the unfair world should uplift the biased veil to see splendors and truth in nature and inhale the aroma of life.

Most significantly, this disintegrated & fragmented picture of modern life and culture strikes the common reader. And the reader experiences the sense of awe and fear, as well as of absurdity and desperations, he experiences it in Kafka and Sartre. In a sense, it is continuation of modernity in post-modern literature. Yet it is seen that Kiran Desai poses the situations implying the need of love, harmony and truth. She describes in the end of the novel hopefully: "The five peaks of Kanchenjunga turned golden with the kind of luminous light that made you feel, if briefly, that truth was apparent. All you needed to do was to reach out and pluck it" (Desai: 2006:324).

WORKS CITED

1. Bhatnagar, M.K., *Post-modernism – An Introduction, Post-modernism and English Literature,* ed., by Bhatnagar M.K. and M. Rajeshwar, New Delhi: Atlantic Publications and Distributors, 1999, p. 3.
2. Deshpande, H.V., *Research in Literature and Language,* Kolhapur: Sukhada Saurabh Prakashan, 2007, p. 21.
3. Desai, Kiran, *The Inheritance of Loss,* Penguin Books, 2006, p. 324.
4. Donne, *Anniversary of the World,* 1611 ref. - in *Post-modernism and English Literature,* ed., M.K. Bhatnagar, New Delhi: Atlantic Publications and Distributors, 1999, p.18.
5. Singh, Avadesh Kumar, *Knowdge Globalization and Third World: An Indian Contextual Discourse, Indian Journal of English Studies,* Vol. XLIV.
6. *Indian Association for English Studies,* 2007, Katak, pp. 32-33.
7. Steven, Cannor, *Post-modernist Culture: An Introduction of The Contemporary,* Oxford: Basil Black Well, 1939, p. 126.
8. Tripathi, A.K., *Dina Mehta: No Rusdie's Child,* ed., Monica Gupta, *Women Writers in 20th Century Literature,* New Delhi: Atlantic Publishers and Distributors, 2008, pp. 33-34.

❐❐❐

15

Immigration is a Line of Attack to Scrutinize Individual Loss : A Bird's Eye View on Kiran Desai's *The Inheritance of Loss*

T. SASIKANTH REDDY

From the perspective of cultural hierarchy, this paper mainly discusses the influence on the Indian people of the novel *The Inheritance of Loss*[1] by Kiran Desai. *The Inheritance of Loss* is the winner of the Booker Prize for 2006. Its author Kiran Desai was born in India. She left for Britain at the age of 14, and moved to the U.S. a year after. She is the third Indian English novelist to win the Booker Prize after Salman Rushdie and Arundhati Roy, and she is the youngest woman winner. Her novel focuses on an Indian family in the 1980s and their struggle between two cultures.

"A magnificent novel of humane breadth and wisdom, comic tenderness and powerful political acuteness,"[2] so said Hermione Lee, the chairwoman of the judges of the Man Booker Prize for 2006, when she announced that Kiran Desai, with her novel *The Inheritance of Loss*, won the prize. The novel may be a sweet and delightful saga of an Indian family, but its humour can hardly cover the bitterness which infuses the novel. Characters in this novel are trapped between two cultures-the dominating Western culture and the 'degenerated' native counterpart-and find it difficult to solve the dilemma.

Along with the continuous cultural domination of the West from colonial days to the current globalizing world, the tension which comes into existence with the colonialism has not been weakened in the postcolonial world. This can be observed in *The Inheritance of Loss* that the cultural tension or conflict is not only between the British and the Indian as the previous colonizer and the colonized, but in a larger scale between the Indian and the Western culture which is now anchored in the United States. Despite the power shift in the Western world after the Second World War from Britain to the U.S., it is always the domination of the western culture that set India in a cultural predicament. Just as Kiran Desai writes in her novel *The Inheritance of Loss*, certain moves made long ago had produced all of them: Sai, Judge, Mutt, cook, and even the mashed-potato car.

In 1835, Macaulay wrote an educational *Minute*, which was to advise the British government of its policy on education in India. One of his statements, frequently quoted in later days, is that "we must at present do our best to form a class [in India] who may be interpreters between us and the millions whom we govern; a class of persons, Indian in blood and colour, but English in taste, in opinions, in morals, and in intellect"[3]. His words are often regarded as the best footnote to the later cultural and educational policies adopted by the British administration in India. In the 1850s, English became the medium of instruction in some schools and universities in India. Through the language of English, the western culture was introduced to and accepted by a class of Indians. And the education of English language and culture re-stratified the Indian society. Those Indians who received western education were recruited into the British administration and thus won a respectful social status.

A similar situation can be found in *The Inheritance of Loss*, where the Judge, who is born in a farmer's family, climbs up the social ladder and become a judge in the Civil Service through hard work in a mission school and then in Cambridge University. It seems that in colonial days, the western language and culture were equated with power, and were therefore greatly admired among Indians. In this way, the re-stratification of Indian society by English education resulted in the establishment of cultural hierarchy-the western culture occupied a predominant position compared to the native culture. The fundamental reason for the British colonial culture to establish itself as superior to the native culture is to justify its dominance in India. On one hand, the British colonists accepted this superiority so as to constitute its imperial power. On the other hand, the imperial centre wanted to instill this kind of cultural hierarchy in its colonizers so that it would sustain the colonial power.

Indian culture might be very difficult for the colonists to understand and appreciate in a short time or probably they did not even intend to understand it at all. For British people, India was a colony, a territory not legally obtained. What they needed was a seemingly right reason to govern this land. Cultural superiority seemed to be the best excuse. Therefore, by setting up a 'degenerated' image of native people partly through imagination or misunderstanding, they convinced themselves that native culture was far less sophisticated and refined than western one. On the other hand, the imperial center attempted to inscribe the thought of cultural hierarchy in natives to sustain the colonial power. The most effective method may be English education. There is an interesting scene in *The Inheritance of Loss* which may reflect the power of English education on establishing cultural hierarchy among natives.

For Indians, the acceptance of cultural hierarchy may be even more troublesome. It leads to some long-lasting personal dilemmas that are hard to resolve. One of them is the identity crisis. The judge Jemubai in *The Inheritance of Loss* may be the best example. As a boy growing up under the colonial project, finishing secondary education in a mission school and college education in Cambridge, Jemubai becomes a faithful follower of Britain. Recruited as an ICS (Indian Civil Service) member, he makes great efforts to be an official 'keeping up the British standards'. The pursuit of British standards shows his admiration toward Britain and his attempts to get into the imperial center. It also reflects his thinking that Britain represents a superior society to India. He studies hard to obtain more knowledge about western culture. In addition, he also keeps up the British standards in his daily life: to have afternoon tea every day, to speak English with an English accent, and to cover his brown skin color with the powder puff. But all his efforts are futile; he cannot be accepted by the center. Even though he is in the ICS, a British-originated institution, he works only to reinforce the domination of Britain, and he is never regarded as equal by the British administrators.

When returning to India, the judge is a 'foreigner' to his family, an awkward man with the habit of powder puffing. The powder puff is the symbol of self-denegation. He uses the puff not for improving his looks or protecting his skin, but for covering his brown skin colour-a cosmetic cover-up resulted from the racial discrimination he suffers during his study in Cambridge. At his arrival in England, the judge cannot find a house for several days, because the house owners do not welcome Indians. Attempting to get into the imperial center, the skin colour becomes the eyesore and the biggest obstacle for the judge. He then figures out to disguise, by the use of the powder puff. But back in India, powder is rarely used and if being used, it is only for the women. The family members cannot understand the judge's behaviour and some even mock him. A big fight bursts out between the judge and his family, especially between the judge and his wife; a sense of estrangement is set up between the judge and others. Therefore, the judge suffers a kind of double isolation. On the one hand, he is cut off from the colonial center. On the other hand, he is cut off from his culture and his family. And the double isolation traps him in the 'identity crisis'.

It is both the cultural difference and identification with the cultural tradition that defines one's identity; and the denegation of either may result in a state of loss. Yet the 'difference' here implies no cultural hierarchy. If the difference indicates a kind of superiority or inferiority, just as what the Judge considers, then it falls into the colonial mentality that all the reality and truth is established by the dominant. Thus the identity is unreal and the real identity is lost. That is why it is from the denial of the cultures as incommensurable and acceptance of the cultural hierarchy that all cultural conflict occurs. The judge's pursuit of British standards and attempts of disguising his skin colour implicates his complicity to the cultural hierarchy which denies the 'difference' as incommensurable. On the other hand, his failure to get into the center and his isolation from the Indian culture and his family corners him that it is impossible for him to form any meaningful cultural identification. He is stuck in an 'identity crisis'. The judge cannot understand that the denial of cultural hierarchy is the power to challenge the dominant, to unsettle the authentic and to disturb the centre. As we observe in *The Inheritance of Loss,* even though the judge experiences racial discrimination in Britain, he is still looking forward to an India dominated by Britain and the British lifestyle. He blames the disorder of India on the Indians and the Indian culture rather than the colonizers.

Kiran Desai in her novel *The Inheritance of Loss* expresses her idea that the fate of the Indians who were trapped in the East and West in the current age of multiculturalism and globalization seems to be doomed since the age of colonialization. This continuous cultural domination of the West nowadays results in the lingering of cultural hierarchy. The idea that western culture is more advanced and refined lingers in India. In colonial days, when the cultural hierarchy was accepted by Indians, they appeared as great admirers of western culture. The idea that the West stands for the civilized while the native does not still widely exist among many Indians. When Biju, the son of the judge's cook, applies for his visa in the U.S. embassy, he is with a group of Indians struggling to reach the counter window. The biggest pusher among them tries hard to impress the U.S. officials that he is civilized:

> He dusted himself off, presenting himself with the exquisite manners of a cat. I'm civilized, sir ready for the U.S., I'm civilized, mam. Biju noticed that his eyes, so alive to the foreigners, looked back at his own countrymen and women, immediately glazed over; and went dead[4].

It is probably one of the most agonizing scenes in the novel. Their eagerness for a U.S. visa results from a fancy image of the West as orderly and civilized. By accepting that the West represents the civil, the Indians actually deny themselves the possibility of being civilized. When Kiran Desai was asked in the interview: "There is certain in your tone when you describe the desperation experienced by Biju and thousands like him as they stand in line for a visa. What inspired you to come up with that particular aspect of the novel? Have you spoken to people like Biju in the US?" She says:

> I have stood in line myself at the American embassy many times and witnessed the scene unfold. I think poverty is so extremely close to us that it's practically the closest thing in our lives although sometimes we refuse to see it. It's every bite of food we eat that's been picked by someone poverty stricken and every item of clothing we wear. I've seen the efforts made on the Indian side to leave India. I get request for help in this matter every time. I return and in the states, in every restaurant and shop, in taxis all over Manhattan, I've heard the story on other side. I used

> to live near a bakery like the queen of Tarts and talked to the people who worked there and I lived with people from Zanzibar in the neighborhood that I describe, so that is also taken from real life[5].

The older generations of Indians who are inscribed with colonial mentality unconsciously become the helpers to spread the western culture and reinforce the western hegemony. Lola and Noni who live in the same village with the judge in Kalimpong are typical Anglophiles. They grow broccoli with seeds procured in England, wear Marks and Spencer panties, listen to BBC, read nineteenth century British novels, keep an empty jam jar with 'By appointment to Her Majesty the queen jam and marmalade manufacturers' written on its coat. Lola is so proud of her daughter being an anchor at BBC and she asks her to seek residency and not to come back ever after.

The cook always tells his son Biju his American dream of obtaining sudden wealth and living a modern life and makes every possible attempt to send Biju to the U.S. The judge asks Noni to teach Sai instead of sending her to a public school in Kalimpong because he believes that Sai will learn the Indian-accented English in public school. The older generation passes down their colonial mentality to the young. Though it does not mean that the young will think as exactly as the older, the colonial thought is to some extent passed down. In postcolonial world, in the eye of the West, the Indians, the people from the Third World remain at the bottom of society; their rights have not been guaranteed. In the basements of New York restaurants, as depicted in *The Inheritance of Loss*, are full of illegal immigrants form the Third World. The wage is little and the dream of wealth remains far away. They are being exploited, but they are unable to change their status.

In *The Inheritance of Loss*, we can perceive the attempt to resist western domination from the young people such as Biju, Gyan, and Sai, though the resistance is hardly effective. They are a little different from the judge and the cook who accept the existing cultural hierarchy whole-heartedly and make no effort to resist. They try to resist but they are still trapped by the influence of the West. Biju is sent to the U.S. by his father with a traveling visa. After his visa is expired, Biju works illegally in the basements of New York restaurants with many other illegal immigrants from the Third World. Biju comes to the U.S. with his, or rather his father's 'American dream', since it is always his father who tells Biju how modern the U.S. is and how easy to get rich there. Throughout the novel, Biju is fond of the modernity of the U.S. which he does not have the chance to experience though he is in the States. However, being in the west reveals to him another side of it, that is, the disorderly and the uncivilized side. The presupposed cultural reality of the west begins to collapse. One day, Biju amazingly discovers that Indian men in New York restaurants order beef without hesitation. The behaviour is certainly against Hindu observance, but it seems that they do not care at all. He at once feels repulsive towards this disorderly situation "One should not give up one's religion, the principles of one's parents and their parents before them. No, matter what. You had to live according to something"[6].

Biju's reaction or resistance toward the uncivilized of the West is a little more forceful when later Biju understands that he, with many other illegal immigrants in the restaurant, is actually being exploited. He has a fight with his boss, but what seems pathetic is that his fury about the imperial exploitation does not reduce his fondness of the modernity in the western society. Before Sai comes to live with her grandfather, she studies in a convent school where English is the teaching language and the English culture is what she learns. She leads a relatively lonely life in her grandfather's mansion in Cho Oyu until she meets Gyan, the Nepali tutor. The different backgrounds in which they grew up lead to diverse attitude towards the western culture and finally threaten their relationship. Gyan is aware of their different backgrounds when first dining with Sai, because Gyan uses his hands without a thought and Sai eats with a fork. Gyan is not familiar with the western way of eating. Later when he dines at the judge's house, his awkwardness with the fork and knife is shown again. Interestingly, he feels ashamed about it.

The sense of inferiority surging in Gyan is a result of his fondness of the western style yet his unfamiliarity with it. Annoyed about feeling inauthentic in the western culture which Sai and her grandfather are immersed in, Gyan retreats to his own culture so as to refuse the approaching any other culture. Joining GNLF (Gorkha National Liberation Front), he submits to "the compelling pull of history and found his pulse leaping to something that felt entirely authentic"[7].

Among Nepalese, he recovers a feeling of identification by

mocking on the judge's mimicry of the western lifestyle. In fact, even those participants in insurgency are not un-influenced by the western culture. They wear T-shirts of American brand and admire Bruce Lee, an icon of martial arts in Hollywood. As nowadays, more and more parts of the world are cross-related, rendering cross-cultural exchanges and influences inevitable. Gyan's relationship with Sai breaks up in a series of quarrel beginning from Christmas, which indicates his own dilemma in the encounter of two cultures. Sai sharply points out Gyan's fondness of the West and it is hypocritical and stupid for him to take refuge in the Nepali culture for a sense of authenticity. When fighting on Christmas day, Gyan argues that it is completely nonsense for a non-westerner to enjoy such a holiday, while Sai insists that it is only an excuse for a party, which shows her broad-mindedness toward a different culture. Grown up in the convent school, Sai, like her grandfather, speaks English better than Hindi and has a lifestyle more English than Indian. But that does not mean she is an Anglophile like her grandfather.

She refuses to accept the idea that the Indian culture is inferior. She feels humiliated and angry after she reads a paragraph written by an English writer, which advises all the Indian gentlemen, whether or not they have required the habits and manners of the European, not to enter into the compartment reserved for Europeans. The writer suggests that Indians should enter the one set apart for them because of their race. This is a piece of writing full of the sense of superiority as the colonizer intending to inoculate Indians with the colonial mentality, Sai feels angry about it and at the same time realizes the lasting domination of the western culture after the independence. She has grown up in the hybridity of two cultures and she accepts the difference of them peacefully.

In colonial India, culture difference indicates a kind of superiority or inferiority. From the denial of the incommensurability of cultures and the acceptance of cultural hierarchy, cultural dilemma like identity crisis occurs. The denial creates the superior and the inferior, the centre and the periphery, the dominating and the dominated, order and disorder, the authentic and the inauthentic, the powerful and the powerless. In the postcolonial world, this colonial mentality has to be rooted out, and the central position of the West destructed. Otherwise all the reality and truth will be established by the dominant center just as in colonial days. Kiran Desai, with her novel *The*

Inheritance of Loss, challenges the dominance of the West and the 'reality' of an orderly, civilized 'center' told by the West. In her novel, the depiction of New York City, the center of the center, reveals its disorder-the basements filled with illegal workers, and its uncivilness-religious people taking no notice of the religious disciplines. By showing the same 'disorderly' and 'uncivilized' state both in the center and the periphery, Desai unsettles the western hegemony and destructs the reality of center. The West no longer has the privilege to tell reality. The East has its chance to tell its version of reality and truth.

The Inheritance of Loss ends with the depiction of nature: 'The five peaks of Kanchenjunga turned golden with the kind of luminous light that made you feel, if briefly, that truth was apparent. All you needed to do was reaching out and pluck it'. Kiran Desai in the interview says:

> The second book isn't a book that is set entirely in India, but one that tries to capture what it means to live between East and West and what it means to be an immigrant. On a deeper level, it explores what happens when a western element is introduced into a country that is not of the west, which is what happened. Of course, during colonial times and is happening again with India's new relationship with the states. I also wanted to write about what happens when you take people from a poor country and place them in a wealthy one. How does the imbalance between these two would change a person's thinking and feeling? How do these changes manifest themselves in a personal sphere, a political sphere, over time? These are old themes that continue to be relevant in today's world the past informing the present, the present revealing the past[8].

For those Indians who have been silenced since the dominance of the West, they seem to get the chance to tell their version of reality. Though their voice may be brief, it is a meaningful attempt.

WORKS CITED

1. Desai, Kiran, *The Inheritance of Loss*, New Delhi: Penguin Books, 2006.
2. Harleman, Ann, *Luminous Family Saga bridges eras, cultures,* Atlantic

Monthly Press, 4, Jan, 2006.www.Boston.Comlbonsai_fba/file_ Based_ Image_ Resource.

3. Childs, Peter, ed., *Post-Colonial Theory and English Literature: A Reader*, Edinburgh: Edinburg University Press, 1999.
4. Desai, Kiran, *The Inheritance of Loss*, New Delhi: Penguin Books, 2006, p.183.
5. Malvea, Anushka, *Human warmth is such an innate part of India*, News letters, 30, Jan, 2006.Rediff.com/news/2006/jan/30.html.
6. Desai, Kiran, *The Inheritance of Loss*, New Delhi: Penguin Books, 2006, p.136.
7. *Ibid.*, p.160.
8. Malvea, Anushka, *A Passage of Loss: Conflict & Isolation under Globalization*, www.fdurop.fudan.edu.cn/stu/docs.

❑❑❑

16

Kiran Desai's *The Inheritance of Loss* Versus the Inheritance of Writing

LT. SATENDRA KUMAR

Newcomer Kiran Desai, who was born in India in 1971 and educated in India, England and the United States, is the daughter of highly praised Indian novelist, Anita Desai. Kiran Desai was fifteen when she left India -- she lived in England for a year and has been in the US since then -- and it's tempting to pigeonhole her as another NRI writer obsessed by themes like dislocation (something that certainly runs through *Inheritance*). In person, however, she comes across as someone who's never really felt out of place no matter where she's been. She's pleasingly unselfconscious about the topic of immigrants, joking (again from the outside, as if she isn't personally involved) about the various kinds there are: "Those who throw up their hands at the difficulties -- and, at the other end of the scale, those who are expert at playing the ethnic card, accentuating the character traits they are expected to have, and thereby making a success of their lives'. Desai feels 'no alienation or dislocation".

Kiran Deasi has written two novels *Hullabaloo in the Guava Orchard* (1998) and *The Inheritance of Loss* (2006). Desai wrote the novel, which is based partly on her family history, in her mother's house in Cold Spring, New York, in 'a completely happy atmosphere of stillness and peace', she said, speaking in a soft, Anglo-Indian lilt. 'The light in her house seems golden'. Mother and daughter worked side-by- side on their separate manuscripts during the day, then cooked together at night, Desai said, and drank rum. When she finished the first draft of *Inheritance*, 'it was an enormous mess', Desai said. She showed it to her mother. 'She was terrified and I was terrified'.

Indeed, *The Inheritance of Loss* is a rich, expansive work. It's about globalization, immigration and class, and Desai is now among a growing group of prominent young novelists of Indian background, including Arundhati Roy and Jhumpa Lahiri. The present article is a modest attempt to decipher at hatching the graph of the theme of dislodgment and hypocrisy that surely run through the novel. Kiran Desai reveals in one of the interviews:

> I think there are several kinds of loss that happen in this book. It is really a book about characters that have been forced to live half-lives or lives of hypocrisy because of the circumstances that they find themselves in. I found that when I writing it, everyone had that half-story to tell, which together added up to a picture that I felt was whole[1].

In the words of Roxana Robinson:

> A Whirlwind of a novel, rich and sad and funny. Kiran Desai moves between New York and the northeast corner of India; between the sense of loss and the sense of possession; between the big notion of colonialism and the small notion of intimacy. Desai's enchanting - often hilarious - descriptions are a pleaser to read'[2].

This majestic novel of a busy, grasping time -- every moment holding out the possibility of hope or betrayal - which is devoted to her mother who gave her the blessings (in disguise) of the inheritance of writing, opens with the following lines:

> All day, the colours had been those of dusk, mist moving like a water creature across the great flanks of mountains possessed of ocean shadows and depths. Briefly visible above the vapor, Kanchenjunga was a far peak whittled out of ice, gathering the last of the light, a plume of snow blown high by the storms at its summit.

> Sai, sitting on the veranda, was reading an article about giant squid in an old *National Geographic*. Every now and then she looked up at Kanchenjunga, observed its wizard phosphorescence with a shiver. The judge sat at the far corner with his chessboard, playing against himself. Stuffed under his chair where she felt safe was Mutt the dog, snoring gently in her sleep. A single bald lightbulb dangled on a wire above. It was cold, but inside the house, it was still colder, the dark, the freeze, contained by the stone walls several feet deep[3] (1).

Set in the mid-1980s in Kalimpong, high in the north-eastern Himalayas, *The Inheritance of Loss* centres on three people and one dog living together in an ancient house named Cho Oyu. There's the embittered, reptilian judge, lost in his chessboard and in his memories: of a youth spent at Cambridge many decades earlier; of humiliation in a foreign land. Staying with him (in this order of affection received) are his beloved dog Mutt and his 17-year-old granddaughter Sai, who was orphaned as a child. The judge's cook, who manages the household, and a few neighbours scattered around the area, round off the cast. As the story unfolds, insurgency is growing in the region: the Indian Nepalese want their own country or state, a Gorkhaland where they will not be treated as servants; young boys, trying to be men, roam the mountainside looting houses, collecting ammunition. Their predicament is contrasted against that of Indians settled abroad (the cook's son Biju, stumbling from one job to the next in the US, in a humorous parallel narrative).

Like Sai, the teenager in the novel, Desai attended a convent school in Kalimpong, where her family also had a summer home. In the novel, Sai falls in love with the impoverished Gyan, whose Nepalese family once provided cheap labor for tea plantations. The novel takes place in the 1980s, when ethnic Nepalese rebelled. 'They didn't have political and economic power', she said. 'It suddenly skidded into violence'. The Nepalese immigrant story, she said, parallels that of Biju in America, and of immigrant groups everywhere

Sai, who was studying in St. Augustine's Convent, heard the news of the death of her parents who were crashed by the local bus wheels, made her orphaned and compelled to take haven in the house of retired Judge residing in isolated house at the foot of Mount

Kanchenjunga in Himalayas. Judge was served by a faithful cook who was always lost in memory of his lovable son Bijju illegally immigrant in New York for job. The Judge first appointed Nonita or Noni as a tutor to teach Sai-Science to Shakespeare. It was only when Noni's abilities in Maths and Science began to falter when Sai was sixteen that the Judge was forced to hire Gyan twenty years old pal to take over these subjects.

It was Feb. 1986, Sai was seventeen and her romance with Gyan the mathematics tutor was not even a year old:

> Could fulfilment ever be felt as deeply as loss? Romantically she decided that love must surely reside in the gap between desire and fulfilment, in the lack, not the contentment. Love was the ache, the anticipation, the retreat, everything around it but the emotion itself (2-3).

When Gyan came to teach Sai the very first day his eyes rested directly upon her as if he were eating her alive in an orgy of the imagination. That night Sai sat and starred into the mirror: "Sitting across from Gyan, she had felt so acutely aware of herself, she was certain it was because of his gaze on her, but every time she glanced up, he was looking in another direction" (74).

Over the days, she found herself continually obsessed with her own face, aware that she was meanwhile whiting her aptitude for something else. When Sai became interested in love, she became interested in other people's love affairs, and she pestered the cook about the judge and his wife. She was more interested in traverse than in studies as the novelist revealed:

> Books were making her restless. She was beginning to read, faster more until she was inside the narrative and the narrative inside her, the pages going by so fast, her heart in her chest-she couldn't stop (68-9).

The novelist depicted the conversation between Gyan and the Judge (retired) when he came to teach Sai but Gyan found himself perplexed when he was quizzed by the Judge:

> 'So what poets are you reading these days, young man?'...Gyan racted his brains. He never read any poets. 'Tagore', he answered uncertainly, sure that

> was safe and respectable. 'Recite us something, won't you?'
>
> 'Where the head is held is high, Where the knowledge is free, Where the world has not been broken into fragments by narrow domestic walls...Into the heaven of freedom, my father, let me and my country awake' (109).

Hearing this Judge laughed in a cheerless and horrible manner. The novelist depicted the lives of their hypocrisy step by step in the novel in an exotic manner as if the novelist might have experienced in her life. In the drawing room sitting with newspapers, Sai and Gyan were left alone, quite alone, for the first time. 'For the first time his eyes rested directly upon her as if he were eating her alive in an orgy of the imagination-aha! At last the proof' (113). Their eyes read on industriously, but their thoughts didn't cleave to such discipline, and finally Gyan, unable to bear this any longer, this tightrope tension between thεm, put down his paper with a crashing sound, turned abruptly toward her, and blurted:

> 'Do you put oil in your hair?'
>
> 'No', she said, startled. 'I never do.'
>
> After a bit of silence, 'Why?' she asked. Was there something wrong with her hair?
>
> 'I can't hear you – the rain is so loud', he said, moving closer.
>
> 'What?'
>
> 'Why?'
>
> 'It looks so shiny I thought you might'.
>
> 'No'.
>
> 'It looks very soft', he observed. 'Do you wash it with shampoo?'
>
> 'Yes'.
>
> 'What kind?'
>
> 'Sunsilk'.
>
> Oh, the unbearable intimacy of brand names, the boldness of the questions.
>
> 'What soap?'
>
> 'Lux.'

'Beauty bar of the film stars?'
'Let me see your hands. They are so small.'
'Are they?'
'Yes'. He held his own out by hers. 'See?'
Fingers. nails.
'*Hm.* What long fingers. Little nails. But look, you bite them'.
He weighed her hand.
'Light as a sparrow. The bones must be hollow' (114).

So they played the game of courtship, reading, retreating, teasing, molesting, intoxicating and fleeing. '*Kiss me!*' He pleaded. 'No', she said, delighted and terrified. Moments clocked by precisely, and finally she couldn't bear it – she closed her eyes and felt the terrified measure of his lips on hers, trying to match one shape with the other. And there was a flood of kisses one after another without a moment's delay:

'Nose?' He kissed it.
'Eyes?' Eyes.
'Ears?' Ears.
'Cheek?' Cheek.
'Fingers'. one, two, three, four, five.
'The other hand, please'. Ten kisses.
'Toes?' (125)

Thus Gyan and Sai's romance was flourishing. The novelist captured the moment in the novel pornographically:

> She picked up the judge's powder puff, unbuttoned her blouse, and powdered her breasts. She hooked up her blouse again and that puff, so foreign, so silken, she stuffed inside; she was too grown-up for childish thieving, she knew, but she was filled with greed.[...]He clamped down on her, tussled her to the floor, and as more of that perfect rose complexion, blasted into a million motes, came filtering down, in a dense frustration of lust and fury - penis uncoiling, mottled purple - black as if with rage, blundering, uncovering the chute he had heard rumor of - he stuffed his way ungracefully into her.[...] Your eyes

> are lovely, dark and deep. [...] Drink to me only with thine eyes (166-69).

The novelist did not forget to reveal the inner soul of the protagonist Gyan after playing the act of sin:

> In the spare room, Gyan was wondering what he had done-had he done the right thing or the wrong, what courage had entered his foolish heart and enticed him beyond the boundaries of properties? It was the bit of rum he had drunk, it was the strange food. It couldn't be real, but incredibility, it was. He felt frightened but also a little proud (120).

On the other hand Sai too felt the same feeling in her heart as the novel unlocks: "Sai thought of how she turned to water under Gyan's hands, her skin catching the movement of his fingers up her and down, until finally she couldn't tell the difference between her skin and his touch" (129). At later stage Sai found herself bewildered when:

> Sai thought of how it had been unclear to her what exactly she longed for in the early days at Cho Oyu, that only the longing itself found its echo in her aching soul. The longing was gone now, she thought and the ache seemed to have found its substance (223).

Sai recapitulated the moment how she embarked on the path of blind curve and bog from where there is no return:

> In the end what Gyan and Sai had excelled at was the first touch, so gently, so infinitely, so they had touched each other as if they might break, and Sai could not forget that.
>
> She remembered the ferocious look he had given her in Darjeeling, warning her to stay away which she could not resist.
>
> One last time after refusing the acknowledge her; Gyan had come to Cho Oyu. He had sat at the table as it in chains.
>
> A few months ago the ardent pursuit and now he behaved as if she had chased and trapped him, tail between his legs, into a cage.

> What kind of man was this? She thought. She could not believe she had loved something so despicable. Her kiss had not turned him into a prince; he had morphed into a bloody frog (249).

The character of Gyan is depicted by the novelist like the butterfly tasting and sipping the pollen from different flowers and resting no where. In one of the scenes Gyan was found by Sai red handed in voluptuous critical situation: 'Does Gyan live here?' Sai asked despite herself (256). Suspicion shadowed the girl's face. It was an old, unsurprised sureness of ulterior motives, a funny look in a child. 'He's my mathematics tutor', answered the other girl (256). Still looking as if someone like Sai could only mean trouble, she set down the pot and went back into the house as the rooster rushed forth to peck the grain stuck at the bottom, climbing right inside, giving the hens a reprieve. At that moment, Gyan came out, caught her expression of distaste before she had a chance to disguise it, and was outraged. Gyan said: "How dare she seek him out to find her indulgence in pity! (256). He had been feeling guilty about his extended silence, was considering returning to see her, but now he knew he was quite right. The rooster climbed out of the port and began to strut about. He was the only grand thing around, crowned, spurred, crowing like a colonial: 'What do you want?' asked Gyan (257). She saw his thoughts recast his eyes and mouth, remembered that he had abandoned her, not the other way around, and she was bitterly angry:

> Dirty hypocrite.
>
> Pretending one thing, living another. Nothing but lies through and through (257)....How dare....How dare you not...?Why shouldn't I have....Her tantrums and fits....Her mean tears....Her crying, enough for all the sadness in the world, was only for herself. Life wasn't single in its purpose...or even in its direction....The simplicity of what she'd been taught wouldn't hold. Never again could she think there was but one narrative and that this narrative belonged only to herself, that she might create her own tiny happiness and live safely within it (322-23).

Above everything else, though, *The Inheritance of Loss* is a tender meditation on loving and loss. It is about how, in all our different ways, we wish to fit in. The fact of exile and how that exile affects the notion of home, how it colors perception and how it heightens the sense of wanting to belong are strong currents that run through this novel and make it a parable of times.

In a generous vision, sometimes funny, sometimes sad, Desai presents the human quandaries facing panoply of characters[4]. Whatever be the love and deportment of Gyan to Sai but Sai thought with a burst of hope. A message: 'I will love you after all' (324) and the novel sums up happily as Sai looked out and saw two figures leaping at each other as if the gate swung open: "The five peaks of Kanchenjunga turned golden with the kind of luminous light that made you feel, if briefly, that truth was apparent. All you needed to do was to reach out and pluck it"(324).

Besides the glimpses of the romance and sex which is the natural need of the youth the novel, beyond doubt, is replete with the Indian vernacular words sprinkled here and there in galore besides Gujarati and Punjabi words with acuteness and mindedness of which a few are as under:

> *nakhra* (5), *pakora* (6, 7, 11), *huzoor* (7, 45, 47), *hamara kya hoga, hai, hai hamara kya hoga* (8), *bar bar karta rehta hai* (11), *mithai* (12), *mia-bibi* (13), *pitaji, angrezi khana* (14, 16), *Oi, koi hai? Khansama? Uth, koi hai. Khansama?* (19), *salwar, desi* (22), *sooar ka baccha, uloo ka patha* (23), *kamala hai* (24), *baap re* (25), *laddoos, dhotis* (30), *pallu* (38), *aayiye, baethiye, khayiye, dhanyawad. Shukriya* (50) *o yeh ladki zara si deewani lagti hai* (51), *chapattis, jalebis,* (53, 56), haveli (56, 302), oo aaw, oo aaw (57), *kakas-kakis- masas-masis-phois-phuas* (58, 167), *chokra, murga-murgi* (60), *bania* (61), *dhobi* (63), *puja, hai hai, hamara kya hoga, hamara kya hoga* (72), *hubshi* (76, 101, 184, 185), *atta* (86, 103), *srikhan* (90), *bhai, dekho, aesa hai* (95), *peepul, choolah* (103), *angrez ke tarah, angrez jaise* (105), *rasata rook* (107), *ai yai yai ai yai yai* (120), *phata-phat* (131), *choli, lehnga, bilkul bekaar* (139), *kishmish, kaju* (140), *sala* (149), *puja* (153, 181, 238), *sunno kahani* (146), *paan, loki, tinda, kathal, kaddu, patrel saag* (176), *balli, amavas, hota hai hota hai* (179), *bhai* (182, 316), *bandar, yaar* (185), *rishi* (188), *Prasad* (189), *tamasha* (191), *chappals, durries* (203), *ghas phoos* (212), *kya*

cheez, gas maar raha hai (217), *goondas, chalo yaar* (218), *mujhe jaaane do* (222), *lathis* (225), *dehati* (234), *nimboo* (246), *salwar kameez, susu & potty* (254), *bhaiya* (261), *kheer* (268), *chaandni rate, pyaar ki baate* (273), *jawan* (276), *dalda saag* (281), *intezaam* (287), *ke liya jaenge, bhel puri khaenge* (298), *ekdum bekaar* (300).

Just see the use of Gujarati and Punjabi words like *kem chho* (Gujrati, 137), *wahe guruji ka khalsa, wake guruji ki fateh* (Punjabi, 286-87). As per the demand of the situation the novelist could not prevent herself by using pornographically words to suit the occasion like *machoot sala oloo ka patha chaar sau bees* (190), *bhenjoot* (287), *saala machoot* (289, 314), *kutti,* (289). The budding novelist also used compound words to decorate the novel with her acute use of these which are as under: hanky- panky, crick-crack (17), wishy- washy, lush-lashed (33), knick-nack (44), poky- poky (98), honky- tonk (106), lotions-potions (146), whoo-hoo (152).

In *Stone Town* the novelist made her characters eat *samosas* and *chapattis*, jalebis, pilau rice...Saeed Saeed could sing like Amitabh Bachhan and Hema Malini. He sang *'Mera joota hai japani...'* and 'Bombay *se aaya mera dost-Oi'*. He could gesture with his arms out and wriggle his lips, as could Kavafya from Kazakhstan and Omar from Malaysia and together they assailed Biju with thrilling dance number. Biju felt so proud of his country's movies he almost fainted (53).

Salman Rushdie, a family friend, describes their divergent styles this way: 'Anita is a deceptively quiet writer. Kiran is a little bit more showy as a writer. There is a little more flamboyance in the prose'. Unlike her mother, Desai said she doesn't think of marrying or having children. 'The isolation of writing settles in too deeply. It becomes part of your personality and your life', she said. 'If I had a child, I'd have to break out of it and be sweet. But as a writer I am trying to understand hate and anger'. Lately, Desai said, she has been longing for the solitude of writing to pull her back in. She glanced wistfully outside at the rain and the wet landscape, reminiscent this afternoon of Kalimpong[5]. At the age of 35, she became the youngest woman ever to win Britain's Man Booker Prize, for her novel *The Inheritance of Loss* - a career-stirring event for any budding novelist, but particularly so in her case, because it is an honour that has eluded her celebrated mother, Anita Desai, who has been a finalist three times for the prize.

Ergo, the novel depicts and reveals the secret that it is not the inheritance of loss rather the inheritance of writing which she acquired from her mother and achieved the place which her mother could not get as she is an inborn novelist. That is why the thirsty readers are waiting for her next novel to be in their hands *anon* in future.

WORK CITED

1. In one of her interviews published in the *Sunday Hindustan Times* dated 22 January 2006. Desai herself unlocked, 'I have really tried to capture the patterns- the emotional and historical patterns that I have witnessed. It has been a history that is caught between East and West and travelling back and forth'.
2. Quoted by Roxana Robinson, Kiran Desai, *The Inheritance of Loss,* New Delhi: Penguin Books India Ltd., January 2006, cover page.
3. Desai, Kiran, *The Inheritance of Loss,* New Delhi: Penguin Books India Ltd, January 2006. (All the citations are quoted from the same edition.)
4. Quoted by Binnie Kirshenbaum, Kiran Desai, *The Inheritance of Loss.* Cover page. He further unearths: 'A nation's tragedies, great and small are revealed through the hopes and the dreams, the innocence and the assonance, the love betrayed and the all - too human failings of a superbly realized cast of characters'.
5. *Inheritance* her second novel, was much harder to write than 'Hullabaloo', she said, taking 'seven years of my being determinedly isolated'. It almost didn't get published in England. 'The British said it didn't work', Desai said. Nearly 10 houses rejected it until Hamish Hamilton bought it.

17

Alienation, Anger and Angst in Kiran Desai's *The Inheritance of Loss*

KANWAR DINESH SINGH

Kiran Desai's *The Inheritance of Loss*[1] deals with several themes which include globalization, multiculturalism, nationalism, violence, inequality, class division, religion, immigration, different forms of love and relationships, besides colonial consciousness and postcolonial chaos, but throughout the novel there prevails a sense of alienation that keeps every character disconcerted. The cause of alienation is, however, unique in individual case. Dislocation, nationality, (im)migration, Eurocentrism, racism, fundamentalism, capitalism, class system, community, marginality, religion, education, gender, status, position and background - all are causes of alienation in one form or another.

Etymologically, the word 'alienation' relates to the Latin word *aliçnus* which means belonging to another person or place, from the root word *alius* meaning 'other' or 'another'[2]. Thus, as used in English from the 14th century, it refers to 'an action of estranging or a state of estrangement'[3]. There are several interpretations for the term given by psychoanalysts, psychologists, social thinkers and philosophers. But, in any case, alienation is a state of being emotionally separated from others and from one's own feelings. It is a powerful feeling of isolation and loneliness and in contemporary times, it also relates or (cross) refers to a feeling of loss, disillusionment, disappointment, cynicism, fear, angst, anger, radicalism, violence and several other forms of emotional maladjustments and psychological complexities. According to some psychoanalysts, alienation also stems from inconveniences caused by man's impotence, incapacity, limitation or helplessness to cope with surroundings and circumstances and his/her need to overcome that inability and powerlessness. Many a time, it is subjectivity that gives rise to alienation. An alienated conception or determination of conveniences and inconveniences forms alienated emotional states, alienated needs and alienated actions, and at times develops egoistic features of the character that are manifest in the form of greed, ambition, fanaticism, violence and fight for survival[4].

In the specific context of *The Inheritance of Loss,* the reasons for alienation in the characters are many - social, political, economic, cultural and psychological. Jemubhai, Biju, Sai, Gyan, Lola, Noni, et al - all have their personal as well as social reasons for their feeling of alienation, anger and angst in their respective milieus. Jemubhai Patel leaves for England for the first time and suffers from disillusionment with his image of England and at the same time gets alienated from his native land, culture and mores. In England, he feels isolated as he has difficulty in adapting to the western culture and civilization. He feels inferiority complex, humiliation and anger at the opinionated and colonial attitude of the Britons towards Indians. But, when he returns to India, he finds it difficult to accept the Indian ways as he is sophisticated and conditioned to be an Anglophile with the English mannerisms now. Cambridge-educated Jemubhai Patel who has worked as Judge in India decides to settle after retirement at Kalimpong near Darjeeling in a house called 'Cho Oyu', where he finds himself as a foreigner in his own country, distant from all. He is seen as bogged down by the dilemmas of postcoloniality. Since he was educated in England, his deportment is very much English, but at the same time he finds it hard to jettison the irons of the Indian tradition in which he has had his initial grooming and conditioning.

Jemubhai never forgets the day he voyaged as a student from India to England for the first time for his studies in law: "Many years had passed, and yet the day returned to him vividly, cruelly" (IOL: 35). The word "cruelly" refers to the nasty colonial experience he had during the period of his sojourn in England. He was moved at the very beginning of his journey to England by the discrimination that the colonizers showed against the colonized, when at the Bombay dock he found benches labeled "Indians only" and "Europeans only" (IOL: 36). On board, he started feeling ill at ease with his Indian ways as he found it difficult to get into the habit of the English. He finds the meals packed by his mother with love and care for him as inappropriate at the point in time, and "he lacked the courage to go to the dining salon on the ship, given that he couldn't eat with knife and fork ..." (IOL: 38). He felt humiliated and so he "picked up the package, fled to the deck, and threw it overboard...Undignified love, Indian love, stinking love, unaesthetic love - the monsters of the ocean could have what she had so bravely packed getting up in that predawn mush" (IOL: 38). Thus, Jemubhai's alienation from the native tradition, custom and milieu starts with his movement to England itself.

However, when Jemubhai reached Liverpool and further moved to Cambridge, he found himself shocked by the enormous difference between the foreign country and his own. He had in his mind a grandiose image of England, the country of the colonizers, which instead, appeared to him too small and congested and he was "unimpressed" and "It took him by surprise because he'd expected only grandness, hadn't realized that here, too, people could be poor and live unaesthetic lives" (IOL: 38). At this juncture, he started comparing the nation and the alien nation, where he became a victim of racial discrimination. He became upset by the behaviour of the foreigners toward him, including segregating and humiliating treatment by the ladies, as "even the hapless - blue-haired, spotted, faces like collapsing pumpkins - moved over when he sat next to them in the bus...The young and beautiful were no kinder; girls held their noses and giggled, "Phew, he stinks of curry!"" (IOL: 39). As nobody spoke to him, "he retreated into a solitude...The solitude became a habit, the habit became the man, and it crushed him into a shadow" (IOL: 39). He was all unsettled. Kiran Desai describes his condition in a poignant way:

> Jemubhai's mind had begun to warp; he grew stranger to himself than he was to those around him, found his own skin odd-coloured, his own accent peculiar. He forgot how to laugh, could barely manage to lift his lips in a smile, and if he ever did, he held his hand over his mouth, because he couldn't bear anyone to see his gums, his teeth...He began to wash

> obsessively, concerned he would be accused of smelling, and each morning he scrubbed off the thick milky scent of sleep...To the end of his life, he would never be seen without socks and shoes and would prefer shadow to light, faded days to sunny, for he was suspicious that sunlight might reveal him, in his hideousness, all too clearly (IOL: 40).

Eventually, Jemubhai "felt barely human at all" and dreaded and agonized over even necessary dealings at shops, as, for instance, in dealing with the fat woman who ran the corner store: "What can I get you? Say that again, duck...she said to his mumble, leaned forward to scoop up his words, but his voice ran back and out as he dissolved into tears of self-pity at the casual affection" (IOL: 40).

Albeit, Jemubhai attained success in making it into the Indian Civil Service and returned to India to serve His Majesty as a Judge. Having experienced an awful dislocation in England, he now finds he cannot make a place for himself in India - he is too English. He has been sent back to India equipped with a snake-bite kit, a twelve-bore shotgun and a tennis racket. Despite a glorious reception, he finds his wife repulsive and his people alien. He rejects his wife, his baby, his family, their ways and becomes more English than the English - trying (and failing) to hunt animals with his gun, eating toast for breakfast and crumpets for tea, and pouring all his love into his relationship with his dog, Mutt. He is a tragic and lonely figure even more than he was in England. With lingering of the colonial thought, Jemubhai is, thus, doomed to be always alien in his own country.

Another character in the novel, Biju, the son of Jemubhai Patel's cook, experiences a tough time as an immigrant in the New York City of the Unite States of America. Biju lands in America on a two-week travelling visa, but stays there for years as an illegal alien. He represents the underclass of illegal immigrants in the U.S. who make their living by doing cheap labour. He works in the basements of restaurants in New York with many other illegal immigrants from the Third World countries. Biju moves from one restaurant to another for a living, and at "Le Colonial" he gets "the authentic colonial experience": "On top, rich colonial, and down below, poor native ..." (IOL: 21). It is ironic that on top the restaurants have flags of America, France, Italy, etc. but below in the kitchen it is Mexican, Indian,

Pakistani, Guatemalan, Colombian, Tunisian, Ecuadorian, Gambian and so on and so forth. In another instance, when after a year in the U.S., Biju starts working at "Pinocchio's Italian Restaurant", he experiences racial discrimination, which Desai describes movingly:

> "He smells," said the owner's wife. "I think I'm allergic to his hair oil." She had hoped for men from the poorer parts of Europe – Bulgarians perhaps, or Czechoslovakians. At least they might have something in common with them like religion and skin colour ...The owner bought soap and toothpaste, shampoo plus conditioner, Q-tips, nail clippers, and most important of all, deodorant, and told Biju he'd picked up some things he might need ..." (IOL: 48).

But, Biju's "smell" does not improve and he is fired even from there. In all, he undergoes an anguish of isolation/loneliness in the alien land, and finds himself wedged between his longing and belonging: "Biju couldn't help but feel a flash of anger at his father for sending him alone to this country, but he knew he wouldn't have forgiven his father for not trying to send him, either" (IOL: 82). Thus, on the one hand, he feels "a pang for village life" while, on the other, he has to wait for the green card in any case. He can be seen on the horns of dilemma, whether to stay in America or return home.

While working in different basement kitchens in New York, Biju happens to meet people of different nationalities from across the world. From most of these people he comes to know of his country as their respective countries are full of Indians, and that it is difficult now to get rid of them. He is proud of his nation, but he is disappointed to see Indian people abroad eating beef. However, he solaces himself by telling that foreign cow is different from Indian cow, and so, it hardly matters: "The cow was not an Indian cow; therefore it was not holy?" (IOL: 76). While working in an alien nation, Biju becomes somewhat fanatical about his national identity, especially when it comes to dealing with the Pakistanis. The (stereo) typical antagonism of India and Pakistan is roused between Biju and a Pakistani as they happen to encounter at a restaurant, though both are working as waiters there. Whatever viewpoint Biju and his father have had about India earlier, he becomes an unyielding nationalist when he compares his nation with the alien nation. He shows hatred toward a Pakistani and even fights with him, because of which both of them are fired.

Feeling alienated in the foreign milieu, Biju hates being in the U.S. any more. He finds a number of people in the U.S. who "lived in the fake versions of their countries" (IOL: 267). He is disillusioned with the glamour of the alien land and desperately longs to return to India where he actually belongs, where he had the gracious company of his father, and where he was truly loved and valued. Although, the travel agent, from whom he inquires about returning to India, persuades him to stay in America and asks him not to be swayed by the soft feelings:

> But Biju said: "I have to go. My father..."
>
> "Ah, soft feelings, they will get you nowhere. My father, so long as he was alive, he always told me, 'Good, stay away, don't come back to this shitty place'"...
>
> "Don't say I didn't warn you".
>
> Then he grew more thoughtful. "You know," he said, "America is in the process of buying up the whole world. Go back, you'll find they own the businesses. One day, you'll be working for an American company there or here. Think of your children. If you stay here, your son will earn a hundred thousand dollars for the same company he could be working for in India but making one thousand dollars...You are making a big mistake..." (IOL: 269).

However, Biju is resolute to go back to his native country where he really enjoyed the prime of his life with the country boys. He has been fond of the modernity and affluence of the United States, which he does not find any chance to experience, though he is in the States. Conversely, like Jemubhai, he is disenchanted by the unruly, oafish and rough-edged side of the West. However, when Biju arrives in Calcutta, the unruly scene of the Indian life perturbs him and he confesses that leaving the U.S. was the biggest mistake he had ever committed. Thus, migration, besides poverty, is the cause of alienation and anger in Biju. He resorts to menial jobs in the U.S. for fulfillment of his ambition, but he becomes irate at the inhumane conditions of living and exploitative attitude of the unscrupulous restaurateurs. In the foreign country, he suffers from inferiority complex and harassment and faces enormous difficulty in coping with the circumstances; but, when he returns to India, he is disillusioned even by the lack of peace, integrity and harmony among Indian people. Despite disconcerting situation in India, he finds consolation with his father and his native land and people as and what they are. Biju's feeling of alienation is, thus, short-term, related to his travail of (im)migration.

Sai, the female protagonist of the novel, the granddaughter of Jemubhai Patel, is a young girl who, at six, was sent to St. Augustine's, a residential convent school, where she learned English and Western values, culture and way of life and that anything English was superior to anything Indian. The kind of education she gets at the convent does not fit in the society she enters when she is sent to Jemubhai, her maternal grandfather, at Kalimpong after her parents die in a car accident. Her maladjustment is also because of her dislocation, both physical and emotional, right from her early days. She comes from a broken family. Her parents worked in Russia leaving her in a residential school, and later on, when they die in a car accident, she is handed over to her maternal grandfather, her only contact in case of emergency, whom she has never seen before. So, Sai has been bereft of parental love and care and her childhood joy is shattered. She has her own emotional inconveniences and tensions, hard to recuperate. Besides, she feels alienated in her own country with the exotic education, "the flat creed", she has got: "cake was better than *laddoos*, fork spoon knife better than hands, sipping the blood of Christ and consuming a wafer of his body was more civilized than garlanding a phallic symbol with marigolds. English was better than Hindi" (IOL: 30). Nonetheless, Sai is delighted to leave the strict convent:

> "Good-bye," said Sai, to the perversities of the convent, the sweety sweety pastel angels and the bloodied Christ, presented together in disturbing contrast. Good-bye to the uniforms so heavy for a little girl ...Good-bye to four years of learning the weight of humiliation and fear, the art of subterfuge, of being uncovered by black-habited detectives and trembling before the rule of law that treated ordinary everyday slips and confusions with the seriousness of first-degree crime... The system might be obsessed with purity, but it excelled in defining the flavour of sin. There was titillation to unearthing the forces of guilt and desire, needling and prodding the results..." (IOL: 29).

Sai's grandfather understands that she would be a misfit with the people around because of the mannerisms she has learnt at the St. Augustine's and, therefore, engages Noni as tutor for her as he supposes if he sends her to a government school, she would "come out speaking with the wrong accent" (IOL: 34). She finds it strange at Cho Oyu, and describes her grandfather as "more lizard than human" and his dog as "more human than dog" (IOL: 32). But, later on, when Sai comes in contact and falls in love with her mathematics tutor Gyan, a Nepalese, she understands the real beauty of free breathing and values the new social circle she is exposed to out of her cocoon in the rigid and stern convent school as well as out of the clogged and claustrophobic air of her grandfather's house. Noni, her tutor has "looked her over critically" and discusses it with Lola "how bad it was for Sai to continue to grow up like this":

> "She won't pick up social skills... nobody her own age... house full of men ...."
>
> ....
>
> The way she'd been abandoned to the cook for years... If wasn't for Lola and herself, Noni thought, Sai would have long ago fallen to the level of the servant class herself" (IOL: 66).

Noni and Lola ask Sai to keep an appreciable distance from the servants and tell her about their tendencies, but she feels embarrassed to see the cook living in extreme poverty, in a wretched condition, stripped of all his pride, self-esteem and human dignity. He is no less an alien for her as they have different class levels and their relationship is all fake: "when she did come searching for him and enter, he was ill at ease and so was she, something about their closeness being exposed in the end as fake, their friendship composed of shallow things conducted in a broken language..." (IOL: 19). Even in verbal communication, they seldom get into deep conversations, "for she was an English-speaker and he was a Hindi-speaker..." (IOL: 19); yet she is moved by his caring and tender approach to her.

As Gyan gets imbued with the revolutionary spirit of a group of young men including his college friends associated with GNLF, the Gorkha National Liberation Front, he all at once becomes disgusted by Sai, her affluence and western ways and her family background and tells her that they are all like slaves to the Whites: "You are like slaves, that's what you are, running after the West, embarrassing yourself. It's because of people like you we never get anywhere" (IOL: 163). But, soon, Gyan realizes his mistake and apologises to Sai and "She too turned from this thought into his kisses" as he tells her, "I can't resist you, that's the problem..." and "She, the temptress, laughed. But human nature is what it is. The kisses were too soppy. A few moments more, the apology turned from sincere to insincere, and he was angry at himself for giving in" (IOL: 175). At the same time, "Sai at Cho Oyu also sat contemplating desire, fury, and stupidity. She tried to suppress her anger, but it kept bubbling up; she tried to compromise her own feelings, but they wouldn't bend ... "You bastard," she said to the emptiness. "My dignity is worth a thousand of you"" (IOL: 175). Thus, love, "so fluid a thing" between the two, begins to fall apart. Kiran Desai provides with the rationale for Gyan's decision to abandon Sai in a comprehensive way:

> Why should he not betray Sai?
>
> She who could speak no language but English and pidgin Hindi, she who could not converse with anyone outside her tiny social stratum.
>
> She who could not eat with her hands; could not squat down on the ground on her haunches to wait for a bus; who had never been to a temple but for architectural interest; never chewed a *paan* and had not tried most sweets in the *mithaishop* ...used paper to clean her bottom; felt happier with so-called English vegetables, snap peas, French beans, spring onions, and feared – *feared – loki, tinda, kathal, kaddu, patrel,* and the local *saag* in the market.
>
> Eating together they had always felt embarrassed – he, unsettled by her finickiness and her curbed enjoyment, and she, revolted by his energy and his fingers working the dal, his slurps and smacks. The judge ate even his chapattis, his puris and *parathas,* with knife and fork. Insisted that Sai, in his presence, do the same (IOL: 176).

He turns upset by her sheer lack of Indianness and "unnerved by how easily she gave herself" which is so "unsavory" of her (IOL: 175). In fact, he is confused altogether; he is swayed by the mass revolt and he incurs a strong feeling of alienation with the non-Gorkha people and takes a decision to become a martyr for the cause of the Gorkhas instead of wasting his life for Sai and people with and around her: "It was a masculine atmosphere and Gyan felt a moment of shame remembering his tea parties with Sai on the veranda, the cheese toast, queen cakes from the baker, and even worse, the small warm space they inhabited together, the nursery talk - It suddenly seemed against the requirements of his adulthood. He voiced an adamant opinion that the Gorkha movements take the harshest route possible" (IOL: 161). He discloses about the guns and other things at the Judge's residence to the revolutionaries, which leads to the gun robbery at Cho Oyu and things start worsening thereafter. Gyan is fraught with guilt for his actions - for his betrayal to his family, Sai and the Gorkha revolution, all three that fill him with a trilemma of which direction to choose. Gyan is, in fact, affected by the pressure of the revolutionaries, which makes him difficult to adjust with Sai. As a result of his association with the insurrectionists, he starts self-discovery, and ponders deeply over differences of backgrounds, financial conditions and social status, which alienate him from Sai and her world. It becomes difficult for him to adjust with Sai any more. Because of incompatibility, the bond of love between Gyan and Sai slackens before burgeoning any further.

Kiran Desai depicts the discontent of the Gorkhas among the non-Gorkha land in an engaging manner. She depicts how they feel dissatisfied and alienated in India as they are politically motivated for a separate Gorkha-land. They voice their strong resentment:

> We are laborers on the tea plantations, coolies dragging heavy loads, soldiers...We are kept at the level of servants... We are soldiers. Our character has never been in doubt. And have been rewarded? Have we been given compensation? Are we given respect?
>
> "*No!* They spit on us" (IOL: 158).

And the leaflets flooding the hillsides say: "Brave Gorkha soldiers protecting India - hear the call. Please quit the army at once. For when you will be retired then you may be treated as a foreigner". And promised that "The GNLF would offer jobs to its own, and a 40,000 strong Gorkha army, universities, and hospitals" (IOL: 160).

The members of the GNLF turn insurrectionary to have a peaceful separate country of their own but resort to violence and robbery to create it. At the outset of the novel, the GNLF boys, mostly in their teens, dressed in guerrilla fashion break and enter the Judge's house. In a later instance, these GNLF boys are found as having built camps on the property of the two women, Lola and Noni. One night, some of them broke into their house and forced them to feed them. The two sisters ask them to leave but they did not move. The sisters turn angry but helpless as they are, they lock themselves in a room, pushing a trunk up to the door. The boys only laugh and tease them, and mockingly tell them not to worry as they are now far too old for them. With such activities of the insurgents, there is distrust and anger growing among the residents of Kalimpong toward the Nepalese. Lola and Noni look even at their watchman with suspicion for the sole reason that he is a Nepali. Nonetheless, teasing, violence and anger, all stem from a feeling of alienation among the Gorkhas. It is their dissatisfaction with the political system and norms that get manifest in their alienated needs and actions.

The two sisters, Lola (Lalita) and Noni (Nonita) at 'Mon Ami' are living in the postcolonial chaos. Even at home, they are living as aliens to their surroundings. They do not mingle with local people and abhor their crude and countrified ways. They have a penchant for the English mannerisms and have loathing for the Indian things. Lola's daughter, Pixie, works as a news reporter for the BBC and Indians poke fun at her British accent. Annoyed by the Indian people, Lola asks Pixie to leave India and never look back. Noni has got education at a Catholic school, where, as she realizes now, her spirit had been demolished long before, and presently she starts seeing herself in Sai when she comes to her. She gives her instructions regarding how to behave as a lady and how to deal with the servants and low class people. They have their own predicaments making them estrange the indigenous ways. They are teased by the localists who despise them for their rude and alien attitude. Both are, in fact, maladjusted and full of psychological complexes, because of which they do not fit in the society.

The Cook, Biju's father, is no less alienated in the slavish employment at the Cho Oyu. He is lowly paid and is shown the least of human concern by the Judge: "Compressed childhood, lingering old age. A generation between him and the judge...There was age in his temperament, his kettle, his clothes, his kitchen, his voice, in the undisturbed dirt, the undisturbed settled smell of a lifetime of cooking, smoke, and kerosene" (IOL: 19). But he remains faithful and obedient to him. However, he has the worst feeling about the fact that he has been working for a family that has the least appreciation for him. At times, he becomes jealous of servants who were treated well by their employers. Upset by the kind of circumstances he has been coping with, he sends his son, Biju, to the U.S. for a better living and keeps supporting him by earning through extra work: "...selling his *chhang* ... He had first started a liquor business on the side for Biju's sake, because his salary had hardly been changed inn years. His last raise had been twenty-five rupees" (IOL: 54). Poverty and class discrimination are the cause of his angst, alienation and silent anger, which make him dream about a better world in the west. He becomes proud of his son working in the U.S. as he believes that "since his son was cooking English food, he had a higher position than if he were cooking Indian" (IOL: 17). All the same, his high imaginings of the west are shattered, when he comes to know of the realities of the west from Biju. And he consoles himself with the lot he is destined to.

In all, almost every character in *The Inheritance of Loss* suffers from a feeling of alienation and has some kind of angst as well as anger towards individual circumstances. All the characters are maladjusted in their respective milieus and have to cope with tensions, confusions and dilemmas. All have tug-of-war situations to struggle with. Almost all the characters are moving through trying situations of life, where they find humiliation and misery. Although all of them survive their tribulations to a considerable extent, yet they carry with them pains and peeves of their dismal and distraught past. Besides, all have unfulfilled desires leading to losses or inconveniences of some sort, besides differences of class, community, race, creed, gender, nationality and monstrous growth of globalization, which result in discontent, frustration, regret, anger, angst, and alienation.

WORKS CITED

1. Desai, Kiran, *The Inheritance of Loss*, New Delhi: Penguin Books, 2006. (All subsequent references to this work have been parenthetically incorporated in the text.)
2. Toad, T.F., ed., *The Concise Oxford Dictionary of English, Etymology*, Oxford, New York: OUP, 1996, p. 11.
3. Williams, Raymond, *Keywords: A Vocabulary of Culture and Society*, Fontana: Crook Helm, 1976, p. 29.
4. http://www.sarovic.org.

□□□

18

Kamala Markandaya : *Between the Two Worlds*

SHUBHA MUKHERJEE

> Kamala Markandaya (Purnaiah Taylor, 1924-2004) is an insider-outsider in that she is an expatriate, who has been living in England for a number of years. Markandaya's fiction evinces a much broader range and offers the great variety of setting, character and effect, though her quintessential themes are equally few – viz., the East-West encounter, the woman in different life-roles. The East-West encounter takes two forms – first a direct relationship between Indian and British characters, and secondly the impact of the modern urban culture brought in by the British rule on traditional Indian life [*A History of Indian English Literature,* p. 236].

Most of Kamala Markandaya's novels persistently present the picture of India struggling against odds and trying to surmount them. She confronts a tradition-oriented society and learns to live under the twin forces of heritage and modernity: "a fundamental dualism in her novels – she tries to criticize the tradition which she has inherited, but at the same time in a sense tries to renew it" [*The Novels of Kamala Markandaya, Reassessing Feminine Solemnity,* p.137].

Markandaya confines herself to the life lived in the villages and cities of South India. She is also critical of the traditional attitude towards women in this male dominated society. In *Some Inner Fury* the novelist refers to the silent barriers against women:

> There is a tradition not only in India that women should not be worried, that the best way to ensure this is to keep them as far as possible in ignorance. Certain domains belong to men alone, the Indian women learn early not to encroach [*Some Inner Fury*, p.117].

She dwells upon the theme of urbanization in Indian villages and its disastrous impact on human life in India. The coming up of a tannery on a rural society produces stress on the people and Markandaya is concerned about the impact. K.R.S. Iyengar has rightly pointed out: "Markandaya's writing is very suggestive and feminine. If her writing is less rich in imagery it has more ease and partakes more of life's fitful fever."

Kamala Markandaya feels the crisis of her generation on her pulse. Her response is feminine and, so, very deep. She perceives the pain of transition: from rural culture to urban set-up, from the complacence of a dependant nation to the sense of responsibility or irresponsibility that comes from newfound independence, from agricultural pattern of life, from superstitious acceptance of what is given to scientific challenge, from fear of society and God to an existential mode of thinking; in short, from tradition to modernity.

Nectar in a Sieve, Markandaya's first novel, is lyrical and moving and can be read on a variety of levels. On the most basic level, it is the story of a rural peasant life in a south Indian village. On another level it is the tale of indomitable human spirit that struggles with poverty and unending misfortune. Finally, it is a novel about the conflict between a traditional agricultural culture and a burgeoning industrial capitalist society. The novel touches on several important social phenomena: the importance of traditional cultural practices, people's reluctance to change and the impact of economic change.

In *Nectar in a Sieve* Markandaya takes us to the heart of a South Indian village where the tradition-bound villagers still depend on agriculture as their source of living. The story moves around Rukmani, the female protagonist, who has been the source of perennial love and solace for her family. Married as a child bride to a tenant farmer,

Nathan, she comes to her husband's village and works side by side in the field with her husband to earn a living from the land. Rukmani and Nathan are the product of a culture where the birth of a son is a blessing and that of a daughter a sort of curse. Rukmani, though quite liberal in her views, is not free from this bias. As luck would have it, her first child is her daughter Ira. She is sad and her sorrow is expressed in her words: "I turned away and, despite myself, the tears came, tears of weakness and disappointment; for what woman wants a girl for her first born?" [*Nectar in a Sieve,* p.19]

Nathan does not express his disappointment. His behaviour, however, shows his preference for a son: "He wanted a son to continue his line and walk beside him on the land, not a puling infant who would take with her a dowry and leave nothing but a memory behind" [*Nectar in a Sieve,* p.20].

After the birth of their daughter Ira, Rukmani fails to conceive further and seeks modern medical assistance from Kennington, the kind-hearted British doctor and social servant. She is then blessed with one son after another but she keeps her meeting with Kennington a secret even from her husband because she knows that the tradition-loving people of the village will never accept her bold step.

Gradually the condition of her house deteriorates and they have to fight hard for survival. With remarkable fortitude and courage Rukmani seeks to meet changing times and fight poverty and disaster. She sees one of her infants die from starvation, her daughter becoming a prostitute and then giving birth to a son who resembles a foreigner. Then she learns of her husband's infidelity. Although it is a traumatic event for her it does not uproot he; rather it strengthens her to withstand this emotional upheaval with greater courage. Her sons, except Selvam, leave the land for jobs, which she does not approve of and yet she somehow survives.

Nathan's infidelity hurts Rukmani but like a traditional Indian woman she accepts it with courage and self-control. For a modern woman it is difficult to accept an unfaithful husband as a result of which homes break away, stress and strain over-rule one's personality and hatred reigns everywhere. Markandaya tries to show that there is power in acceptance and familial bond strengthens with this power. The love, faith and trust that Rukmani and Nathan have for each other invest them with a stoic calm to face the worst in their life. The matrimonial bond between Rukmani and Nathan rests serenely on the solid foundation of trust, faith and understanding.

Gradually industry and modern technology invade the village in the form of a tannery and from its impact sinister consequences issue. It is very difficult for the tradition-bound village folk to adapt the modern industrialization with its changing values and wavering culture. Some, no doubt, accept it hoping for a better future but in most, including Rukmani, a sense of insecurity, fear and despair crop up: "Fear, fear of the dark future, fear of the sharpness of hunger; fear of the blackness of death" [*Nectar in a Sieve*, p.83].

But change is a must and either willingly or unwillingly one has to cross the barrier and step into the modern world of industrialization. Even when Nathan and Rukmani leave the village they meet with frustration and the only hope that they get is from Puli, their adopted son. A tenure of thwarted hopes, deprivations, hunger and tragedies, take toll of Nathan's life. Their last moments of togetherness are poignant and touching. They forget the gruesome realities of their unhappy existence, pangs of regret, repentance and sorrow, and sit together enveloped in thoughts of joy and married bliss they had. There lies the superiority of a traditional woman - to find peace of mind in the most inconvenient situation. Finally after the death of Nathan Rukmani returns with Puli to her village home and Selvam and Ira are overjoyed. There grows some hope in the forlorn heart of Rukmani as her own children as well as her adopted son rebuild their lives on the graves of the past, in the hope to retrieve traces of nectar in the sieve of life.

In *Nectar in a Sieve* Markandaya is mainly preoccupied with the sufferings of peasants in colonial India. She, therefore, views the problem of human relationships in this novel, in the context of economic forces, social evils and vagaries of cruel nature. She also celebrates the basic virtues of traditional Indian women - love for husband and children, a sense of sacrifice for the betterment of family, and delight in fertility. These are the qualities modern women seem to have little regard for, and therefore, the hearts of such women are devoid of simple pleasures of life to which Rukmani belongs. Gradually, of course, as the novel concentrates on the suffering of Rukmani and Nathan at the hands of rapid industrial growth, the fertility symbol, which is dominant in the beginning, becomes dimmer and dimmer. The coming of the tannery symbolizes industrialization and urbanization but on the other hand it also represents artificiality and unnaturalness of life and it becomes the embodiment of all the evils that money brings.

The central theme of the novel is the identity crisis resulting from a clash between western value systems and Indian value systems. The symbol of progress, the tannery, with all its pollution and corruption which it engenders, stands for western value system of materialism and agro-industrialism, while the idyllic rural life as depicted by Rukmani stands for Indian rural value systems. The Indian peasant is conditioned to work without hope, to leave everything in the hands of God and bear all sorrows and sufferings with a sense of fatalism which a Westerner cannot accept.

In *Some Inner Fury* Markandaya's thematic concern is the encounter between the tradition-loving East and the fast changing world of the West. The narrator heroine of the novel, Mirabai, belongs to a traditional Hindu home but she has been brought up in an anglicized manner. The novel recounts the tragic love story of Mira and an Englishman, Richard. Richard respects Indian culture and despite certain obstacles he is infinitely tender in his love towards Mira. Mira breaks all bonds of convention and surrenders herself in the arms of Richard. Mira's successful attempt to come forward to assert her individuality and adulthood creates a disapproving rustle among her elders. She herself is astonished at her courage to throw off the shackles of her conservative upbringing. This is not something very unconventional for Richard, as he is born and brought up in an altogether different cultural and social milieu. Mira gets an opportunity to see the variety of life in Richard's company as for the first time distinction between 'dos' and 'donts' is obliterated. Although she enjoys this freedom, her traditional background keeps her rooted. But in the company of Richard she tears off all bindings and searches for her own identity. Later, however, she takes up a journalistic career and engulfs herself in the fervid flames of patriotism and very courageously sacrifices even Richard for 'her people'. At this juncture she is a complete woman, traditional and bold enough to proclaim her values and priorities in life fearlessly.

Premela, the other unfortunate woman, is totally engrossed in Indian culture and tradition. She is married to Kit, the anglicized brother of Mira, and as is expected of an Indian wife she makes a sincere and desperate attempt to adopt herself wholly to her husband's personality and her inner self revolts. Finally she releases herself from all social constraints and involves herself in humanitarian service where her life takes a new meaning.

The third female protagonist in the novel is Roshan who is a non-conformist and unlike her counterparts, is Westernized and sophisticated. But her non-caring Western attitude becomes unacceptable in society and therefore Markandaya very cleverly implants a patriotic zeal in her. Roshan's rebellious nature is transformed and she destroys her foreign goods and restores to homespun sarees. The author endows Roshan with a spiritual power and embellishes it with an aura of patriotism. Therefore, Roshan will survive in society but has to compensate for it with her individuality. Although Roshan was a divorcee and Mira was 'living' with Richard, there is something common in both the women: they both shed their individual selves and engross themselves in their pre-destined roles that have been traditionally bestowed on them.

A Silence of Desire narrates the story of a Swamiji around whom revolves the conflict of religious belief and scientific reasoning; tradition vs. modernity. Dandekar, a senior clerk, is happily married to Sarojini and has three children. Sarojini is traditional and superstitious but her husband is modern and questioning. The smooth happy life of the couple is shattered when Dandekar comes to know about Sarojini's visits to the Swami. She then discloses to her husband that because she has a growth in her womb she visits the Swami to get it healed. She reveals that she has kept her visits to the Swami a secret only because Dandekar will not understand her:

> But I do not expect you to understand – you with your western notions, your superior talk of ignorance and superstition ... And mine is a disease to be cured and so you would have sent me to hospital and I would have died there [*A Silence of Desire,* p.88].

Dandekar wages a war against abstractions like the superstition of his wife and the 'immense spiritual power' of the Swamy. To fight a man would have been easier for him but to wean away his credulous wife from the firmly grounded faith is very difficult. It is a clash between faith and reason, superstition and science. C. Paul Verghese rightly remarks:

> The conflict between the husband and the wife is

treated in the novel as a part of the conflict between Science and Superstition. The novelist in presenting the conflict does not make an outright condemnation of superstition or faith healing Swami. She attempts to strike a balance between Science and Superstition.

Possession focuses attention on the strange love-hate relationship that exists between the East and the West and emigrants' quest for her identity. The relationship between Valmiki, an Indian goat-herd keeper and born painter, and his mentor, the rich English heiress Caroline, is the encounter between the tradition-loving East and the materialistic West in the context of human relationships.

Caroline who represents Western materialism, fails to possess Valmiki, who in the initial stages is lured by the luxuries but is finally drawn to India where his spiritual roots lie. The clash between the East and the West - between their respective cultures, values, traditions, convictions, and most important of all, between human beings who personify their virtually irreconcilable worlds - remain the focus of attention throughout the novel.

A Handful of Rice is conflict between traditional Indians and modern affluent. Men like Ravi abandon the traditional village life; comes to the cities in search for a living, and finally fail to sustain themselves in this high demand competitive world. Still they cling on for they cannot go back to the past. They struggle hard in the city, hope for a better future ahead and finally succumb to starvation.

Ravi's life, from birth to the close of the novel, has been a prolonged search for better existence, a hectic seeking after his own identity. He is simply one of the hapless, hopeless angry young men of this century. Throughout he is in search of a decent life, lost in the perplexing question of self-identity in the midst of dehumanized urban surroundings and people.

The novel *The Coffer Dams* centres on issues relating to tradition and modernity, scientific attitudes and human values, a rational approach to nature and an emotional response to its changing moods and freaks. The conflict is even symbolized by the death of the tribal chief at the emergence of scientific and technological knowledge and at the establishment of new factories and industries, dams and buildings. The dam becomes a symbol of modernity, encroaching slowly and steadily over the tradition-bound and unenlightened village in the lap of nature.

Like *A Handful of Rice,* Two Virgins also depicts the clash of values between village and city life, tradition and modernity. The novel is about two sisters, one of whom trades away her body and soul lured by city splendor while the other watches the city from a distance but feels safe to return to the lap of nature. Typical of modern youths educated in public schools, Lalitha, the elder sister, begins to criticize Indian religion and culture in an attempt to prove her liberal attitude to life. She leaves for the city without her parents' permission and the film world finally disillusions her. Saroja, the younger sister, on the other hand, despite her desires, remains a 'virgin' for the simple reason that she is in the hard grip of fear and distrust.

Lalitha and Saroja both are in search of identity and they pursue two different directions in this search. Lalitha pays heavily for belonging to the city; she is totally exploited and wrecked yet she feels that it is the city that she belongs to. Saroja, on the contrary, is quite disciplined and practical and thus saves herself from the dangerous clutches and corrupting influences of the city. Saroja symbolizes the dewy freshness and innocence of village life, gradually withering in the aftermath of India's rapid industrialization. She looks yearningly to the city and to the West, has a taste of urban life, but feeling disappointed she comes back to her rural life, where lay real happiness for her - all else being ephemeral. She is also conscious that the village cannot remain permanently insulated from urban influence and that innocence and virginity could be spoilt by the acid touch of the city.

The theme of East-West encounter becomes more persistent and pervasive in the *Nowhere Man.* It is the story of Srinivas who ultimately belongs to no place, neither to the land of his birth nor to the alien country where he settles down; he can go back neither to traditional India nor accept modern England. A 'nowhere' man his heart shuttles between the conventional and the contemporary.

The Golden Honeycomb recounts India's struggle for freedom and it reveals the nationalist's deep love for her motherland. In the novel we come across a series of touching events, pitiable strikes, baffling agitations and lockouts and Kamala Markandaya turns her attention to the historical events that affected India during the British rule.

In *Pleasure City* Markandaya focuses on the encounter between the East and the West on the one hand and the clash between tradition and modernity on the other. It is the slow and steady spread of Western science and technology on the remote coastal regions of India lying on the lap of nature and enjoying a calm, quiet beauty of their own that forms the central theme of the novel. If the fishing village represents poverty and backwardness, Shalimar the holiday complex represents progress and industrial development brought about by the scientific approach of engineers and technocrats.

Set in the 1980s, *Bombay Tiger* tells the story of Ganguli -- who arrives in Bombay with little more than ruthless ambition, and becomes the city's biggest industrialist. Ganguli is the representative of a changing India, post the era of high socialism and beginning to be transformed by private enterprises. Unfortunately, the multifaceted world of Bombay business that Markandaya attempts to expose, a world characterized by Ganguli, does not convince the readers and Markandaya comes off sounding vague.

Kamala Markandaya's novels depict balanced and harmonious man-women relationships. Her protagonists are average men and women who do not run after individually and want to remain united to face poverty, social change or political fanaticism. The external factors of their existence are so threatening that intimate familial ties assume crucial importance for their lives. In their struggle for survival, on the physical level, their emotional bonds become their source of strength, security and happiness.

Like Jane Austin, Kamala Markandaya works within the family fold the primary ties within the family fold are esteemed and cherished. Nevertheless, in the modern age these fundamental bonds have become fragile under the pressure of in-built personality traits, a quest of identity and external stresses, economic and political upheavals. Consequently, temperamental properties influence even basic human relationships. When relationships break, there is a crisis. This crisis is not only psychological but also social. Kamala Markandaya tries to explore the nature of this crisis.

In the context of Indian culture, marital and filial bonds assume great significance since the familial ties are considered sacred in our country. All relationships - whether matrimonial, filial or sibling - are based on the idea of doing one's duty ungrudgingly. All successful and satisfying bonds are based on a spirit of sacrifice and self-denial. However, the changed temperament of the age, when a distinctly individual identity is the cherished dream of every individual, has dealt a severe blow to the traditional concept of primary relationships. These ties are being seen from a different perspective altogether. Subtle cultural and intellectual changes, responsible for a shift in emphasis, from a collective destiny to an individual identity, are causing great upheaval in the psychic ecology of the contemporary man. The modern man is therefore living in a psychologically tense, socially dynamic and economically uncertain milieu which is not conducive to the establishment and development of gratifying interpersonal relationships.

When Kamala Markandaya looks at the West through the eyes of the East, it is a traditional Indian woman viewing the modern culture which has come from the West with suspicion, awe and temptation, and when she looks at the East through the eyes of the West it is a modern person viewing Indian tradition with skepticism and, more often than not, hatred. She brings out clearly the barriers of arrogance, colour and cultural differences that kept the East and the West apart. In the words of C.D. Narasimhaiah:

> Generally her novels reflect her strong penchant for Indian values as against the spiritual impoverishment of the English society, but Indians are not spared. Actually her good men and women come from both cultures.

In each of her novels there is a crisis, a tension, and an attempt to come out of it through the sacrifice of the 'good'. The basic message is religious, as in a successful tragedy. Human nature, social set-up and fate: each is a character playing a complex role and finally it is the moral victory of the person who has sacrificed the most. In the Indian social tradition she sees much that is evil and also discovers strength enough to generate resistance against deviations, and in industrialization and other things with which we associate 'modernism' she sees economic prosperity as well as the pain of uprooting. Her ambivalence makes the drama of conflict most appealing. Her sympathies are with tradition, particularly the age-old values, but she accepts the inevitable change as an aspect of history. Though herself not a hard core feminist, her keen perception of the plight of a woman has inspired many writers to go much ahead of her – towards feminism.

WORKS CITED

1. Naik, M.K., *A History of Indian English Literature,* Sahitya Academy, 1982.
2. Geetha, P., *The Novels of Kamala Markandaya, Reassessing Feminine Solemnity, Between Spaces of Silence: Women Creative Writers,* ed., Kamini Dinish, New Delhi: Sterling Publishers Private Limited, 1994.
3. Iyengar, K.R.S., *Indian Writing in English,* New Delhi: Sterling Publishers Private Limited, 1993.
4. Narasimhaiah, C.D., ed., *Indian Literature of the Last Fifty Years: 1917-1967,* Mysore: The University of Mysore, 1970.
5. Markandaya, Kamala, *Some Inner Fury,* London: Putman, 1955.
6. Markandaya, Kamala, *Nectar in a Sieve,* USA: A Signet Book (Penguin Group), 1956.
7. Markandaya, Kamala, *A Silence of Desire,* Putman, London, 1960.
8. Markandaya, Kamala, *A Handful of Rice,* New Delhi: Orient Paperbacks, 1985.
9. Markandaya, Kamala, *Two Virgins,* New Delhi: Vikas Publishing House Pvt Ltd, 1983.
10. Markandaya, Kamala, *The Nowhere Man,* Sangam Books, 1974.
11. Markandaya, Kamala, *Bombay Tiger,* New Delhi: Viking (Penguin Books), 2008.
12. Markandaya, Kamala, *Possession,* New Delhi: Jaico Publishing House, 1994.

❑❑❑

19

Human Relationships and Political Upheaval with Special Reference to Minor Characters in Kamala Markandaya's *Some Inner Fury*

SHISHU PAUL

Kamala Markandaya (1924-2004) is unquestionably one of the most outstanding among the women novelists who have enriched Indian fiction in English. She has to-date ten novels plus one published posthumously to her credit. The centripetal force in these novels is India racked by confusion, violence, economic disparity, convulsive social and political changes, political conflicts, the Independence struggle, Quit India Movement, the East-West conflict, cultural disparity, political rebellion, disorientation of values, etc. As a creative writer Kamala Markandaya "provides variety and vividness to these themes..." (Dodiya: 2).

Her novels have sociological interest as they allude to several features of Indian society. One refreshing feature of these novels is the transcending of the barriers of region and caste. The novelist is simply not interested in a person's caste and she does not emphasize regional characteristics. As a keen observer of life in India, she must have noticed the continuing hold of casteism and regionalism on our society. As an artist and thinker, she has exercised her right of selection and deals with her characters as individual Indians and not as representatives of any narrow section or creed. It can be confidently said that her India is a united India with a culture and soul of her own.

Her fiction is of particular interest within the context of the modern Indian novel because it crystallizes various literary directions that the quest for identity has taken since the 1930s. Two main directions – philosophical and sociological – are clearly discernible. Markandaya's novels, noted for Indian ethos, portray India in throes of social change. She succeeds in arresting in fictional forms the Indian mind in its conflict between the old and the new; the traditional values and the Westernized modernity. In this respect, Shiv K. Kumar aptly observes:

> Of all the Contemporary Indian novelists writing in English, Kamala Markandaya is the most accomplished, both in respect of her sensitive handling of a foreign medium and her authentic portrayal of the Indian Scene. What distinguishes her most incisively from Other Indian novelists is her acute awareness of a gradual shift in values that has been taking place in this Sub Continent during the past two decades or so (qtd. in Singh, 1).

Markandaya's disastrous experiences and hardships of the National Movement affected her emotionally and imaginatively. Her vision always remains objective and positive. R.S. Singh opines that she is "to a large extent unbiased and balanced; her aim is to display how various attitudes [and human relationships] and ideologies shaped the human destinies in the context of the British regime in India" (qtd. in Arora: 16). Basically, "she is an impressive explorer of human...intimate interpersonal relationships ..." (Bhatnagar: 1).

Markandaya's second novel *Some Inner Fury* is "...set against the backdrop of political unrest of the 40s reverberates the essence of the east west conflicts of that era" (Indianetzone) and it is "primarily a political novel dealing with the straining of human relationships in the wake of Quit India Movement" (Nawale). Besides, the three distinct attitudes to Western political and cultural domination through various characters, especially Kit, Roshan, Premala and Govind and also the encounter between the East and the West is also being explored in the love story of Mira and Richard which is set against the background of the national freedom movement and where conflict of loyalties leads to the final parting of the lovers. It is true that the "central concern of the novel is the clash between passion and patriotism" (R.S. Singh, 138). The plot of this novel is woven around the Quit India Movement of 1942. Actually, in 1942, "the Indian National Congress passed the famous Quit India Resolution, asking the British to leave India. As India was the brightest jewel in the British Empire, the British were against the Independence Movement. However, in 1947, they had to leave India" (Nath: 4). The novel also shows the effect of political upheaval on human relationships. Besides, the novel "represent[s] the problems and prospects of establishing intimate and meaningful relationships between two racial and cultural groups" (Aithal: 84).

The unnatural and savage hatred for the British ruler felt by most people in India during the days of struggle is graphically depicted in the novel as it "presents an India caught up in the maelstrom of her sanguine struggle against the British rule" (Kumar: 207). Govind incites his followers to violence. He makes them set fire to the newspaper office where he himself worked for twenty years. He is disappointed to hear that the English man who had been his boss has escaped. Banners put up in the streets have messages of hate: "...a hate such as only an occupied country can generate" (165).

Markandaya depicts, in this novel, how, when freedom is suppressed, resentment spreads among people and resistance gets organized on a large scale. It also "describes how the rich young men and women like Roshan, Mira and Govind, plunge themselves into the vortex of the national movement" (Raizada: 145). When a country is engaged in a painful struggle for liberation, it is quite natural that either some individuals within themselves or individuals and groups with one another experience a conflict of loyalties. Markandaya shows the conflict as creating divisions in one and the same family – that of Mira. Mira is in love with an Englishman and has experienced complete union with him, but she is also averse to Western ways of life and the British as masters. When they come to part their ways, Richard automatically joins the group of Englishmen, and Mira, with the same spontaneity, joins her compatriots. She is "torn between passion and India's independence ..." (Ramesh, 146). The final parting between Mira and Richard is clearly symbolic of the parting between India and Britain. Mira herself confesses that for them there was no other way, the forces that pulled them apart were too strong. But, nevertheless, the "freedom-struggle is clothed in the haze of romantic love ..." (Naik: 19).

The theme of cultural clashes assumes multi-dimensional aspects in this novel. The novelist highlights two important aspects of India's confrontation with Britain – the impact of the Western education and civilization on the outlook of Indians and the conflict between India and Britain arising out of its political dominance. In this connection Roshin George rightly maintains: "Kamala Markandaya is a writer who often took for her themes the Indian societies under the influence of the West" (70). India's contact with Western culture and civilization led to the emergence of the three distinct types among educated Indians. One, there were extreme fundamentalists who stuck blindly to the old Indian tradition and values. They were solely averse to the British ways of life. They were deeply hostile to the British rule in India. They thought British rulers a scourge in India and did not hesitate to resort to violence and conspiracy to drive them out of the land. On the other extreme were those who had been greatly influenced by the English education. They found nothing valuable in their ancient Indian culture and way of life. They were completely anglicized. These people occupied high positions in the British administration in India.

Between these two extremes stood the middle group of people. This group had drawn inspiration from the liberal and democratic values. They had developed cosmopolitan and broader international outlook on life. This group was deeply concerned about the freedom of their country and the large number of national leaders belonged to this group. These three different attitudes to the Western way of life and the British relations with India find expression in the characters of Govind, Kitsamy and Roshan.

Govind, the adopted brother of Kitsamy and Mira, has a deep hatred for the British rulers. He is a fanatic in his love for his country. His attitude to the Western influence is well expressed in these lines: "To him it was the produce of a culture which was not his own – the culture of an aloof and alien race twisted in the process of transplantation from its homeland, and so divorced from the people of the country as to be no longer real" (107).

He does not appreciate even the well meaning English missionaries who are engaged in selfless service of the poor masses. He is a revolutionary and does not hesitate to use violence, conspiracy and bloodshed to emancipate his country from the alien rulers. Premala, the wife of Kitsamy, also nourishes Indian values and respects people like Govind. She "champions the traditional Indian woman who fails to transmute her entreaty for brazenness into her daily life" (Ramesh: 146). She often escapes from the house of her anglicized husband to help Hickey in his humanitarian work. Kitsamy is a different sort of man. He is just the opposite of Govind in his approach to the West. His education at the Oxford University has changed him in everything except his name. He holds the high position of a District Magistrate and is a votary of the Western culture. His outlook makes him an alien in his own country.

Roshan is portrayed as a liberated woman of modern India. Having been educated in England and on the Western values, she has a dual citizenship and feels quite at home in both the worlds. Bubbling up with vitality and free spirit, she has only one object in her life and that is to fulfill her personality in her own way and for this no stake is too dear for her. In her pursuit of freedom, Roshan, the rebel, breaks the bonds of marriage.

Though she has sympathy for the West and is on intimate terms with individual Westerners, yet she is truly Indian at heart and actively participates in the political struggle against Britain. On her release after serving a term of imprisonment, she tells Mira confidently: "... 'What do you think? Of course I'm not sorry! I'd rather go to the devil my own way than be led to heaven by anyone else. And I wouldn't give up being free like that for anything...it hasn't always been that way – no, not even for me!'" (145).

Roshan, further, does not believe in using violent means for the freedom movement. When Govind, who belongs to the terrorist, approaches her for help, she replies: "... 'Everybody is interested in freedom ...only, we do not all agree on the means to the end, as I think you know too'" (94). She believes: "There is no power in violence...only destruction'"(94). Finally, looking at him steadily, she says: "'I am not really interested in destruction'" (95). However, she helps Govind when he is imprisoned for subversive activities. She not only pays the fees but also provides an alibi for him. She "testified for him too, at the last minute... swore he'd spent the night with her. It was cleverly done..." (131).

She possesses a strong stamina for the advocacy of the New Woman and symbolizes the resurgence of Indian women in the wake of the National Movement. She resembles Rajeshwari (K.S. Venkataramani's Kandan, the Patriot), who renounces the comforts of her luxurious life to dedicate herself to the cause of India's struggle for independence.

This novel, moreover, dramatizes the lives of young people lost in political confusion of the Independence struggle. It is the story of Kit, Premala, Govind, Roshan and Mirabai, educated, sophisticated, Westernized Indians, and Richard, a British visitor to India and Mira's lover. It is not a novel simply depicting the East-West confrontation as in *The Nowhere Man*; it is about national struggle, and the havoc it causes in the private lives of individuals.

Kamala Markandaya is at bay in imparting socio-psychological colour to her novels. Unlike Mulk Raj Anand and other Indian-English fiction writers, she has endeavoured her best to present how diverse shades of socio-psychological colour affect the strings in making or marring human relationships, how sundry desires of giving and receiving love are not translated into action and remain unfulfilled and how the lack of mutual understanding leads to frictions and social disintegration. "As an artist, Kamala Markandaya," says S. Krishnaswamy, "sincerely believes in the universal sisterhood/ brotherhood of man and that her writing systematically espouses the cultivation of warm, caring human relationships cannot be denied" (167).

Kitsamy, thoroughly Westernized son of a moderately forward family from London, brings with him the British mannerisms, Oxford gossip and a British acquaintance, Richard Marlow. The family, consisting of the reticent father, the quietly 'Amma,' the young Mirabai, the silent Govind, the garrulous Uncle and the ubiquitous Dodamma, is forced into receiving Richard with courtesy and good grace. Mira, the youngest and the ablest to withstand the heat and the strenuous outings, is made to accompany Richard on his sight-seeing trips. This leads to an intimacy between the two which the mother would fain prevent, but does not know how without appearing rude.

After Richard leaves to take up his assignment, the family gets busy over selecting a bride for Kit. Premala is, made to go through the unorthodox process of reverse courtship in which the girl comes to stay with the young man's family in order to be tested and approved by him. Premala is by nature, shy and conventional and basically Indian in spirit. She bends backwards in order to become a suitable mate for Kit. She endeavours to mould herself according to his Ultra-modern tastes. Their marriage is performed with a lot of fanfare, but it reaffirms Premala's personal simplicity and religiosity, and Kit's popularity as well as casual impracticality.

Kit takes up a job, settles down in a state capital, and invites Mira to visit him. One major inducement for her is the simultaneous visit of Richard. The mother slyly delays Mira's journey long enough to ensure that she would just miss Richard. Mira gets acquainted with Roshan and her work; likes it, decides to stay on and work for Roshan's paper. She is asked to report on a peasant resettlement in the neighbourhood.

By virtue of his temperament and position, Kit is frequently at the centre of social activities, but Premala is unable to fit into that world wholeheartedly and badly hurts his social sensibilities by her indiscretions. Kit suggests that she might find distraction or amusement in a visit to the village in Mira's company. Thus, Premala gets involved in the progress of the school building, to share in the dreams of Hickey, the missionary, and to adopt an orphan.

Some Inner Fury, according to K.R. Chandrasekharan, is fundamentally a "novel with an entirely political theme" (qtd. in Prasad, Hari Mohan: 163), for it is set against the background during the Second World War when Quit India Movement was in full swing. Personal relationships operate on many levels and it studies the impact of the troubled national spirit upon the love relationship of Richard and Mirabai who belong to the different races – the ruler and the ruled; as well as between Kitsamy – a Westernized husband, and Premala typical Indian wife. The undeclared war is between the freedom-seeking, colonized Indians and the colonizing British. The racial prejudices do not let the Indians and the British stay together harmoniously, even on individual level.

On the one hand, the novel is replete with the cautious love between Mira and Richard and, on the other, with rather cold relationship between Premala and Kitsamy. As its title shows, the novel deals with some inner fury – the passion, love, anger – of Mira for Richard as also with the fury of the Indian freedom fighters up in arms against the colonizers. As the gale of the freedom movement lashes the subcontinent, personal relationships between Indians and the English are swept away, leaving nothing concrete and intact. Yet some inner fury is intensely felt but remains inadequately articulated.

The influence of the idealistic national movement is so far-reaching and unrelenting that it prompts K.R. Srinivasa Iyengar to deem *Some Inner Fury* "...a tragedy engineered by politics...." (440) and "... undoubtedly, a fury against the British people who oppressed the Indian people during the struggle for Independence" (Arora: 16).

In contrast to Mira-Richard relationship which is based on love without marriage, the relationship of Premala and Kitsamy could be termed marriage-without-love, being no more than yoking together of two disparate individuals into matrimonial alliance. Premala, who is brought up in the conventional Hindu tradition, lives in a world defined by her parents and society. She is made to deny her impulses and is forced to live according to an abstract set of ideals far off from reality. Her family has protected her from the realities of being a woman. Her mother wishes Kitsamy to be her son-in-law but, being influenced by the Western ideas, he refuses to marry a girl without first knowing her. His love for a silk-haired English girl called Sylvia could not have been materialized into a marriage. His opposition to marry Premala arose in the absence of his acquaintance with her.

The first phase in their relationship is when in order to facilitate marriage, Premala comes to stay with Kit's family. She knows, of course, the object of her coming: "...no woman, after all, goes lightly to her marriage, there are always shadows before" (35).

The second stage begins with the marriage of Premala and Kitsamy and then the latter's efforts to modernize her. It is seen that she is by nature coy and conventional and basically Indian in spirit. It is here that their contrasting natures begin to surface. Vigourlessly and candourlessly, Premala is like a damped matchstick that falteringly burns and lights only to be extinguished even before its function is over. Kit likes playing tennis; Premala does not. He asks her to put on shorts for which she has no liking. She, even then, endeavours to mould herself according to his ultra-modern tastes. She comes to Mira to borrow her shorts, which she puts on only to satisfy Kit's likings. Her blushing is meaningless and curries no favour with Kit. She prized honesty which for Kit signifies nothing. Her desire of playing on Veena is contrastly to Kit's lack of interest in classical music. She knows the Gita, which Kit has forgotten. Their natures are as diametrically opposed as those of Maya and Gautama in Anita Desai's *Cry, the Peacock* (1988) except that whereas Premala strives vigorously for adjustment, Maya does not. What Premala search in life is quite different from what Kit wants her to be. It is evident that the "Indian husband, even when educated, does not treat his wife as a companion but as a subordinate. However, he expects her to behave like a modern wife" (Shirwadkar: 57). But, "... a woman must be companion as well as wife to her husband" (36). Gentle and unassuming, Premala agrees to give many more tries for adjustment but fails.

She wins everybody's heart in the family. There was no one who could not speak of Premala with affection, "for she was gentle and unassuming, and had tender pleasing ways" (38). Mira, who also likes Premala, praises her saying: "And Premala? ...A lovely face, tenderly moulded, which never lost its tenderness because she could never learn to be tough..." (107-08). Even Iyengar compliments her: "Of all the characters ...Premala is the sweetest, even the most heroic ... whose silence is stronger than all rhetoric ..." (440).

In the third phase, Premala's dampened yet sparkling love for Kit is extinguished in the absence of her husband's reciprocal gesture before it could turn into a flame the way it had become in Mira-Richard relationship in the second stage. Mira reflects at Premala's quite-pained bewilderment and her lost face which gave up the lights and colours of happiness, one by one. It is seen that in any case, Premala's love has been one-sided; it was because of her love that she tried so hard to please him. The bubbling enthusiasm of Kitsamy in modernizing her also cools down substantially. Premala becomes quiet and withdrawn in the parties. Her awkward behaviour before the guests invites Kit's wrath. Her "...seeming capacity for resignation is the true measure of her measureless strength" (Iyengar: 440).

In the fourth step, the absence of her husband's love breeds frustration in Premala. It is also evident that within a year of her married life, she and her husband drift apart. Being Indian to the core, she cannot adjust completely to Kit's lifestyle – though not for lack of effort on her part. The failure of Kitsamy is not providing for Premala's physical comforts as in starving her soul hungry for love. Premala is a misfit in the world of Kitsamy and, hence, fails miserably. She grows lonely without an outlet for her pent-up affections. Both her wifehood and motherhood remain incomplete in the absence of a child. Having none of her own, she adopts an orphan girl without caring for her husband's disapproval of it. For K.R. Srinivasa Iyengar, Premala "... is symbolic of the Mother – Mother India who is compassion and sufferance, who must indeed suffer all hurts and survive all disasters" (440). The child that pleases Premala irritates Kit being mistaken as a bastard.

Premala has sympathy for the children who are fighting for scrapes. As she sees their compassionate condition, she is moved to pity. Dodamma and Kit are against this sentimentality and ask her not to be emotional. She says: "It is neither emotional nor sentimental to call children children ..." (44). She is innocent, modest, utterly unpretentious and universally loved. "To her, goodness of heart was almost the sum of perfection and little else of consequence: for there are many keys that unlock the gates of men's liking, and each is differently fashioned" (117-18).

She rebels: the bringing up of the orphan girl is the first act to make her husband realize that she is not mere property or possession at his disposal but a woman who has her own identity. She enjoys many a pleasure of unfulfilled motherhood in the possession of the orphan girl.

Her unsatisfactory marriage is responsible for Premala's social service. She becomes busy in her social work, as she needs an outlet. If Kit had really loved and accepted her as she was, without forcing her personality into rigid and inhospitable moulds, the question of her becoming a reformer would not have arisen.

Govind is the only man who reads the closed book of her heart. He touches the chord of her heart but her traditional twist will not allow her to accept him to be her lover. She has fire but this fire cools off as soon as she realizes herself and sublimates her feelings. She puts up a heroic struggle between her instinctual urge and the demands of the group. She votes for the group making her busy in its social work. Her preference to serve the group makes her a new woman and this step of hers also symbolizes the step of the Indian woman towards liberation.

The fifth step comes in the sudden awakening of Kit's love for Premala once danger and death threaten her. On learning of the danger to Premala's life, Kit hurries to the school. Her failure to find a meaning in life drives her to death. But Premala remained virtuous in her life and also in her death, she was looking more beautiful. Iyengar aptly observes: "And after she is dead, having apparently fought hard for her breath, for life, her face is as serene as ever, with no trace at all of the struggle or the pain" (440). Death, that did not have the courage to touch and destroy her beauty, helped a lot in making her more beautiful. Mira reflects about her death: "... I could not believe she was dead. The feeling would not come, then. I looked at her and she had always been beautiful and she was beautiful now" (186).

For people, like Premala, who scatter love around, death means nothing. Iyengar points out how she "looks transfigured through suffering...." (440). In Premala's face, before death, Mira had noticed a glow and serenity which did not exist before. Premala, as her name suggests, is an embodiment of love - prem — and she, like a reformer, must lavish on her husband, on Govind, on the adopted child as also on the entire village, but who in the pervading violence and hatred, cannot survive and must inevitably die.

She becomes a martyr without a cause. She sacrifices herself at her attempts to be an ideal wife and later when she rushes to protect the school, which she has helped to build, which to her, perhaps, symbolizes the reason for living, she is consumed with dignity in the real fire. It is then that Govind blames Kit for driving her to her death: "'She loved you,' he said. 'You never loved her — you do not even know the meaning of love. You gave her nothing — not even a home. You drove her to the village — you drove her to her death'" (187). Since Premala had identified herself with the village and its school, for her the destruction of school must have meant the absence of meaning in life and as such the destruction of her ownself. Kit, on the other hand, charges Govind with her destruction considering him as guilty of her death as if he had strangled her with his hands. The fact is that, to some extent, both, Kitsamy and Govind, have been responsible for her death - Kit by not loving her enough and Govind by being a leader of a group of nationalists who destroyed the village school and caused her death. But, Mira's brother Kit also passes away after Premala in the novel. This novel, in the opinion of P.P. Mehta, is, thus, also, a story "of violence and destruction" (qtd. in Prasad, Hari Mohan 163).

One perceptible effect of growing Westernization and urbanization has been the gradual collapse of warm and sincere love relationship and the birth of commercialized love. Nathan and Rukmani in *Nectar in a Sieve* continue to remain models of loving husband and wife, but in *Some Inner Fury*, the cold love of the arranged, ill-matched marriage and the warm love outside it ends up in sterility and death. Mira's love, being short even if intense, could neither be converted into marriage nor result in the birth of a child. With Premala, love is silent – a typical husband-wife relationship without exhibitionistic fireworks. Nothing concrete comes out of the love between Mira and Richard; Premala and Kitsamy; and even between Premala and Govind except death. Premala's adopted child vocalizes the failure of Kitsamy's love, challenges his manhood and invites his ire. The world of *Some Inner Fury* is the world of filtered love not in its primitive state but like that of a castrated man and that too becomes subordinated to the violence caused by the Quit India Movement of 1942. Westernization has desexed the whole generation of which Kitsamy seems to be a good specimen. In this connection, Mark Spilka's words seem significant when he says that his "condition represents a peculiar form of emotional impotence" (127).

Kitsamy is a grafted plant of modernity on the roots of tradition making the latter painfully subservient to the former. With his arrested maturity, Kitsamy can be called an emotional adolescent. Tied by Westernized codes of behaviour, he goes with what a society expects and accepts, suppressing real emotions. Considering him a representative of "the generation of Anglophiles," A.V. Krishna Rao compares him with Harish in Sahgal's *A Time to be Happy* in his, "denationalised individuality and in his demonstrative unorthodoxy" (6). In such a society, exhibition of external forms rather than restrained feelings of love, religion and manhood are emphasized. His death is the death of his wholesome nature.

Human relationships, by and large, are affected by the life and style of Westernization in case of Kitsamy especially. Kitsamy does not have unadulterated sensibility which Premala has. It is so because the dead albatross of Westernization and modernity curse him which he is doomed to wear round his neck and which Premala's pure love fails to remove. Rather than confronting the British and their manners, he passively succumbs and forces them on Premala. His art of forcing Premala to learn empty forms is an example of hamartia that brings about his tragedy.

Govind provides the third element in a love triangle in both Mira-Richard and Premala-Kitsamy relationships. Mira's love relationship with Govind remains rather mysterious. When he takes up a job and goes away, Mira misses him more than she missed her real brother

Kit. This mystery thickens when her adopted brother Govind is charged with the murder of Kitsamy while she defends him vigorously.

Govind's love for Premala is more intense than his love for Mira. Mira's love could be that of a sister for adopted brother, it is altogether of a different kind. But it is seen that though Govind did love Premala, his love certainly did not go to a point where he could have murdered Kit for her. He did even scold Premala for feeding the poor children and realized that his love for her made him wish to hurt her so much which was more in anger against others than against Premala herself. His protest against the steady erosion of her individuality is another instance of this hidden love. Govind thought no one could have better wife than her.

Premala's love for Govind is certainly warmer than Mira's. Govind's act of holding on to Premala's hands while remaining oblivious of Mira's presence shows that the love between them was mutual. Even Kit does not fail to notice how excited Premala was on seeing Govind.

In short, in *Some Inner Fury* the effect of the political upheaval of the Quit India Movement on human relationships is seen mainly between the Oriental and the Occidental and as well as among other minor characters.

Kit is an Anglophile; Govind an Indophile. Kit is loyal to the alien rule whereas Govind is a revolutionary. There is again a conflict between the two races accompanied by inter-racial frictions.

Further, Kitsamy is married to Premala – out and out a traditional Indian woman. Due to the growing of the Westernization, there is a collapse of warm love relationship. It shows the forced marriages of the East and the West bound to be sterile and mutually destructive.

WORKS CITED

Aithal, S. Krishnamoorthy and Rashmi Aithal, *Indo-English Fictional Experiments with Interracial and Intercultural Relationship, Alien Voice: Perspectives on Commonwealth Literature,* ed. Avadhesh K. Srivastava, Lucknow: Print, 1981.

Arora, Sudhir Kumar, *A Study of Kamala Markandaya's Women,* New Delhi: Atlantic, 2006.

Bhatnagar, M.K., *Kamala Markandaya: A Critical Spectrum,* New Delhi: Atlantic, 2002.

Dodiya, Jaydipsinh K., *Cultural Conflicts in Kamala Markandaya's Novels, Indian Women Writers: Critical Perspectives,* ed., Jaydipsinh K. Dodiya and K.V. Surendran, New Delhi: Sarup & Sons, 1999.

George, Roshin, *De- or Re-colonisation? Kamala Markandaya's Pleasure City as a Postcolonial Novel, Postcolonial Readings in Indo-Anglian Literature,* ed., K.V. Dominic, New Delhi: Authorspress, 2009.

Indianetzone, 6 January 2009, 30 April 2010. indianetzone.com/16/some_inner_fury_kamala_markandaya.htm.

Iyengar, K.R. Srinivasa, *Indian Writing in English,* 1962, New Delhi: Sterling, 1984.

Krishnaswamy, S., *Kamala Markandaya: Autonomy, Nurturance and Sisterhood of Man, The Woman in Indian Fiction in English,* New Delhi: Ashish, 1984.

Kumar, Shiv K., *Tradition and Change in the Novels of Kamala Markandaya, Indian Fiction in English,* ed. P. Mallikarjuna Rao and M. Rajeshwar, New Delhi: Atlantic, 1999.

Markandaya, Kamala, *Some Inner Fury,* 1955, New Delhi: Penguin, 2009. (All the textual references are from this edition.)

Nawale, Arvind M., *Indian English Fiction: An Appraisal,* March 2009, 27 May 2010, literature-study-online.com/essays/indian-english-lit.

Naik, M.K., *Indian English Fiction 1864-1980: The Emergence and the Peaking, Twentieth Century Indian English Fiction,* Delhi: Pencraft, 2004. Print.

Nath, Rajendra, *Why did independent India and Pakistan retain British generals?, Rev. of War and Diplomacy in Kashmir 1947-48,* by C. Das Gupta, *Tribune: Spectrum* 12 May 2002: 4.

Prasad, Hari Mohan, *The Quintessence of Kamala Markandaya's Art, Response: Recent Revelations of Indian Fiction in English.* Bareilly: Prakash, 1983.

Raizada, Harish Chandar, *Impact of Mahatma Gandhi on Indian English Fiction, Alien Voice: Perspectives on Commonwealth Literature,* Ed. Avadhesh K. Srivastava, Lucknow: Print, 1981.

Ramesh, V., *Kamala Markandaya's Indian Women – The Principles and the Principals – A Feministic Elucidation, Indian Journal of Postcolonial Literatures* 9.1, 2009, pp.144-51.

Rao, A.V. Krishna, *Continuity and Change in the Novels of Kamala Markandaya, Perspectives on Kamala Markandaya,* ed. Madhusudan Prasad, Ghaziabad: Vimal, 1984.

Shirwadkar, Meena, *Image of Woman in the Indo-Anglian Novel,* New Delhi: Sterling, 1979.

Singh, R.A., *The Novels of Kamala Markandaya: A Study*. Bareilly: Prakash, 2005.

Singh, R.S., *Soulful East and Ratiocinative West: Kamala Markandaya, Indian Novel in English: A Critical Study*, New Delhi: Arnold-Heinemann, 1977.

Spilka, Mark, *The Death of Love in The Sun Also Rises, Hemingway: A Collection of Critical Essays*, ed., Robert P. Weeks, Englewood Cliffs N.J.: Prentice-Hall, 1962.

❏❏❏

20

Kamala Markandaya's Experience of the Indian City Life in Her Novel *A Handful of Rice*

PRADNYA VIJAY GHORPADE AND J.A. SHINDE

Apart from the 'big three' like M.R. Anand, Raja Rao and R.K. Narayan, we can mention such names as Bhabhani Bhattacharya, M. Malgaonkar, K. Singh, Arun Joshi, Kamala Markandaya, Ruth Prawar Jhabwala, Anita Desai, etc. who attempt a wide variety of themes: such as, social change, encounter between east and west, struggle for independence, inter-communal marriage, horrors of partition, problems of women, etc. Stephen Ignatius Hemenway (1975:52) has rightly stated: "Kamala Markandaya is definitely one of the most productive, popular and skilled Indo-Anglian novelists and a superb representative of the growing number of Indian women writing serious literature in English".

Kamala Markandaya is recognised as a powerful creative writer with the publication of her very first novel *Nectar in a Sieve* in 1954. She is mainly concerned with the theme of conflict between traditionalism and modernism, eastern and western values and reveals a remarkable variety and profundity within her limited range. As A.V. Krishna Rao (1972: 64) observes: "The purposive direction of her creative sensibility endows her novels with a certain representative character that marks them out as a significant entity in Indo-Anglian fiction".

A Handful of Rice (1966) is Kamala Markandaya's fifth novel and it is a realistic novel like *Nectar in a Sieve*. As K. Venkata Reddy (1984: 154-55) points out: "Whereas *Nectar in a Sieve* is purely a novel of rural problems, depicting the poverty and hunger of the rural masses. *A Handful of Rice* deals with urban life with its struggle for survival". This novel is about the urban India and its problems. Markandaya has provided a complete picture of the society. Besides, it focuses on the nightmares of urban poverty, the exodus from the village to the town, the destruction of artisans by industry and also some major social problems like unemployment, crime, marriage, class system, etc. As Kai Nicholson (1972: 117) remarks in *A Handful of Rice*: "Markandaya uses the village as a pretext for her hero, Ravi, to flee the countryside and plunge into the turmoil of urban life". By depicting the urban India and its problems, here, Markandaya provides a complete picture of the society.

Ravi, the protagonist of the novel, is the son of a poor peasant. Tired of rural hunger and poverty he joins the general exodus to the city. Having neither work nor money, he joined a gang of loafers whose business was to deal in smuggled or stolen goods. One day he was caught drunk and while trying to escape from the police he was resting against the house of an old tailor, Apu. The tailor asked him to go away. In his drunkenness, he breaks the bars of a window of the house of Apu. Then Ravi slept there and the wife of the tailor, Jayamma, tied his hands and feet while he was asleep. In the morning he confesses that he was hungry and he was also drunk. She took pity on him, fed him and allowed him to go. Ravi who gets a glimpse of Nalini, the daughter of Apu, gets attracted to her and falls in love. At the advice of Damodar, he goes to Apu's house in the daylight and offers to replace the bars that he had broken. Though Jayamma at first hesitates, allows him later to do the job. Having won their confidence, Ravi tries to win Nalini also. Apu, an aging man, alone has to work for the family. Ravi decides to work as an apprentice with Apu. Ravi married with Nalini. When Apu falls seriously ill, his son-in-law, Puttanna who is good-for-nothing person, steals away all the savings of Apu and run away. When Apu dies, Ravi becomes the head of the family. But as he is not a skilled worker, his business declines. Irritated by this, he often beats Nalini. As a result of serious quarrel, Nalini leaves the house. Ravi caught in the web of all these problems. This affected his temper also. His son, Raju dies of poverty. Ravi approaches Damodar to get out of his problems. But Damodar refuses to give him work. Then Ravi joined a crowd that was attacking rice godowns for a handful of rice. He feels that the innocents have always suffered and violence is the only way. When his chance comes, he doesn't dare and turns back. Thus the story is the story of the decline and fall of Ravi's fortunes. As P.P. Mehta (1979: 303) observes: "This novel completely deals with the life of the poor classes in the city of Madras". The crowded conditions of lower middle class and poor families have been realistically described in a simple and straightforward style.

The joint family system in the city is also presented by Markandaya. Ravi's family in the village is a joint family. Even Apu's family in the city is no exception to this. Apu's family stands as a good example to show the demerits of the joint family system. In this family, at first, Apu is the only bread winner. Ravi joins him later to shoulder his responsibilities to some extent. The innumerable relations, that the Indian family have and the family ties are difficult to be understood by the English Memsahib. When Ravi explains his delay in delivering Memsahib's clothes, on account of Apu's death, she fails to understand him. She thinks: "These people with their innumerable uncles and aunts and cousins who seem to be forever dying - really they are impossible people inhabiting in an impossible country" (p.153). Compared to the mud huts, the middle class people of the city figures out better. Apu's house is small. He had one room- perhaps twelve feet square - for himself, another big room, which he used as workshop and a kitchen which seemed the purpose of bedroom for the newly weds. The workshop also became the sleeping cabin for all the hangers – on at night. A little shelter arranged on the roof of the house becomes for Ravi, a place to dream about the happy future without anybody's interference. He can only view with awe and jealousy the big bungalows of the memsahibs, rich people and even that of Damodar, his one time accomplice. The family that is portrayed do lack the attachment, love and affection. Ravi's mother, stands as an exception and worries about her children who desert her one by one. Love and affection is totally absent in between Apu and Jayamma. Jayamma doesn't recognise the existence of her husband until he falls ill. This lack of love is conducive to lack of sexual satisfaction. The relation between Thangam and her husband do lack love and affection.

Money plays an important role in establishing and keeping the relations in this novel. Such emphasis on money and the prestige attached to it can no doubt be found in the urban society. Ravi loves his wife, Nalini. But the financial problems make him a fretful man and in his moods of anger, he beats her and even his son Raju.

In urban India the major problems are unemployment and underemployment. Particularly in joint family, where many parasites are found depending on the sole or the very few bread earners, the economic conditions deteriorate very quickly. In Apu's house half a dozen people depend on only two earning members, viz. Apu and Ravi. When Nalini is saved from a possible abortion, Ravi is forced by the poverty to think, "... if the disaster so narrowly averted would not in fact have been a blessing" (p.189). But in the end, Ravi's son dies, not because of fever or illness, but because of poverty, which doesn't allow the family to arrange a proper medical treatment. Arrival of more children in a family forces a poor man even to think to such an extreme: "I want to put my hands round their necks and squeeze until I know I'll never again have to think about feeding them" (p.126). Though it has become quite like a custom to wear new dresses on festivals, Apu and to decree: "There were...be no new clothes for anyone this Deepavali" (p.64). Ravi's anger, when he sees Memsahib spend fifty rupees for one little jacket for one of her little girls, is well justified because his family, "...of late... not been able to afford a few vegetables for the evening stew" (p. 86).

Markandaya deals with the unemployment problem in the cities, of which she had given a microscopic view. The village youth who find their future dark in the villages, join the general exodus to the city. But their dreams are shattered the moment they land up in the city. Ravi finds the situation in the city very frustrating: "... was no job. The city was full of graduates...the college turned them out in their thousands each year... looking for employment so what chance he with his meagre elementary school learning?...his education didn't allow Ravi to compete against the gaunt, shabby, genteel graduates who hung around the streets..." (pp.26-27). Ravi had seen the queues that every vacancy produced, "the long waiting lines, the fine-drawn patience that suddenly snapped, turning these mild, well-bred men into screaming agitators" (pp.206-09). Such unemployed youth, forced to hunger and then to frustration, finally get a "passport to a world shot with glitter and excitement" (p.27) i.e. the underground world. In the city, Ravi has been initiated by Damodar, his friend, "a city slicker, born and bred in the streets of the city" (p.15). Into the rules of jungle which govern life here and he can so far play only this game that life in an Indian city is, Ravi has learnt from Damodar and from his own experience here by now that "life was a battle in which the weak always went under..." (p.15). And once while Ravi is ruminating on the city life he communes with himself: "...ah yes, the jungle, its darkness, its lawlessness, where a man's strength and courage alone gave him mastery... live by jungle law and then see who survived" (p.33). Ravi is initiated in to this underground world trade by Damodar. Markandaya gives a descriptive picture of one such location, where the underground trade is going on: "George Town...skirted the docks, was its unproclaimed clearing house and into the maze of streets that penetrated in land, poured the products of a thriving industry the world's underground trade" (p.16). Markandaya analyses the reason due to which such an industry thrives. There is a craze among the people for the clothes with a foreign label. Regarding the demand and supply of such foreign cloth, Markandaya comments: "Commercial interests would have catered for their needs, but in these post-British days there were bans, quotas, import restrictions, imposed by a government. More interested in postering national industry than in pandering to the rich. So the black marketers took over" (p.30). Such a profitable industry is controlled by the large operators.

Kamala Markandaya has been successful in depicting certain trends of social changes. Some trends of social changes are working towards the revival and preservation of the traditional values and other trends are working towards modernisation on the pattern of the advanced western countries. The environmental factors like excess of rain, failures of rain, drought etc. which play the major role in this novel. This is the factor because of which many youth of the villages join the general exodus to the city in search of employment. The train which carries hundreds of youths like Ravi, to the city, stands as a symbol of rapid change assuring a journey from hell to heaven to these young aspirants who are in need of employment and regular bread. She has depicted the impact of industrialisation on the individual families in particular and on the society in general. There is organisation of labour, specialisation and fast life. In the business world Apu survives because of his specialised skills and his in-depth knowledge about the business world. Ravi, on the other hand, fails utterly because he lacks these qualities. Industrialisation has given rise to new classes. Ravi tries to revolt against the social injustice. He fails to understand why they get only Rs. 80/- per dozen garments made ready by them, whereas the same are sold by the shoppers at Rs. 25/- per piece in the market. He is surprised to note that the Indian women join hands with the European ladies in harassing the tailors. He is also distressed to note that the tailors are not ready to get united and fight to safeguard their own common interests. He notices the lack of unity: "No wonder they fought, he and they. But the battle had never yet been wages as a joint one, and until it was the day of reckoning would not dawn" (p. 209).

Markandaya highlights on class system i.e. the oppressors and the oppressed, the problems of the lower middle class people. The poor people like Ravi's father, look to the lower middle man like Apu, with fear and respect. Apu, in turns thinks his rich customers to be Gods. He behaves with the memsahibs as if they are goddesses. The petty criminals like Damodar are full of hatred towards the rich people. But once they too become rich then they turn their hatred towards the poor people like Ravi. When Ravi comes from the village, though poor, he is a part of the polite society. At the centre of his being he has had a different sanskara. The author writes thus:

> Ravi respected him (Damodar) for it. He himself, he knew would have gone in for rich food, for silk shirts and enamel cuff links: yet his upbringing had taught him to focus inward, upon the constant light within, to see the raging obscenities and miseries of their life as essentially external and ephemeral; and for all that he angrily repudiated this teaching, shreds of it obstinately clung... (p.113).

But, when he joins the gang of criminals, he becomes an anti-social element. When he decides to marry Nalini, what troubles him more is his inner conflict - to give up the anti-social circle, which provided him freedom and food, and to join the society once again and thus to get entangled in the social ties and responsibilities. He doesn't want to give up the values inculcated in him in his early life in his village. When he remembers it in the city of Madras makes him feel sick. Markandaya writes:

> It sickened him: the misery and the squalor, the ailing babies who cried all night long, the way one was

> always poor and everyone, one knew was always poor too, the desire — the constant nibbling desire — to have a second helping of food, a cup of coffee every morning, a shirt without holes, a shawl made of pure wool to keep out the cold of a monsoon dawn; and to know that one never would (p.49).

But once the decision is made, he regains the respectful place in the society. On the other hand, Damodar, as stated earlier, chooses the life of jungle animals flourishes. To him, money is power. To what extent, money has degraded human life is described in these lines in the novel: "... money was power. Money, he thought, with a craving that crawled like a disease in the bones and marrow of his body, if only, if only... and in his mind it took on the shape of a dark flame over which men crouched like opium-eaters to taste the savours of life" (p.186). The new house that he builds for himself is a living monument of his success. The author describes it thus: "It stood on the site of a dozen tenements, which Damodar had bought and torn down, scattering the dazed inmates without qualm" (p.212). While most of the people accept their status in the society as it is, and thus tolerate all the suffering caused thereby, very few people stand out and protest. Ravi, as a representative of such people, becomes angry when he sees the big merchants taking away the profit margin, leaving them the real workers - a paltry sum. He tries to register his protest by not supplying the products to them and by raising charges etc. Ravi also gets angry when he is kept in waiting by the Memsahibs or when has to pay tips to the attendants to meet the Memsahibs. When Apu and Ravi go to rich houses to deliver stitched clothes to, and secure more tailoring orders from, wealthy ladies in Madras city, Ravi often feels dazzled and awed at the opulence of the interior decorations of these households: "Then they would sail upstairs, the lady, Apu, Ravi and bundle — always in that order — and on the way Ravi would peek into other rooms catching glimpses of silk hangings and tall windows, gleaming floors and fine furniture, and feel an awe of so much wealth" (p.83). Ravi often rebels against this system. He wants "to take revenge, to get even with them, all of those people who ground into the dust with a careless heel weaker men like his father and himself" (p.125). But this sanskara restrains him from throwing the jagged brick, poised level at his shoulder, at the glass pane of the showcase of the fashionable shop named EVE dealing into ladies' garments - the shop which had been exploiting Apu and him. This shop sold ladies' coats Rs. 125/- a piece while Apu and he had stitched these coats for the shop at the rate of Rs. 80/- per dozen. While another man from the retreating crowd throws a brick at the show case and prompts him to throw his also, Ravi's hand drops. The author writes: "Ravi took aim, poising the jagged brick level at his shoulder. But suddenly he could not. The strength that had inflamed him, the strength of a suppressed, laminated anger, ebbed as quickly as it had arisen. His hand dropped" (p.237).

Apart from poverty, unemployment, crime, class system, Markandaya also refers to other social problems like alcoholism, prostitution and corruption. But these problems have not been dealt with in detail in this novel. People like Ravi, drink liquor because they are hungry and want to forget about the dark future. Markandaya refers to 'qreasing the palms', i.e. to corrupt the concerned to get the work done. Even the attenders at the bungalows of the memsahibs are not an exception. Apu could get entry into these bungalows only when he paid same amount to these people. He thought it is essential to survive in the cut-throat competition. All these social problems have become a part of the urban life and Markandaya very realistically depicts them in the novel.

Her deep understanding of Eastern and Western values of human life provides her a unique insight into the cultural codes and convictions of different societies. The presence of two cultures in her mind helps her in making a successful quest for real identity. Like M.R. Anand, Kamala Markandaya has projected the picture of modern India under the impact of intellectual and cultural change. In her creative outputs, she has presented as a sensible novelist, people dehumanised by society or the tyranny of custom, its blind and incessant demands. In this connection S.Z.H. Abidi (1989:27) remarks: "The social realism employed by Kamala Markandaya in this novel is very close to the observed conditions of life". Markandaya shows how Ravi's calamity is not due to only rural poverty but also urban moral sickness. The city life as described in this novel also reflects on her experience of the Indian city life. She very realistically mirrors the Indian life in terms of its socio-economic and socio-cultural changes.

WORKS CITED

Abidi, S.Z.H., *Nectar in a Sieve: A Critical Study*, Bareilly: Prakash Book Depot, 1989.

Hemenway, Stephen Ignatius, *The Novel of India*, Vol. II, Calcutta: Writers Workshop, 1975.

Markandaya, Kamala, *A Handful of Rice*, Delhi: Hind Pocket Books, 1966

Mehta, P.P., *Indo-Anglian Fiction: An Assessment*, Bareilly: Prakash Book Depot, 1979.

Nicholson, Kai, *Social Problems in the Indo-Anglian and the Anglo-Indian Novel*, Bombay: Jaico, 1972.

Rao, A.V. Krishna, *The Indo-Anglian Novel and the Changing Tradition*, Mysore: Rao and Raghava, 1972.

Venkata, Reddy K., *A Tryst with Conscience: A Handful of Rice, Perspectives on Kamala Markandaya*, ed., Madhusudan Prasad, Gaziabad: Vimal Prakashan, 1984.

□□□

21

Finding Happiness Amidst Adversity : Kamala Markandaya's *Nectar in a Sieve*

RACHEL IRDAYA RAJ

Literature in India was a rich and vast collection that included texts written in various regional languages. As early as the sixteenth century Molla was famous for her *Molla Ramayanam*. Muddupalani (1730-1790) was a courtesan in Pratapasimha's court, one of the kings of Tanjavur. She is best known for her *Radhika Santwanam* which was harshly criticized by the literary critics in the later centuries. The English language was introduced in India by the colonial rulers. With the colonial subjects being taught about the literature of England, it strengthened the western cultural hegemony in India. In 1835 'Macaulay's Minutes' stated that they must create a class of people who were Indian in their blood and colour but English in their thinking and intellect. With the social reforms movement English education in India was progressing in the nineteenth century. The social reformers like Raja Ram Mohan Roy encouraged women's education. By 1880 women started to graduate from universities. A lot of changes took place in the literary scenario in the nineteenth century. The impact of the western culture and the emerging of the printing press saw the increase in the number of people who wrote and read literature. Novel as a genre came into existence in the latter half of the nineteenth century. The impact of English Literature was seen on the early novels. The language of the colonial rulers was used by the Indians to talk about their experiences. Unlike earlier when people were hesitant to use the English language because it was forced on them, now the language became a medium through which they expressed themselves and also reached an international audience. Such writers as Mulk Raj Anand, R.K. Narayan and Raja Rao; the first among the Indian writers in English, put India on the global map of literature. As early as the nineteenth century Indian women also started writing novels, thus making writing as their profession. Even prior to that women did compose excellent poetry in their regional languages as mentioned earlier. But traditionally the work of these women writers was undervalued because of the patriarchal attitude in society. Most of the women wrote about the enclosed domestic space and their experiences within that space. The prominent themes that shaped their novels were their expectation of marriage, their roles in their family life, the relationship between husbands and wives and so on. In the twentieth century the writings of the women were about the struggle to find an identity of their own. Writers such as Krupabai Satthianandhan, Nayantara Sahgal, Ruth Prawar Jabvala, Kamala Markandaya, Corenelia Sorabji, Sashi Deshpande, Kamala Das, Anita Desai and Arundathi Roy have contributed to the Indian writing in English.

Kamala Purnaiya Taylor (1924 - 2004), who started writing novels under the pseudonym Kamala Markandaya was born in Mysore in South India. She was educated at the Madras University and later moved to London to pursue a career in journalism. After her marriage, she settled down in England. She shot to fame with the publication of her first novel *Nectar in a Sieve* in 1954. Her next novel *Some Inner Fury* (1955) narrates the story of a young woman who falls in love with an English man. The political unrest in the 1940's forms the background for this semi - autobiographical novel when India was fighting for its independence. The turbulence of the protagonist Mira caught between the east and west is expressed lucidly. *A Silence of Desire* (1960) deals with an office clerk whose marital harmony is disturbed when he finds his wife is away from home in his absence. His trail about his wife's whereabouts leads him to a spiritual guru and his suspicion that his wife is having an affair is laid to rest. The novel deals with the conflict between science and religion and tradition and modernity. *Possession* (1963) again revolves around the conflict between Eastern spirituality and Western materialism, with the story moving from London to a small village in South India. *A Handful of Rice* (1966) is a poignant tale of the protagonist Ravi, who moves from the village to the city in search of a better life, only to be caught in the whirlpool of poverty again. *The Coffer Dams* (1969) is the story of an English couple – Clinton and Helen, who come to India on business purpose. An engineer by profession and the head of an international firm, Clinton had come to India to construct a dam. He is so obsessed with the construction that he has no time for his young wife. Helen finds solace with the local tribals learning about the importance of nurturing human relationships from them. Here again we find Markandaya dealing with conflicting ideologies between the East and the West.

Writers during the 1950's and 1960's often centered their stories on the common man. Rural India was a subject explored by many contemporary writers of that time, with all its beauty and agony portrayed in depth in their writings. Markandaya's novels were also based on the agrarian community, the working class, the conflict between the Eastern and Western ideologies and explored human relationships within this maze. Having lived in India as well as in England, she had a firsthand experience of the mannerism, lifestyle and the value system of both nations. One cannot pin down Markandaya and say that her novels or her characters are of a particular type. Her protagonists are strong women who withstand the pressures of lie, often emerging victorious. Their strength of character and their individual identity are not lost though they are living within the complying standards of a patriarchal society.

Nectar in a Sieve is one such story told by the protagonist Rukmini. It is a story of survival, of hardships endured, of happiness found, of trials and tribulations, sometimes succumbing but always hopeful that there is a better tomorrow. A person reading the novel relives all those emotions narrated by Rukmini and many a times your eyes moisten reading through the struggles that she has endured. Such is the empathy one feels for the protagonist. Markandaya has the knack of weaving a story so close to real life describing the minute details of the peasant life. Rukmini is the epitome of all the virtues of a south Indian farmer's wife. Her elaborate description of her environment around her not only gives us an elaborate picture of rural India but also takes us closer to nature. The story begins with the narrator going back into her past and looking at how far she has come in life. She begins her narration with her marriage to a poor peasant called Nathan. As all young girls who dream of their marriages, she too had many plans of how to have a gala wedding. But it was not to be so as by the time her father - a village head man - got her three older siblings married he was left with almost nothing to give her. So she was married into a humble family with no dowry at all. When she steps into her new home, a small mud hut, it was too much to take in for a twelve year old. But when she sees her husband full of love and affection for her she forgets her miserable condition and resigns to the life of being a farmer's wife. She says:

> While the sun shines on you and the fields are green and beautiful to the eye, and your husband sees the beauty in you which no one has seen before, and you have a good store of grain laid away for hard times, over you and a sweet stirring in your body, what more can a woman ask for? My heart sang and my feet were light as I went about my work, getting up at sunrise and going to sleep content. Peace and quiet were ours [9].

And from there on life for her is one big learning process, every experience teaching her something and also adding memories to her life. Her husband Nathan being a simple man tells her that as long as they have a good harvest they can be happy and content. As a new bride Rukmini learns how to run her home from her neighbours. Soon Rukmini conceives but her joy is short lived when she gives birth to a baby girl, Ira. She has silent tears in her eyes as her first born was not a boy because according to Indian culture the first born in the family is expected to be a male child. Rukmini narrates that:

> They placed it in my arms when I had recovered a little from the birth, in silence. I uncovered the small form, beautiful, strong, but quiet plain, a girl's body. I turned away and despite myself, the tears came, tears of weakness and disappointment; for what woman wants a girl for her first - born?" [16]

On the peripheral she looks happy but underneath she is distraught that she is unable to bear a son. This thought takes on her life so much that she visits Dr. Kenny in secret and pleads him to find a remedy. Dr. Kenny a kind and gentle Englishman has set up a small clinic in their village. Over a period he develops a soft corner for Rukmini and often consoles her in times of misery. Seven years later she gives birth to her first son, Arjun and soon she has other sons - Thanbi, Murugan, Raja and Selvam. As her family increases there is always a shortage of food. Whereas her first two children were fed on milk, butter and rice there was not much left for the latter children with only enough milk for the youngest child. They could not afford curds and butter, and even the vegetables that they grew, but they found solace that they need not starve as some of the other families did.

The serenity of the village is disturbed with the establishment of a new tannery in the nearby vicinity. The tannery acts as a metaphor of all that is evil and sinister and western. Rukmini does not take accept the tannery as progress instead feels that it will somehow destroy the peace in her family. She says:

> They had invaded our village with clatter and din, had taken from us the maidan where our children played, and had made the bazaar prices too high for us... They may live in our midst but I can never accept them, for they lay their hands upon us and we are all turned from tilling to barter, and hoard our silver since we cannot spend it, and see our children go without food that their children gorge, and it is only the hope that one day things will be as they were... [30].

Soon it was time for Ira to be married and Rukmini had been saving for Ira to marry well since her birth. Nature plays havoc in a peasant's life every now and then, whose very life depends on the rain. So also we find in the story that one year there is no rain at all or there are heavy floods washing away the crops. Either way we find there is famine and starvation. That year the monsoons were very harsh and the fields were flooded with water and their harvest was lost. There was such a shortage of grains that the family survived only on water for days together. Five years pass by and one day we find that Ira and her husband come home. But it was not a casual visit in any sense as the husband announces that he has brought Ira back as she cannot bear him children. Her daughter being termed as a barren woman was another tragedy in Rukmini's life. She takes the help of Dr. Kenny but it is too late as Ira's husband has already married for a second time. To make matters worse we find later on that Ira has taken to prostitution to keep her from starvation. Rukmini's son Arjun announces that he wants to work at the tannery. Rukmini was disheartened when her son announced his decision and so was her husband Nathan as his son did not show any interest towards their land. Arjun justifies his decision stating that "I am tired of hunger and I am tired of seeing my brothers hungry. There is never enough, especially since Ira came to live with us" [53]. Soon her second son Thambi follows suit to work at the tannery. Once a week when the tannery was closed both the sons used to help their father on their land. And Nathan was only too happy to teach his sons all about agriculture. Now there is steady flow of income and the family has food to eat. But their joy is short lived as all the labourers call for a strike at the tannery and decided to resume work only their demands are met. This incident leaves Rukmini and her family to survive on her reserve stock of grain. Rukmini's third son Murugan goes to the town to find some work. Thus we find that three of her sons do not take up agriculture as their livelihood. Rukmini is disheartened and tries to convince her sons to work on their land but in vain. Soon Arjun and Thambi leave the tannery and decide to take up work at the tea plantations in Ceylon. With a heavy heart Rukmini bids farewell to her sons knowing well that she will never see them again. She says:

> The tears came, hot and bitter, flowing and flowing as if the very springs of sorrow had been touched in my body. They spoke soothingly - of how much they would earn, and how one day they would return...and it was all a sham, a poor shabby pretence to mask our tortured feelings...Two sons have gone, now the third is going - and not to the land, which is his blood, but to be a servant, which he has never been [70, 71].

Rukmini sees the tannery as a curse upon their lives as it has taken her sons away from her. Her other son Raja is killed at the tannery when they find him trying to steal a hide of a calf. Officials from the tannery come home to tell her that the watchmen were only trying to do their duty and it was done with any kind of mal intention. They said: "He was seen in the yard, where he had no business to be, and when the chowkidars caught him they found he had stolen a calf - skin" [93].

That year there is drought because of failure of rains and the landlord demands the rent on his land to be paid. Nathan and Rukmini have to sell half of their belongings a few mud pots, two brass vessels, the tin trunk, their bullocks and finally her wedding sari to pay the rent on the land. Her personal life turns miserable when her neighbour Kunthi first requests her for food, and later threatens to reveal to her husband of her secret meetings with Dr. Kenny. Added to this, Rukmini finds that her bundle of food grains has been stolen by her husband Nathan. To her utter shock and disbelief Nathan reveals that he is the father of Kunthi's sons. Rukmini is heartbroken but her resilience is not completely broken as she forgives her husband over a period of time. In the mean while there are many changes happening in her children's life but none that could actually give her happiness. Her son Selvam decides to work as an assistant to Dr. Kenny. When he announces his decision Rukmini was disappointed. She says: "Not displeased. Perhaps disappointed, since all our sons have forsaken the land. But it is the best way for you" [114]. Her other son Murugan who had gone to work in the city had got married without the presence of either of his parents. This thought deeply saddened Rukmini but she was helpless as she had no money to travel to the town. The town was more than a hundred miles away and Selvam was earning very little and so they could not afford to travel by train. Also her husband Nathan was not keeping well. He was suffering from rheumatism, and frequent bouts of fever. This made him very weak, so much so that he could not continue with his usual routine of sowing, reaping and tilling and other such tasks needed for a harvest. Rukmini and Ira did as much as they could but the heavy work needed a lot of strength. Dr. Kenny on one of his visits to their home notices that there is no one to help them out in the fields as none of her sons had taken up agriculture. He feels guilty about it but Rukmini tries to reason out with him saying that Selvam would not have been a farmer like his father. She says: "We would not wish for our son other than what he would wish for himself" [133].

A major tradegy to strike Rukmini was to see her daughter become a prostitute. Ira's life as a prostitute did bring in money for the family, but Nathan was displeased and Rukmini was helpless. With this money Ira was able to buy food for her last brother Kuti. Rukmini's last son Kuti was never a healthy child and Ira took care of him as if she was her own son. But the child did not survive for long and his death was another blow to the family. Because of her wayward life, Ira soon conceived and gave birth to an illegitimate child who was named Sacrabani. The child was unusually fair, with pinkish eyes but Ira hardly seemed to notice this. She and her brother Selvam accepted the child as part of the family, though it took some time for Nathan and Rukmini to come to terms with this new development in their family. The greatest misfortune to strike them was when they get to know that the landlord has sold his land to the tannery. There was no scope for any discussion as the deal had been finalized and they were given two weeks time to vacate the place. Rukmini echoes saying:

> Somehow I had always felt the tannery would eventually be our undoing. I had known it since the day the carts had come with their leads of bricks... Since then it had spread like weeds in an unattended garden strangling whatever life grew in its way. It had changed the face of our village beyond recognition and altered the lives of its inhabitants in a myriad ways [136].

She realizes the final destruction caused by the tannery - taking their land away from them, their only hope, their only way of life. What else does a peasant know than the smell and feel of the earth beneath his feet? It is because of the tannery that Rukmini's sons went away from her, her son Raja got killed, her daughter Ira became a prostitute and now she lost her home. Now Nathan and Rukmini decide to go to the town to live with their son Murugan. After a long and tiresome journey they stop by a temple where free food was being served. After they finished eating they realize that they have lost their bundle and the money that they were carrying with them. With nothing much left to do they reach the place where Murugan was supposed to be residing. Upon arrival they are told that Murugan no longer worked there and they are given directions to another place. When they reach the Collector's house they are taken to meet Ammu, Murugan's wife. It is here that they learn that their son had deserted his wife two years ago. The place was so poverty stricken that they could not burden themselves on their daughter in law who did not welcome them. So they decide to return back to their village. But with no money for their return journey, they find their way back to the temple and live there for about a year. Here Rukmini decides to reads letters for others in order to earn some money. But none of the villagers take her seriously and she barely earns two annas on the first day.

But her hope is stirred and she is optimistic that soon they will be able to go home. Here they befriend a small orphan Puli who starts to live with them. A street smart kid that he is, he tells them how to earn more. He takes them to a stone quarry where people are employed for breaking stones. Rukmini adopts the boy as part of her family and loves him dearly. Now they are earning good money that in two months time they decide to go back home. In the mean while we find that Nathan health deteriorates further with no hope of recovery. He soon dies leaving Rukmini all by herself. With no hope of going further Rukmini decides to return back to her village. Such was her joy when she returned to her village and she says: "I felt the earth beneath my feet and wept for happiness" [192].

The story as seen from the narrator's point of view is a poignant tale of woe from the beginning to the end. Kamala has a knack of weaving a story that compels you to empathize with the characters; you actually feel the joy whenever Rukmini is happy and share in every sorrow that she goes through. *Nectar in a Sieve* is a novel filled with adversities that after a point of time it is too much to take in. Yet we find our protagonist holding on to the little moments of happiness in her life, through all the phases of adversity. She is trying to hold on to the nectar that she knows will not stay in the sieve.

Nowhere in the novel do we find Rukmini complaining about her circumstances. Even her disappointment does not last long for soon she is full of renewed hope that situations will change and life will be better. For ever optimistic, she is the pillar of support to her family. Rukmini's statement that, "we are all in God's hands. He will not fail us" [82] aptly summarizes the entire novel and what the story has to tell us. We can pick up a leaf out of this novel whenever we are faced with dejection. Life is centred on hope and faith in God and it is in our hands to be happy and content despite all the adversities that come in our path.

WORKS CITED

Dhawan, R.K., ed. *Indian Women Writers,* New Delhi: Prestige, 2001.

Khatri, C.L., *Indian Literature in English Critical Discourses,* Jaipur: Book Enclave, 2003

Markandaya, Kamala, *Nectar in a Sieve,* 1954, India: Viking – Penguin, 2007.

Mehrotra, Arvind Krishna, ed., *A History of Indian Literature in English,* New York: Columbia UP, 2003.

❑❑❑

22

Kamala Markandaya : A Crusading Spirit for the Welfare of Humanity and the Elevation of Human Suffering

S. RAJIYA SWAMY

Indian Novels are the priceless possessions in the domain of Indian Literature. A novel can be defined in broad terms as a piece of prose fiction, which dramatizes life with the help of characters and situations. It presents some aspect of human experiences and creates real-life atmosphere that is often gripping. The test of a great novel lies in its universal appeal.

There was a time when education was a rare opportunity & speaking English was unnecessary. The Indian English novel erupted and really changed our Nation and now Indian English speaks a global tongue unconfined to any particular culture or heritage. Indian novels have reached a notable status not only in Indian book market, but also globally. They gained a high-flaming fame & earned international acclamation.

The plethora of Indian literary personalities have penned down successive events in their novels and aired their stunning aura of creativity.

The Indian Diaspora raised the curtain on the fantastic mythical realities that were part of domestic conversations. The efforts of several generations of Indian authors writing in English have resulted in international success. The novel was not at first a common form, perhaps because the majority of women had less access to education than men. It was not until prose began to be used in the late nineteenth century by Bengali writers who had been exposed to European culture that the novel form took hold in India. Many Indian women novelists have explored female subjectivity in order to establish an identity. "A number of Indian women novelists made their debut in the 1990s, producing novels which revealed the true state of Indian society and its treatment of women".

The efforts of several generations of Indian authors writing in English have resulted in international success, particularly since the publication of *Midnight's Children* (1981) by Salman Rushdie, and the Indian novel in English has finally been accepted as an important literary endeavour. Indian women writers have begun to gain recognition, largely thanks to Arundhati Roy winning the Booker Prize for *The God of Small Things* in 1997. Behind this success lies a social history, and a body of other work to which little critical attention has yet been paid.

> The Vedas cry aloud, the Puranas shout;
> "No good may come to a woman".
> I was born with a woman's body
> How am I to attain truth?
> "They are foolish, seductive, deceptive –
> Any connection with a woman is disastrous".
> Bahina says, "If a woman's body is so harmful,
> How in the world will I reach truth?"
> [Bahinabai (1682-1700)].

Twentieth century witnessed a creative surge in Indian writing in English in general and women writings in particular. The women have realized that she is not helpless & is not dependent. A woman was no longer content to remain in the shadows of their husbands" As independent India progressed women came out of the confines of their homes & learn to assert themselves and were able to earn on their own. Today is the generation of those women writers who have money and are mostly of western education. Their write-ups encourage the women freedom to flirt and give a glimpse of the unexplored female psyche, which has no accessibility women writers affirmed the existence of women with identities of their own".

Women writers in India sweep you off your feet with just their down-to-earth attitudes. Women writers in India can no longer be claimed as the exclusive property of India. Their work and their art belong to the world. Our women writers have grappled with complex issues such as sensuality, servility, subjugation and society. They have handled them with a sense of balance.

The woman is now modern and bold enough in expressing herself. Women writings were a challenge to male stream. The history of feminism in India can be looked at as principally a practical effort. The women of modern era think on different lines & that is what depicted in their novels. Feminism means "Putting an end to all the suffering of women in silence". The Indian readers (Male & Female) read the novels of the Indian women authors with certain expectations. They look for some "Indian ness in their write ups. "Only the women novelists of India are capable of conveying the message of feminism in an Indian way".

The Indian literature has gifted several talented and really out spoken Indian women novelists like, Anita Desai; Shobha De; Bharati Mukherjee; Kamala Das; Indira Goswami; Dina Mehta; Kamala Markandaya and Namita Kokhale.

The last two decades have witnessed phenomenal success in feminist writings. We see Indian women writers like Shashi Deshpande, Arundhati Roy, Anita Desai, Kamala Das and Shobha De, just to name a few, who hold their own in the woman writer's world of initial rejection, dejection, familial bonds, domesticity and what not. It is amazing to note that these writers have climbed the ladder of success in a slow and painful way.

Authors like Kamala Markandaya, Shashi Deshpande & Anita Desai have chosen the problems & issues faced by the women in today's male dominated world. Some of the novels of Anita Desai portrayed the complexities between a man & woman relationship. A new pattern of Indian novels passed their way into the market and are imbibed with life through both speech & images. Anita Desai for social & economic justice had won the Booker Prize in 1997 for her novel *The God* which hit the deeply human chord. She was awarded the Sahitya Academy Award too in 2006. This fictional novel do sprang from her experiences. She painted vivid picture of the horrors of the caste system in India. *The God* is a stunning typical love story that took place in the communist state of Kerala.

Shashi Deshpande, on the other hand, started out just like any other starry eyed young writer- in- the- making. Like innumerable potential women writers she began her work with national magazines such as *Femina* and *Eve's Weekly*, slowly branched out to more serious literature oriented magazines such as The Illustrated Weekly of India, The Junior Statesman and so on. She has also mentioned that writing is a gift, sometimes like a fountain that spouts out words. Although she had the writer's gene in her system (Her father was a great Kannada dramatist and Sanskrit scholar), she has had her share of writer's block too. There have been times when she would not be able to write even a paragraph! According to her, writing is more like a 'patchwork quilt'. Bits and pieces come together at odd times and places and finally merge as a sequenced whole.

Kamala Das, the controversial writer who had her feet firmly on the ground and could get to the brass tacks in no time at all. She had a child marriage and three children followed. Her husband agreed that she should follow her instincts and in the process, augment the family income. But being a woman, however, she could not enjoy a regular morning-till-night working schedule. Her writing schedule was, on the contrary, a night-till-morning affair when the family had all gone to bed. Her working table was the kitchen table where she would cut up the vegetables, get the table cleared, and then, start typing. Though this working time-table reflected on her health, it did give her time to manage a home as well...a woman's idea of an essential pre-requisite for a job.

Shobha De, a controversial writer, has had diverse career roles ranging from model to columnist. All her published novels have been successful. Currently we have witnessed her make a literary transition from writing-projects based on a rather flashy, elite society with emphasis on its extra-marital affairs, to a more mature and rather philosophical work on life and the myriad of twists and turns in relationships.

Women writers in India are moving forward with their strong and sure strides, matching the pace of the world. We see them bursting out in full bloom spreading their own individual fragrances. They are recognized for their originality, versatility and the indigenous flavor of the soil that they bring to their work. Yes, they are our women writers. Writers first, I must insist. Gender is only incidental...but, one must admit, it does spice up their work. Kamala Markandaya, Shashi Deshpande & Anita Desai have chosen the problems & issues faced by the women in today's male dominated word as the main theme of their books. They tried to explore the psychological aspects.

These women writers have given literary work in India an unmistakable edge. They are able to sensitively portray a world that has in it women with rich in substance. Their women are real flesh-and- blood protagonists who make you look at them with awe with their relationships to their surroundings, their society, their men, their children, their families; their mental make-ups and themselves.

I think that a story is like the surface of water and you can take what you want from it. Its volubility is its strength. "Writing is architecture" and one such great architect is Kamala Markandaya who set her own trend not only through feminine subjectivity but also through her fluid, polished literary style. I would like to come up with such great novelist of the pioneering group of Indian women writers who made her mark through her subject matter.

Kamala Markandaya, one of the most outstanding and eminent Indo-Anglian novelists, shows a broad range and rich variety of setting, characters, and theme. Kamala Markandaya -- was a pseudonym used by Kamala Purnaiya Taylor, she moved to Britan, though she still labeled herself an Indian expatriate, she belonged to the pioneering group of Indian women writers who made their mark not just through their subject matter, but also through their fluid, polished literary style. Her works reflects the contemporary conflict between the Eastern & the Western Values. She was born in a small town in Mysore in the year of 1924. She completed her graduation in Madras University and later pursued a career in journalism from 1940 to 1947. She married a journalist colleague Bertrand Taylor who was an English man & permanently emigrated to Britain in 1948. Boston, 21 May 2004 – Indo-British novelist Kamala Markandaya, whose works were first published in the 1950s, passed away Sunday May 18 at her home in the outskirts of London. Markandaya was 80, and had settled in England since the age of 25, following her marriage to Bertrand Taylor.

Indian American author Shashi Tharoor put it succinctly when he admitted: "Markandaya was a pioneer who influenced all of us with Indian writing in English". As all want fame & success in life & these were earned by her first Novel, *Necter in a Sieve* in 1954. This novel became very popular it stood as the book-of-the month. It gained such recognition for it is surprise to know almost 12 PhD Theses have been written in American & British universities analyzing her writings. No doubts the fame she earned was out of immense strength of her wristings. She was robust enough in sensitive creation of individual characters & her mellifluous & controlled prose style.

Actually *Nectar in a Sieve* is her third novel which was written by her but this is the first to be published by signet classics. This book is of worth and became a best seller around the world & was also translated into 17 languages. She also penned down several novels which helped her in establishing her identity in the writing arena. The novel brims with life and finds an echo in every Indian heart. She is gifted with a fine faculty of fine perception The American Library Association named it as a "Notable Book of. 1955 Her Distinctive Style".

Markandaya, one of the revolutionary group of Indian women authors is remarkable for her polished presentation style. She projected the independent minded women. Intrinsic woes of women were exposed in her works. She also portrayed through her writing that "the very existence of women is tortuous & the condition is same everywhere".

Nectar in a sieve is:

- A short novel which gives a glance of the introduction of western students to life in rural India.
- It shows the changes that occurred during the country's Births colonization.
- A lyrical & Moving.
- A story of an arranged but love marriage rural peasant life.
- A tale of an indomitable human spirit that overcomes poverty & unending misfortune.
- A novel about the conflicts between a traditional agricultural culture & a bargaining industrial capitalistic society.
- A materialistic Novel which all over touches the important social phenomena,

Such as:

- Traditional Cultural practices.
- People's reluctance to change
- The impact of economic change.

Nectar in a Sieve is a remarkable saga of battling with abject poverty. We can examine the themes of the indomitable human spirit, the nature of love & human responses to suffering. *Nectar in a Sieve* is the sad story of a large poverty-striken Hindu family in a remote rural village in southern India. Despite valiant efforts, the family failed to extricate itself from abject poverty caused by hardships of nature and economics. This poverty forced the only daughter into prostitution and caused three sons to leave the village to seek employment. With very little to eat, it was a miracle the family remained alive. Inspite of their hardships, the family exhibited love, contentment, and hope that their situation would improve, but this hope never became a reality.

Nectar in a Sieve is a powerful, depressing, but ultimately hopeful novel of a life lived with love, faith, and inner strength – this is the very moving story of a peasant woman in a primitive village in India whose whole life was a gallant and persistent battle to care for those she loved. Her *Nectar in a Sieve,* said to be reminiscent of Thomas Hardy's novels, was published in 1954 and made her widely known. It is a restrained as well as a touching account of the life of an Indian peasant woman, Rukmani, and her struggle for survival and her abiding love for her husband, Nathan.

How It All Goes Down...We know this by the narrator Rukmani, an elderly woman, looking back over the events of her life. At the very onset Ruku (a nickname for Rukmani) launches into her life-story, describing what it means to be desperate and poverty stricken in rural 20th century India.

Rukmini begins her flashback reflecting on her marriage to Nathan. Ruku was the fourth daughter of a once-important village headman. As their wealth and status dwindled, it was hard to scrape together a dowry for Ruku. As a result this fourth daughter was married to Nathan, a poor tenant farmer with no land, but a noble man nonetheless with heart of gold. Ruku settles into a simple farming life very happily, as Nathan is kind and loving with her. The main problem, though, is that she has had only one child, a daughter named Ira, after six years of marriage.

Ruku desperately wants sons, because giving birth to boys is a point of pride in Indian culture. So she pours her heart out to Kenny, a white doctor whom our protagonist first met when he was helping her dying mother. Ruku undergoes fertility treatment despite the fact that she never mentions it to her husband, Nathan. It must've been pretty potent medicine, as Ruku has five sons in the next few years. The family is happy enough, despite all these new mouths to feed, when money is tight.

As the family grew size, their resources diminished & their problems increased with very little substance to begin with, the family became dependant on a small tract of land they ruted from heartless and lord 'Biswas'

Big changes arrived with the construction of a tannery, where animal skins are cured. The noisy process disturbs Ruku, as she watches her home transformed from a quiet village to a dirty town. Other big changes come as Ira grows older and turns fourteen, for that is the traditional age of marriage. A friendly member of the village, Old Granny, finds Ira a nice match through the common practice of arranged marriage. Ira's groom is the sole inheritor of some land. Irawaddy the only daughter of Ruku, is married at the age of 14 but separates from her husband because she cannot bear him a child.She returned to live with her parents. Poverty forced her into prostitution. How unlucly she was! She eventually had an illegitimate albino son, Sacrabani: "Every Thing is going out nothing is a coming in".

The two eldest sons Arjun & Thambi do not want to work on the land with their father because they saw no hope of improving their situation. They are employed at the tannery & are able to make a financial contribution to the home. For this brief period they enjoyed some degree of prosperity. They lost their jobs at the tannery for instigating a strike. They emigrate to Ceylon (Sri Lanka) to work and have no communication with the family.

The family's home was a mud-walled structure with attached roof & earthen floor. They planted rice & vegetables crops were destroyed by drought & monsoon. They were forced to sell most of their possesions & live extremely frugally. When the family was small, the gap was good and the boys worked in the tannery the family ate well and were able to store some of their rice.

Kensington (Kenny) is a benevolent village white doctor who discharges his functions delight this ambition is to build a hospital with foreign aid in that village. For he kept his heart & soul in their project Kenny became a very close family friend & helped them with money, food & Medicine.

Nathan (Rukus Husband) a hardworking & supportive hopes for better time. Rice cultivation, being very laborious, took a tall on his health. He was very disappointed because the two elder sons understandable did not help much.

The construction of the tannery in the village provided employment for same but increased the price of consumer goods & succeeded in squeezing many of the peasants off the land.

Nathan's land was sold to the tannery, he and Rukmini went to the city in search of their 3rd and Murugun with who they had never corresponded. They failed in finding their son who was married & fathered a son but deserted his son & wife. He was not in touch with his wife or parents.

The city too played its cruel role on the lives of Nathan & Ruku They lost their few belongings & money when they sought refuge in the temple. They survived on handouts of food given as offerings to the God & Goddess in the temple.

Nathan & Ruku yearned for the land from the back breaking work they acquired at a stone quarry with the help of Puli, a destitute but cunning street boy.

Nathan was beaten by poverty and the painful living conditions led him to death. Raja, forth son becomes frail because of malnutrition & is beaten to death by the watchmen when he was found rummaging for food in the vicinity of the tannery. Kuti, the youngest who ws closely attached to Ira. In spite of her efforts to buy him food with money she earned from prostitution keti dies from malnutrition. "Ira unchanged her body for kutis milk and food....but...."

A little ray of hope & life was with Selvam the 5th son. Though the cycle of poverty would continued for the family i.e., the remnants despite severe blows "Ruku, Ira, Puli" relied on Kenny & Selvam for support Selvam built on what his mother taught him & thus become the most educated person in the family. He was apprenticed to Kenny & looked forward to the completion of the hospital.

After the death of Nathan Ruku returned to the village with Poli, whom she introduced as her adapted son and for whom. She expected medical attention from Kenny to rid him of the disease which had eaten away his fingers.

The novel appeals to the modern readers for its sensitive & moving portrayal of the strength of a woman struggling with forces beyond her control. It is a gripping story on one tireless woman's survival of a checked life. Misfortune seemed to have a tight foothold on them. Hope and fear acted like twin forces that tugged at them in one direction and another. "Ruku's life had no parameter for misfortunes".

The living conditions, life struggle, poverty, fragility were depicted here are beyond imagination. In Kamala Markandaya's *Netar in a Sieve* readers will find a determined, remarkable fighter in a women who bears an unfailing faith. The real experience of the central character, Rukmani and her journey through the harsh realities are ideally depicted in the novel. *Nectar in a sieve* has an allusion to the famous Coleridge's poem *Work without hope*. The lines:

> "Work without hope draws nectar in a sieve & hope
> without an object cannot live' finds a divine expression
> in the novel *Nectar in a Sieve*.
> Hope stands as a very important attribute of the lives.
> Thus the title aptly befitted.

Nectar in a Sieve was an "Epic of the Indian Village". Kamala Markandaya was a social-realist and she depicted the realities of life in South India.

In conclusion, the work of Indian women writers is significant in making society aware of women's demands, and in providing a medium for self-expression and, thus, re-writing the History of India. Their work is marked by an impressive feel for the language, and an authentic presentation of contemporary India, with all its regional variations. They generally write about the urban middle class, the stratum of society they know best. Recent writers depict both the diversity of women and the diversity within each woman, rather than limiting the lives of women to one ideal. The novels emerging in the twenty-first century furnish examples of a whole range of attitudes towards the imposition of tradition, some offering an analysis of the family structure and the caste system as the key elements of patriarchal social organization. They also re-interpret mythology by using new symbols and subverting the canonic versions.

The image of women in fiction has undergone a change during the last four decades. Women writers have moved away from traditional portrayals these writers were born after Indian independence, and the English language does not have colonial associations for them. In contrast to earlier novels, female characters from the 1980s onwards assert themselves and defy marriage and motherhood.

The majority of novels written by women writers depict the psychological suffering of the frustrated housewife, the subject matter often being considered superficial compared to the depiction of the repressed and oppressed lives of women of the lower classes. Prior to the rise of the novel, many Indian women composed poetry and short stories in Hindi, Punjabi, Bengali, Urdu, Tamil, Malayalam and Kannada. Women were the chief upholders of a rich oral tradition of story-telling, through myths, legends, songs and fables. Once literacy began to filter through society, those stories were transformed into poetry, drama and later novel form which took hold in India.

The Indian English novel has passed through a tough time. There was a time when Mulk Raj Anand's *Untouchable* was left untouched by British publishers before being recommended by E.M. Foster to Lawrence and Wishart to accept it. The same happened with R.K. Narayan whose *Swami and Friends* had to wait for Graham Greene's recommendation. But today the case is different. Indian English literature is now readily accepted abroad. In fact Indian English novelists have elevated themselves by overtaking novelists whose mother-tongue is English in the race to win major literary awards. An important feature of this period was the growth of Indian women novelists writing in English. Their appearance added a new dimension to Indian English novel. It is only after India gained freedom that they have begun enriching Indian English fiction.

❑❑❑

23

Cross-culture in the Oeuvre of Jhumpa Lahiri

INDU GOYAL

Literature always has its lion's share in bringing, projecting and highlighting the changes in the society. The recent writings in Indian English are full of colour and grandeur, its dimensions extending to life and manners in new civilization and new literature. In the last two decades, there has been an astonishing flowering of Indian women writing in English and the literature of the period is published both in India and elsewhere. The authors are mostly western educated who express in their writing their discontent with the repressive tradition and culture that entrap entire mankind in the shackles of 'unidentified and suppressed individuality'.

In this present era when all the barriers, borders are breaking and this world has become a country. Dr. Malti Agrawal explains about diasporic writings:

> The Diasporic writing which are also known as 'expatriate writings' or 'immigrant writings' largely give voice to the traumatic experiences of the writers when they are on the rack owning to the clash of two cultures or the racial discrimination they undergo. Immigration proves a pleasant experience only to a few immigrants who succeed in assimilating themselves with new geographical, cultural, social and psychological environment[1].

While talking of Indian diaspora fiction in English, so many questions prop up in our mind, for instance, does it have its independent identity, does it possess some unique characteristics that determine its separate status, does it reflect 'Indianness' in true sense, how such writers rule over Indian English writing, and so on and so forth.

Normally diaspora fiction lingers over alienation, loneliness, homelessness, existential rootlessness, nostalgia, protest and assertions and quest of identity, it also addresses issues related to amalgamation or disintegration of cultures, discriminating margins of two different social milieus, internalizing nostalgia and suffering a forced amnesia-we may call it a literary/cultural phenomenon with a distinct melting pot syndrome or that of salad bowl where identity of each ingredient is under question. Surprisingly, the writer has to relocate himself afresh for which he has to undergo penance such as readjustment, adaptation, participation and fulfillment amidst dilemmas and self-imposed ghettoisation.

The recent writers like Jhumpa Lahiri, Kiran Desai, Chitra Banerjee are exploring the cultural clash suffered by Indian woman who is given western education. The experience of being caught between two cultures has remained a prominent theme in their writings. There are many Indian women writers based in USA, Canada, Britain and other parts of the world. Some are recent immigrants, while others such as Jhumpa Lahiri, are second-generation immigrants. These authors write about their situations in cross-cultural contexts-state of 'in- betweenness'. Many of their writings carry their auto-biographical elements. They have explored female subjectivity in order to establish an identity that is not imposed by a patriarchal society. The image of the new woman and her struggle for an identity needs support structures in and outside the family to enable women to survive.

While the first generation migrants like Anita Desai, Shashi Deshpande and Bharati Mukherjee projected the issues like rootlessness, racism, nostalgia and longing, the second generation writers with their weak grasp of actual condition in contemporary India are trying to project their 'imaginary homeland' as they are not directly in contact with reality of India. This 'distance' leads to objectivity and ossification of cultural constructs.

Jhumpa Lahiri explores the fashionable themes of racial and cultural identity. "Its theme of dislocation and the pain of building a new life in a different world shows that in building the new life, something must also be destroyed"[2]. Jhumpa masterfully explores the themes of complexities of the immigrant experience and foreignness, the clash of life-style, cultural disorientation, the conflicts of assimilation, the tangled lies between generations and paints a portrait of an Indian family torn between the pull of respecting family tradition and the American way of life.

Lahiri, the Bostonian, is a true-blood Bengali. Inspite of having lived all her life in the U.K. and U.S.A., she shows the subtle nuances of typical Bengali life and culture, like the back of her hand. While her Pulitzer-winning collection of stories *Interpreter of Maladies* is mainly based on her experience in Kolkata, her novel *The Namesake* powerfully depicts the disillusionment of the Bengali immigrants to the US, whose children grow up rootless-alien to the culture of their country of origin, not completely comfortable in the society in which they actually live. Readers seem to be mesmerized by Jhumpa Lahiri's writings, and their curiosity brings her audience together. As author Jaydeep Sarangi explains, "Jhumpa Lahiri's stories are the gateway into the large submerged territory of 'cross-culturalism'. It is a metaphor to share cultures.....something that will allow them/us to share, instead of dividing, what is on either side"[3].

Author Judith Caesar reasons that, "Americans can learn about themselves and create a richer system of encountering the other foreign custom and ways of thinking of the Indian characters – sometimes without even fully realizing that they have come to understand or the opportunity they have missed"[4]. But in some ways Lahiri herself struggles to understand Indian culture. In an interview with India - West, Lahiri admits: "I'm lucky that I'm between two worlds. I don't really know what a distinct South Asian identity means. I don't think about that when I write, I just try to bring a person to life"[5] and that is exactly what she does through her characters. Writer Nalini Iyer feels, "a story teller is characterization. The people she creates are real, alive, complicated, and individual. She never descends into stereotypes nor does she engage in grand generalization about social and political relationships. Instead, she sweeps her readers through a range of emotions and experiences and lets her characters speak for themselves"[6]. One of the main reasons for

Lahiri's success as a writer is because she writes for herself. Lahiri is able to demonstrate her point in writing merely mentioning the issue that a character is facing. This is a technique that is present in much of her writings. "Jhumpa Lahiri's stories do not revolve around the "Indian ness" of the characters. India is always in the background, but the characters and their emotions are simply human"[7].

Lahiri often toys with the reversal of gender roles, especially as they relate to husband and wife roles within marriages. Whereas in India, a strict set of guidelines dictates how husbands and wives act both publicly, in America, such guidelines are not as clear-cut and, oftentimes, are thrown out altogether. Lahiri's married characters often deal with confusions of marriage roles in relation to cooking, working outside the home, and bearing children. According to Lahiri's generalizations of Indian marital culture, women are solely responsible for cooking and doing household chores, as well as becoming completely domesticated with the arrival of children. Men are, according to such guidelines, responsible for working and providing their families with a monetary income.

Many of Lahiri's characters, specifically the ones in diaspora, must cope with new and sometimes shockingly different gender stereotypes and roles in their new homelands.nearly all of her characters are defined by isolation of some form or the another: husbands are isolated from wives; immigrants are isolated from their families; children are isolated from their parents; and people are isolated from the communities in which they live. In their isolations, these characters feel that they are missing something vital to their identities. It is this missing 'something' that defines them. It seems that few characters in these stories any idea of who they are or where they are going in life. Lahiri's characters defy simple explanations of what their problems are; frequently we are given only a brief glimpse into their lives, a look at one key moment that somehow defines their lack of self-understanding. Generation gaps, culture shock upon moving away from the "homeland" and questions of sexuality play their roles in Lahiri's interpretations of gender and what it means to Indians in Diaspora.

Ketu H. Katrak reads *The Interpreter of Maladies* as reflecting the trauma of self-transformation through immigration, which can result in a series of broken identities that from "multiple anchorages". Lahiri's stories show the diasporic struggle to keep hold of culture as characters create new lives in foreign cultures. Relationships, language, rituals and religion all help these characters maintain their culture in new surroundings even as they build a "hybrid realization" as Asian Americans[8].

Jhumpa's modern approach is evident in her themes as well as narrative style. Some of her stories like the 'The third and the final continent' contain moving pictures of life. The Calcutta boy who gets a job in library at MIT Boston, reminds us of many Indians who by trial and tribulation settle abroad for a better life.

The bond between the landlady Mrs. Croft and the Bengali youth is beyond explanation. It is something to be felt and under-stood. When Mrs. Croft is introduced with his wife, the one hundred and three years old lady spontaneously calls her a perfect lady. The fact of her judgment comes as a surprise and at once ends the strangeness that existed between the newly married couple. It also comes home to us that basically humanity is bound by certain common standards of behaviour and modes of perception.

What is more important is the fact that however deep and wide ranging the experience of meeting different people and living in different places may be, Lahiri in her own inimitable style convinces us through her characters that there is always something new, something unexpected in life. How true the narrator is when he says: "There are times I am bewildered by each mile I have travelled, each meal I have eaten, each person I have known, and each room in which I have slept. As ordinary as it all appears, there are times when it is beyond my imagination"[9].

In an exclusive interview, Jhumpa Lahiri says about the story *When Mr. Pirzada Comes to Dine* that "this story is based on a gentleman from Bangladesh who used to come to my parents house in 1971, I heard from my parents what his predicament was. And when I learned about his situation, which was that he was in the United States during the Pakistani civil war and his family was back in Dacca, I was so overwhelmed by this information that I wrote this story".

Mrs. Sen is a story that defines what emotional exile is. As in the other stories the immigrants experience is at the core of this stirring story too. In addition we also witness this wonderful companionship between two entirely different persons. Mrs. Sen has to fetch a small boy from his house to hers and back as the boy's mother is a working lady. Mrs. Sen expresses her joy and loneliness and shares her Indian memories with great nerve. Eliot listens the variety and uniqueness of her life in Calcutta, India. Her religion, food and the living pattern come alive in her words. When Eliot grows and is stopped by her mother to go to Mrs. Sen, he seems to be missing their togetherness and as a result goes through a kind of void as he watches the gray waves receding from the shore. Once again we see this common human factor well voiced by the writer. It is the emotional dependence that binds Eliot and Mrs. Sen whose only other family members leave them on their own.

In *Unaccustomed Earth* Jhumpa with eight dazzling stories takes us from Cambridge and Seattle to India and Thailand. This book also deals with various male-female relationships-in the context of the immigrant experience. Specifically, Lahiri examines the gulf between first and the second generation immigrants-the expectations, often unmet, dress, achievement and marriage. These stories scrutinize the fate of the second and third generations. As succeeding generations become increasingly assimilated into American culture and are comfortable in constructing perspectives outside of their country of origin, Lahiri's fiction shifts to the need of the individual. She shows how later generations depart from the constraints of their immigrant parents, who are often devoted to their community and their responsibility to other immigrants. The first five stories are thematically related. Each story seems to feature parents who bring their children back to Calcutta each summer to visit relatives; each story features children who struggle to conform to their parents' traditional expectations as well as the cultural demands of an American adolescence. The children often born in United States are more connected to the States. The Bengali culture is slipping away with each succeeding generation. Parents consider India as "Home", while the children only endure those repeated trips back there. "Home" for children is where they now live, a home with a new set of mores, language, dress and relationships. There is a definite generational conflict.

In the title story, a daughter of Indian descent, Ruma, welcomes her unexpectedly widower father with trepidation to her new home in Seattle. Ruma is married to a Caucasian named Adam, and they have a young son named Akash. In every respect the young family is a model of mixed marriage and, in Ruma's case, full cultural assimilation. Nevertheless, her father's visit promises to force Ruma to confront the inevitable fissures that appear between first and second generation immigrant families. Travel to new countries or setting into new lands, postcards of foreign places, the soil in gardening, and measurement of distances all serve in symbolic support to the story's title, but it is a simple misplaced and unmailed postcard that pulls everything together into a poignant ending.

Lahiri's other four stories of this section have similar themes. In *Hell-Heaven*, a young woman recalls her childhood when a fellow Bengali became a family friend and part of her life. The assimilated Bengali-American narrator considers how little thought she once gave to her mother's sacrifices as she reconstructs the tormenting, unrequited passion her young mother had for a graduate student during the narrator's childhood. Usha's mother is left heartbroken when Pranab decides to marry a white woman. At Pranab's wedding, Lahiri depicts various cultural clashes between Bengali and American cultures.

In *Choice of Accommodation*, a middle aged, mixed married couple (Amit and Megan) rediscovers themselves and a bit of their previously unstated history during a friend's wedding held at Amit's old boarding school. Amit feels his parents have left him years ago. Now, as he and his American wife Megan return to his prep school for a reunion, he tells a complete stranger that their marriage has "disappeared". Just as they choose the place where they stay for the weekend, they make accommodation in their lives.

In *Only Goodness*, a model Bengali daughter named Sudha, married and a new mother, tries to cope with her younger brother Rahul's alcoholic failings and her likely role in making him what he has become. Of all the characters in this book, it is Rahul who comes across most powerfully. This story towers over others in the collection, not only because of Lahiri's skilful, succinct prose, but also because the author liberates her writings from simplistic cultural baggage and allows her characters to breathe as individuals.

And in *Nobody's Business*, a American graduate student pines for his Bengali-American roommate, a graduate-school dropout who entertains no romantic feelings for him, spurns the polite advances of "perspective grooms" from the global Bengali singles circuit and considers herself engaged to a selfish, foul-tempered Egyptian historian.

In this collection of stories, each story creates a unique, self-contained world. Yet, there is always the metaphor of disconnection, disengagement with life in America. And, despite the clear Bengali frame of reference on which each story is hung, these are universal themes: the loss of a parent or spouse, the sense of not fitting in, being ill at ease in a strange society.

Jhumpa Lahiri introduces us to people who left behind family and friends and the familiar heat and bustle of Indian to build a new life in America — a cold, bleak land of strangers and new customs. Lahiri's sweet, sometimes deep, sometimes quirky first novel *The Namesake,* picks up on these themes and then expands on them, following the Indian-American immigrant experience through to the next generation as she tracks the member of the Ganguli family.

The story begins in 1968, shortly before the birth of one Gogol, whose parents Ashima and Ashoke, have only recently moved to Cambridge, Massachusetts, from Calcutta. For Ashoke, who is studying for his Ph.D. in electrical engineering at MIT, his new life in United States and his new baby son represent a personal rebirth of sorts. Having miraculously survived a terrible train wreck back in India in his teenage years — the others in the train all perished, but he, having stayed up late reading stories by Nikolai Gogol rather than retiring to his sleeping birth, was spared-Ashoke has vowed to see the world.

But as Ashoke relishes the strangeness of his new home, his young wife Ashima whom his parents have arranged for him to marry, initially mourns the life she has left behind. Yet for her, too, her born - in - the USA baby, Gogol represents the new life she will build in her adopted home, the new roots she will plant and cultivate in America even as her old roots in Calcutta begin to wither and die.

Writing in the long form, Lahiri is able to do what she could not in her short stories: follow her characters beyond one pivotal moment in their lives and track their development and growth. And if some of the recent immigrants in *Interpreter of Maladies* seemed almost unbearably sad — their pain all too exquisitely conveyed — Ashima's similarly depressed state lasts only a chapter or two before relenting as she begins to build a new community around her and to fit happily into her new life.

In her first novel *The Namesake* Lahiri again displays her deft touch for the perfect detail-the fleeting moment, the turn of phrase-that opens whole world of emotion. *The Namesake* takes the Ganguli family from their tradition bound life in Calcutta through their fraught transformation into Americans. On the heels of their arranged wedding Ashoke & Ashima settle together in Cambridge, Massachusetts. An engineer by profession, Ashoke adapts far less warily than his wife, who resists all things American and pines for her family. She remains the typical lady in spite of her physical location in Cambridge, for so many years. At the beginning, when she is in the labor and her water breaks, Ashima calls out to Ashoke, her husband. However, she does not use his name because this would not be proper. According to her: "It's not the type of thing Bengali wives do… a husband's name is something intimate and therefore unspoken …cleverly patched over"[11]. From the statement we are shown how important privacy is to Bengali families. Ashoke is forward-thinking, ready to enter into American culture if not fully at least with an open mind. His young bride is far less malleable. Isolated, desperately missing her large family in India, she will be at peace with this new world.

Soon after they arrive in Cambridge, their first child is born. According to Indian custom, the child will be given two names: an official name, to be bestowed by the great-grandmother, and a pet name to be used only by family. But the letter from India with the child's official name never arrives, and so the baby's parents decide on a pet name to use for the time-being. Ashoke chooses a name that has particular significance for him: on a train trip back in India several years earlier, he had been reading a short story collection by one of his most beloved Russion writers, Nikolai Gogol, when the train derailed in the mid of the night, killing almost all the sleeping passengers onboard. Ashoke had stayed awake to read his Gogol, and he believes the book saved his life. His child will be known, then, as Gogol.

But Gogol, because of some circumstances cannot adjust between these two cultures, resulting it always haunts him to be called Gogol. He finds his strange name a constant irritant, and eventually he changes it to Nikhil. Gogol knows only that he suffers the burden of his heritage as well as his odd, antic name.

Awkwardness is Gogol's birthright. He grows up a bright American boy, goes to Yale, has pretty girlfriend, becomes a successful architect, but like many second generation immigrants, he can never quite find his place in the world. There's a lovely section where he dates a wealthy, cultured young Manhatten woman who lives with her charming parents. They fold Gogol into their easy, elegant life, but even here he can find no peace and he breaks off the relationship. His mother finally sets him up on a blind date with the daughter of a Bengali friend, and Gogol thinks he has found his match. Moushumi, like Gogol, is at odds with the Indian-American world.

Like every American kid, Gogol eventually moves away from home. He does not hate his parents. Far from it, he is very devoted to them. But the things they say do not interest him and their Indian way of life means nothing to him. He detests the way they hold on to Indian tradition and functions that are of no importance to his American mind. He hates it when his parents whisk them off to Calcutta. A place the couple still consider home, for months together, disrupting his entire schedule. Inspite of his yearly sojourns to Calcutta, he does not feel bound to India as they are.

Unfortunately his parents fail to understand him too, though they do try to give him the best of both worlds by religiously celebrating every Indian and American holiday. But the host of Bengali acquaintances he meets at these gatherings tends to put him off and distances him further. There are a few poignant moments that involve Ashoke and Gogol, but beyond that the feelings seem to be lost in the humdrum of daily lives. Ashima is a perpetually depressed character who goes through the motions of life without any enthusiasm. Is she sad because feels lost in this new country? Is she sad because she has not that intimate relationship with her husband she was expecting for? Do her children and her husband never sit together and have fun?

Like his American friends, Gogol drinks, smokes pot and has more than one romantic relationship and is able to dissociate himself from the memories of his girlfriend, though with great difficulty. He goes about his life without a sense of purpose, going where fate leads him. Gogol never thinks to do otherwise. He does take a few drastic steps in his life, but they are motivated more by his rebellious streak against his upbringing rather than a genuine desire to swim against the current. His unfortunate choice in marriage stems from an instinctive desire to cling to his Indian roots.

Is Gogol's life a prototype? Do all Indian immigrant children face the same predicament? Do they all go through a similar reckless phase in their lives, sleeping with every random girl they just meet because it is forbidden? Do their American values clash with their Indian culture, so much that they almost end up being zombies like Gogol? Do they all feel the same indifference towards their parents? Are their relationships ill fated just because they have two conflicting cultures deeply embedded in them? Do they all struggle hard to hide their Indian side from their American peers?

Finally, which way of life or thinking does Lahiri Advocate for a 'successful' immigrant experience? Lahiri's book is less of an insightful study and more of an autobiographical description of the Indian immigrant experience and how it can sometimes go awry. Lahiri's essays and interviews suggest that she herself is a victim of the 'humiliating', her own adjective, process of immigration.

But like Gogol, Lahiri says she herself has now reached the stage in her life where she thinks that bicultural upbringing is a rich, even though imperfect thing. Yet, by her own admission a part of her years is to be completely American, call it a contradiction of sorts, just like any other contradiction in Gogol's life.

The Namesake is about this perpetual dilemma faced by immigrants as they struggle to maintain their identities while trying to shake them off at the same time. It is about the series of distressing choices they are faced to make every day as they try hard to avoid being misfits in a foreign land. *The Namesake* might not be the most authentic portrayal of the Indian-American experience, but even with its one dimensional approach, it manages to make a profound impact.

Jhumpa tries to relocate her cultural space and identity mediated by significant cross- cultural influence. She confessed to Radhika S Shankar:

> When I began writing fiction seriously, my first attempt, for some reason, was always set in Calcutta which is a city, I know quite well from repeated visits with my family, sometimes for several months at a time[12].

Inspite of such strong emotional nourishment, Lahiri at the same time also does not fail to mention the typical immigrant phenomenon of belonging nowhere that even in India, she did not feel at home. She also stresses the dichotomy of growing up in two cultures-how it bothered her when grew up that there was no single place to which she fully belonged.

Jhumpa Lahiri, a recent entrant into the world of Indian writers, tackles the much debated topic of cultural identity of India in a far off land. 'The Namesake' is an ambitious attempt to chart the lives of a family of immigrants through the eyes of a young boy. Both her books have received brickbats as well as accolades but she deserves a mention for tackling a subject long ignored by other Indian writers.

WORKS CITED

1. Agarwal, Malti, *Voice of Indian Diaspora: A Book-review in English Literature*, ed. Atlantic Publishers and Distributors, New Delhi, 2009, pp. 41-42.
2. Quoted in the beginning of the novel *The Namesake* — a review in the *Spectator*.
3. Sarangi, Jaydeep, *The Enigma of Cultural Multiplicity: A Study of Interpreter of Maladies, Jhumpa Lahiri, the mater of stiry teller: A Critical Response to Interpreter of Maladies*, Ed., Suman Bala. New Delhi: Khosla Pub. House, 2002, pp.116-121.
4. Caesar, Judith, *Beyond Cultural Identity in Jhumpa Lahiri's 'When Mr. Pirjada came to dine', North Dakota Quaterly* 70.1, 2003, pp.82-91.
5. Tsering, Lisa, *The Essence of Identity; Jhumpa Lahiri Straddles Too Worlds in The Namesake*, India-West Sept 12, 2003: B1.
6. Iyer, Nalini, *Stories Emphasize Indians' Encounters with American*, International examiner Oct 20, 1999:7.
7. Vasthare, Mekhala, *"bbee"-a book review*, Ann Arbor, MI United States-June 26, 2000.
8. Katrak, Ketu H., *The Aesthetics of Dislocation, The Women's Review of Books*, XIX, no.5, February 2002, 5-6.
9. Lahiri, Jhumpa, *Interpreter of Maladies*, Houghton Miffin, Boston, 1999.
10. Farnsworth, Elizabeth, An Online Newshour Interview, April 12, 2000.
11. Lahiri, Jhumpa, *The Namesake*, Houghton Miffin, Boston, 2003, p.2.
12. Shanker, Radhika, *R. Lahiri's first Book Gets Raves.*
13. http://www.rediff.com/new/may22/1999.

24

Immigrant Voices in Jhumpa Lahiri's *Unaccustomed Earth*

ANJU BALA AGRAWAL

Jhumpa Lahiri belongs to a new generation of the writers of the Diaspora who deals with the themes of immigration, assimilation, exiles and émigrés. Lahiri portrays the tensions of Indians abroad who have immigrated from their homeland and try to integrate themselves into their adopted homeland while adhering to their native culture. She focuses on characters moving from one place to another, meeting each other, or separating and in their subtle tensions and conflicts rediscovering moments of happiness or pain. In her latest work, *Unaccustomed Earth*, we have another brilliant collection of short stories with a similar pattern of movement as in the earlier works, The Pulitzer prize winning *Interpreter of Maladies* (1999) and *The Namesake* (2004), but here the reasons are more personal, of family dynamics, death in the family or starting families where the children of the first generation of immigrants struggle with tangled filial relationships and identity. Lahiri, herself of Bengali descent but born in London, raised in Rhode Island and now living in Brooklyn seems to be telling that it is not necessary that the place one is born in, is the one which provides the strongest attachment, but the place that allows one to become yourself. It is in the land of *Unaccustomed Earth* where one strikes new roots to thrive and flourish. Jhumpa Lahiri has an uncanny gift for turning 'unaccustomed earth' into a familiar habitat of fiction where she consorts with upwardly mobile immigrant

Bengalis enacting their exquisite little dramas of belonging and un-belonging, of losing and finding themselves all over again.

The last two decades have seen high levels of emigration from Asian countries thereby giving rise to cultural alienation that forms a major theme of Indian English writing. As expressed by Salman Rushdie, immigrants are always at a loss to understand which culture is actually theirs. "Migrants straddle two cultures...fall between stools, who suffer from a triple dislocation, comprising the loss of roots, the linguistic and also the social dislocation"[1].

Self-exile and cultural alienation is a complex evolutionary process that brings forth cross cultural shifts, loss of mother tongue and a conflict between one's own native element and a dominant foreign ethos. Diasporic writing brings out the cross cultural concerns that come out of the challenging encounters between two cultures that are completely antithetical in their attitudes and values. It is this that Jhumpa Lahiri's writing is all about. She knows from first hand experience what it is to be pulled in two directions. In an interview she said:

> I think that for immigrants, the challenges of exile, the loneliness, the constant sense of alienation, the knowledge of and longing for a lost world are more explicit and distressing than for their children. On the other hand, the problem for the children of immigrants those with strong ties to their country of origin - is that they feel neither one thing nor the other[2].

The underlying theme of Jhumpa Lahiri's sensitive new collection of stories, *Unaccustomed Earth* is that America is still a place where the rest of the world comes to reinvent itself – accepting with excitement and anxiety the necessity of leaving behind the constrictions and comforts of distant customs. The eight stories in Lahiri's new book, a genre she has refined since her debut Pulitzer Prize-winning *Interpreter of Melodies*, are on transformations intrinsic to the immigrant experience when seemingly rooted people are transplanted into the American soil. The eight stories in this splendid volume expand upon Lahiri's epigraph, a metaphysical passage from "The Custom-House," by Nathaniel Hawthorne, which suggests that transplanting people into new soil makes them hardier and more flourishing. Human fortunes may be improved, Hawthorne argues, if men and women "strike their roots into unaccustomed earth"[3]. It's an apt, rich metaphor for the transformations Lahiri oversees in these pages, in which two generations of Bengali immigrants to America – the newcomers and their hyphenated children – struggle to build normal and secure lives. But Lahiri does not so much accept Hawthorne's notion as test it. Is it true that transplanting strengthens the plant? Or can such experiments produce mixed outcomes? The eight stories are longer than those in her previous collection but just as absorbing and as beautifully written. The stories are set in various locales, from Seattle and Cambridge to India and Thailand, but all concern Bengalis struggling to adapt to new homelands and ways of life. The stories stem from migration or an exploration of Bengalis' dual identities. However, it would be really short-sighted to just focus on ethnic identity because they reflect back to us the way love and relationships function in our life -- be it romantic or familial and that is universal to us all.

Lahiri shows that people may be felled at any time by swift jabs of chance, wherever they happen to live. Uncontrollable events may assail them – accidents of fate, health or weather. More often, they suffer less dramatic reversals: failed love affairs, alcoholism, even simple passivity - the sort of troubles that seem avoidable to everyone except the person who succumbs to them. Again and again, the reader is caught off-guard by the accesses of emotion and experience that waylay Lahiri's characters, despite their peregrinations, their precautions, their concealments.

Five stories comprise the first part; three stories, featuring the same central characters comprise the second part. All eight stories, but the first five especially, are thematically related. They trace the lives of Bengalis who have moved to the United States. They experience a disconnection in their new lives. Many adults struggle to hold on to what they once knew, their circle of friends being largely other Bengali expatriates who are strangers in a strange land. The children, often born in the United States, are more connected to the States. The Bengali culture is slipping way with each succeeding generation. Parents consider India as "home," while the children only endure those repeated trips back there. "Home" for children is where they now live, a home with a new set of moves, language, dress, and relationships. There is a definite generational conflict. The children seldom read or speak Bengali. They serve as "cultural translators" for their parents in this new land, a phenomenon that is happening among any number of immigrant families in schools today.

The title story clearly demonstrates this theme of loss. The central character of this story, the first in the collection, is Ruma, a lawyer and second- generation Bengali living in the USA. She is married to an American. They have a child, Akash, who is three, and she is pregnant again. She is very isolated. Her husband's work has moved them to Seattle, where she knows no one, and Ruma has given up work to look after Akash before he goes to school. Despite herself, she finds herself living the life she was determined to rise above: "Her mother's example - moving to a foreign place for the sake of marriage, caring exclusively for children and a household - had served as a warning, a path to avoid. Yet this was Ruma's life, now" (11). Ruma's husband is away for the week on a business trip.

Ruma's father, now widowed, comes to visit them after his travels in Europe; he started traveling after Ruma's mother died. Her father has been traveling since his wife's death, always sending postcards to Ruma, but "never a sense of her father's presence in those places" (4). When he comes, Ruma is afraid he wants to move in with them, something that had been common in Bengali families. She has to face this issue largely alone, because Adam is away on a business trip. Ruma is disengaged with her community, with life outside her home, and her father is keeping a secret from her. As her father forms a deep connection with his grandson through the planting of a garden, Ruma reconnects with her father, asking him to move in with her family, he declines the offer. However, her father has gotten used to living alone. What is more, recently he has started dating Mrs. Bagchi, a Bengali widow he met while traveling. While he is there, Ruma's father puts in a garden. Just before he leaves, he writes a postcard to Mrs. Bagchi in Bengali. Her young son Akash ends up taking the postcard. Ruma realizes her father is dating someone, even though she cannot read the message.

The story contains moments of aching poignancy as memories rise up and as Ruma and her father seeks to find comfortable common ground. The story switches seamlessly between their two points of view, and between story present and memory. Lahiri explores with great tenderness what it is to be pulled in different directions in the small struggles that surface for them both each day of her father's short visit. Lahiri knows about children. Akash is a wonderful little character, the perfect catalyst to allow his mother and his grandfather to discover things about each other that they do not want to reveal openly. There are many types of unaccustomed earth, literal and metaphorical. Ruma's garden, untended and bare, is planted by her father during his visit, with help (both hilariously and movingly) from Akash.

The nurturing force field of pregnancy shields Ruma from the sting this reflection might be expected to provoke, but it doesn't protect her widowed father. When he visits her in Seattle from his condo in Pennsylvania, he asks her a very American question: "Will this make you happy?" (36) Urging Ruma not to isolate herself, to look for work, he reminds her that "self-reliance is important" (38). Thinking back on his wife's unhappiness in the early years of their marriage, he realizes that he had always assumed Ruma's life would be different. But if his daughter chooses a life in Seattle that she could have led in Calcutta, who's to say this isn't evidence of another kind of freedom? What Lahiri captures beautifully is the landscape of three very different generations - father, daughter, and grandson. We find an estranged, septuagenarian father pulled by the novelty of a relationship with another woman after the passing away of his wife, and drawn to sharing the joys of his only grandson at the same time. The pain of seeing children drifting away is powerfully expressed in a father's rumination.

> He remembered his children coming home from college, impatient with him and his wife, enamored of their newfound independence, always wanting to leave. It had tormented his wife and, though he never admitted it, had pained him as well... That loss was in store for Ruma too; her children would become strangers, avoiding her. And because she was his child he wanted to protect her from that, as he had tried throughout his life to protect her from so many things (54).

The story does not ponder upon life and death but merely touches them in passing. Yet Ruma's awe in her son, and the deep loss she feels in the absence of her mother, manage to evoke something profound. "With the birth of Akash, in his sudden, perfect presence, Ruma had felt awe for the first time in her life... It had caused Ruma to acknowledge the supernatural in everyday life. But death, too, had the power to awe, she knew this now-that a human being could be alive for years and years, thinking and breathing and eating, full of a million worries and feelings and thoughts, taking up space in the world, and then, in an instant, become absent, invisible" (46). It is portals such as these that elevate the story above its predictable, cloistered theme. Lahiri's unencumbered prose touches a reader in the recognition of the universal, in way that is simple and powerful.

The isolation and disempowerment of Ruma sets the theme for the collection. In *Hell Heaven*, we have a switch to a first person narration in a much shorter story, exploring the narrator's role as chaperone to her own mother when the mother becomes infatuated with a visitor. Here it is the mother's isolation that takes centre stage. This story tells about the relationship between Pranab Chakraborty and the narrator Usha's family. A rather ordinary love triangle, spiced up by Lahiri's writing style of course, in which an adult recalls her mother's one-sided love affair with a younger man. Pranab, a lonely but academically brilliant young man meets the narrator's mother and subsequently her father and gets vaguely adopted by the family as a younger brother. Pranab spent all of his time with this family, eating "boudi's" Bengali food, arguing passionately about Indian movies and Indian actors. The narrator's father is of course depicted as a typical introvert highbrow scientist, with little time or inclination for such frivolous discussions. Neither the narrator nor her mother bothered to take the time to draw him out of his shell, proceeding instead, to fall in love, the mother with Pranab, and the daughter with Pranab's girlfriend Deborah. The narrator's father, true to his stereotyped character, doesn't miss any opportunity for neglecting his lonely and bored housewife, who falls deeper and deeper in love with Pranab.

After meeting Deborah, the blissfully ignorant Pranab has little time for his adopted family. Deborah makes some effort to get closed to his adopted family, appearing a little too good to be true at times. The narrator's mother keeps waiting for the affair to blow over and for Pranab to come back to her for consolation. However, Pranab opts to marry Deborah, with a show of callous disregard for the wishes of his parents back in India. This is where the reader gets the second proof of Pranab's irresponsible nature. The narrator's mother does not lose any opportunity for bad mouthing Deborah. The reader rather pities the narrator's father for having to put up with this petty wife of his. Deborah gradually weanes Pranab away from all his Bengali friends, all the while paying pretty lip service to these friends, including the narrator.

Fast forward fourteen years and we see the marriage at an end– Pranab having been unfaithful to Deborah, contrary to all built up expectations for the reverse. Cultural divides are not easy to bridge in trans-cultural marital unions. "I was so horribly jealous of you back then, for knowing him, understanding him in a way I never could," (82) the American woman confesses to the Bengali woman. The narrator's mother has miraculously transformed into a broad minded educated mature woman, thanks to her degree in library science, a university education apparently being the panacea for all that ails a lonely, bored and unhappy housewife. With Lahiri being in her usual haste to end the story, the reader finds mother and daughter reconciled, husband and wife having "grown fond of each other", (81) and the now mature narrator happily embarking on one affair after another with American men, all in the space of a single paragraph.

As with the previous story, the bond between a mother and her child runs strong throughout the narration. The reason is perhaps Lahiri's own recent motherhood. The reader hears nothing further about the middle-aged Peter Pan Pranab. Deborah is seen unaccountably clinging to Pranab's adopted Boudi instead of her own close-knit family. The narrator's mother reveals the story of her own closure towards Pranab to her daughter as a proof of the close bonding between mother and daughter in the last few lines of the story.

In *A Choice of Accommodation* the central character is Amit, who returns to his old boarding school with his American wife, for a wedding. Amit had been the "only Indian student" at the school, "...he was crippled with homesickness, missing his parents to the point where tears often filled his eyes, in those first months, without warning" (97). His own marriage is stale. The wedding is that of a girl he once had a crush on. This story has a dreamlike quality that contrasts with Lahiri's usually straightforward narratives. Initially we don't sense much wrong between Amit and Megan beyond the ennui that can settle in after several years of marriage, but soon little details accumulate: they are disappointed by the hotel they have booked for their two-day stay; a tear in Megan's dress seems like a bad omen; the setting recalls the loneliness of Amit's youth and his failure to pursue the things he was really interested in; at the wedding, he forgets the name of an old classmate and upsets someone with a casual remark about how most marriages "disappear" after some time; he goes back to the hotel room to make a call and falls asleep, leaving his wife alone. Here, as in Lahiri's most subtle work, nothing is spelt out but we sense how interior lives can impinge on mundane daily routines and threaten relationships. In *Hell Heaven* and *A Choice of Accommodation*, the final scenes are surprising, upping the relatively quiet tempo of both narratives.

Only Goodness explores how haunting – and sometimes tragic – our own shortcomings can be. Lahiri portrays a family's gradual erosion as questions of guilt, the burden of responsibility, and the paradox of when to hold on and when to let go surface. *Only Goodness* captures two siblings, Sudha and Rahul, whose parents travelled from India to London and finally to Massachusetts. As the older sibling, Sudha is doting and protective of Rahul, concerned with providing a picturesquely American beginning for him. At the same time, Sudha's parents rely on her as a cultural intermediary. While Sudha matures into an independent and successful woman, Rahul flounders in early adulthood. Sudha weathers the realities of her brother Rahul's alcoholism as it tears up her childhood family. As Rahul begins to rely on alcohol, Sudha is consumed by the memory of giving Rahul his first beer when he visited her university. Rahul's downward spiral accelerates, and Sudha's feelings of responsibility persist. Her parents continue to rely on her as a guide for Rahul, though all efforts prove futile.

Sudha eventually marries a man named Roger in London and has a child. Still plagued by a sense of responsibility for Rahul, Sudha is surprised to receive correspondence from Rahul and hear that he's confronted his drinking problem. She invites him to London to meet his nephew. Building trust over the week that he visits, Rahul unexpectedly lapses back to drinking when Sudha has put her fullest faith in him. In a nearly tragic turn of events, not only is Sudha's belief in Rahul shattered, Roger's trust of his wife is similarly tainted. Uninformed of Rahul's drinking problem, Roger is appalled when the full, dark truth exposes itself. Despite her faith and the best of intentions, Sudha is left with a brother she can't trust and the question of whether her husband will trust her. Only Neel, too young to be cognizant of the fissures swelling beneath the surface, is able to imagine pure goodness. Lahiri's not an original stylist – no mysterious Hawthornian symbolism or Marquezian flights of fancy – but she captures these moments with clarity and grace, a tangible knowledge of how souls twist in the wind.

Deviating from Lahiri's usual style, *Nobody's Business,* is a story about a Bengali girl, from the point of view of her American housemate. Sangeeta, or Sang, with all her American education, her rebellion and her deliberate distance from her conventional parents, falls into the same vicious cycle of the typical Indian housewife - she falls in love with Farouk, cooks, cleans and irons for him in an effort to keep him dependent on her. She keeps making excuses for Farouk's various shortcomings and keeps pretending to be unaware of the fact that Farouk treats her with callous disrespect every day of their time together. Paul, intrigued and half in love with Sang, watches it all from a distance until circumstances force him into a more active involvement. A woman calls up, searching for Sang, and claiming to be Farouk's girlfriend. The reader is rather surprised here at Farouk's ability to make not one but two smart, intelligent women fall in love with him. Deirdre tells Paul the same story of being desperately in love with Farouk, of taking care of his needs, of not wanting to lose him. Later on she tries to talk to Sang, and something in her voice brings Sang face to face with the realities about Farouk that she had long tried to ignore. Paul tries clumsily to help things along, but can't bring himself to reveal that he knew everything about Farouk's double life. The story climaxes with Sang confronting Farouk, getting into a fight with him and finally leaving the country and Paul. *Nobody's Business* is a very well written and well finished story by Lahiri, where the reader sees the shortcomings of each character, and yet sympathizes with Sang, and with Paul. In this story, characters seem extraordinarily well-behaved in stressful situations.

The eight stories in *Unaccustomed Earth* fall into two groups. The first five share only themes; the characters and settings are independent of one another. The last three can be read independently, but work better as they are designed: as a triptych telling the story of Hema and Kaushik. In her three beautifully told stories, grouped together as *Hema and Kaushik,* the demons of love and longing wrestle with implacable realities of the present, making the reunion of lovers an inevitable prelude to a final tragic rupture. The first story focuses on their meeting as children; the second follows Kaushik when his father remarries; the third focuses on their reunion as adults. The good news is that the book ends on a strong note with the elegiac three-chapter novella *Hema and Kaushik,* which brings together many of Lahiri's ideas about lives that have been set adrift. Kaushik is a photojournalist who travels around the world but for whom unaccustomed earth, the place where he feels most like an outsider, is his own home in Massachusetts, where his father's new family has supplanted memories of his late mother. It's another reminder that sticking the Diaspora tag on these stories amounts to limiting them, even if most of the characters are Indians abroad.

Hema and Kaushik, as the title suggests, is a love story, but one quite unconventional. It begins in the manner of many of her narratives-Hema's first person reminiscence of her childhood, when Kaushik and his parents put up in their home upon their return from India. There's a notable difference, in the inclusion of the second person, addressed to Kaushik. Chapter two of the three section novella shows a totally different point of view-with the adolescent Kaushik now in the first person, as we discover the upheavals in his life in progression. The concluding segment then switches to third person universal, where the principals in their adulthood, having grown up to be very different individuals yet similar in never having found the love of their lives, temporarily converge before the final, heartbreaking end. The final epilogue, barely a page, returns to Hema again, her realization of a permanent loss. The shadow of Kaushik in her life is obliterated by fate, as she herself steps into the mundane, by choice.

Here is a writer breaking out of the mould, with the freshness of an experimentation that is both controlled and assured. And in the loosely linked trio of stories closing the collection, the lives of Hema and Kaushik intersect over the years, first in 1974 when she is six and he is nine; then a few years later when, at 13, she swoons at the now-handsome 16-year-old teen's reappearance; and again in Italy, when she is a 37-year-old academic about to enter an arranged marriage, and he is a 40-year-old photojournalist.

The first part, "Once in Lifetime", is a first person narration, one character addressing the other, and one character tells the other about their own past. It became too transparent a device. "Your parents were seasoned immigrants ... they had left India in 1962 ... your father had a PhD, he drove a car, a silver Saab with bucket seats to his job at an engineering firm in Andover..."(224). The first part, "Once in

Lifetime", tells the story of Kaushik Choudhuri's parents and their relationship with Hema's parents, narrated by Hema. Both sets of parents used to be close until the Choudhuris moved back to India. The families gradually drifted apart until the Choudhuris announced that they were returning. Hema's parents invited them to stay until the Choudhuris found a suitable house. The Choudhuri's turned out to be appalling houseguests. Kaushik, a moody boy of sixteen, made little effort to get along with his hosts. Mrs. Choudhuri rarely helped Hema's mother in her housework. But underneath these obvious reasons for dissatisfaction, there were a few less obvious factors at work. Dr. Choudhuri was obviously more successful, professionally and financially, than his hosts. He openly indulged his wife's every whim and fancy. Mrs. Choudhuri for her part, had transformed into a glamorous woman of the world, casting into shadow Hema's mother. The story ends with the revelation that Mrs. Choudhuri's mother was dying of cancer, hence the move to America, and hence the indulgence shown by Dr. Choudhuri towards a wife - every act of theirs was now a once in a lifetime event.

The second part, "Year's End" shows that Kaushik's mother is dead. Dr. Choudhuri, no longer able to face life on his own, marries a widow nearly twenty years younger to him. Kaushik returns from university on his vacation and tries to adjust to a step mother and two young step sisters. But at every step, he finds it difficult to accept the changes wrought by Chitra, not only in his home, but also in his father. In a way, the late Mrs. Choudhuri had created and nurtured both their house and her husband. Removed from her influence, Dr. Choudhuri, an indulgent if somewhat indifferent husband, gives in to Chitra's old fashioned values and gradually becomes a stranger to his son. The story ends with Kaushik driving away from his father's home, lonlier than when he had arrived.

In the third part, "Going Ashore" a series of coincidences brings Kaushik and Hema face to face at a party. They embark on an impulsive and short term affair; each wanting more than the other could give. Hema has recently ended her relationship with a married man and has become engaged to a conservative man of her parents' choosing. She goes to Rome for a last adventure before her marriage and finds everything in Kaushik that was lacking in her relationship with Julian and her fiancé Navin. Kaushik, for his part, finds himself drawn to Hema initially because of shared childhood memories of his mother, and later because of a budding need for growing roots after a gypsy like existence. Lahiri ends this story and the book on an unexpected note, leaving the reader with bittersweet memories of the characters that seem to continue living beside the reader long after the stories are over and the book is finished.

It is one of the best collections of short stories in *Unaccustomed Earth,* these stories focus partly on the back stories of the previous generation, related through the eyes of the "children". This device allows us to see the distances that have been traveled, geographically and culturally, in order for the characters to have arrived at the narrative present, but it sets up a mild dissonance for me. Its success rests on the readers acceptance that the parents are characters who would be open to their children about events in their past.

Unaccustomed Earth is so powerful because it does not use the Happily Ever After crutch to provide comfort to the reader. Lahiri does away with the boy meets girl, girl meets boy, they fall in love, are pulled apart and reunited, in love, forever and actually what she writes is what life is like: that we marry the wrong person even when love stares us in the face, we are bound by family, responsibility and other people, that sometimes we stay silent when we should speak and things happen to us whether we like it or not. It is these traits that determine our self destructive natures.

However, no matter how distinct the plot twists or character circumstances in any of the stories, as a collection *Unaccustomed Earth* is markedly unified. All stories focus on members of Bengali families dealing with England or America. All are richly detailed, painting portraits of the complexity of these families' lives; all deal with making and remaking lives, loves, and identities in the wake of radical disruptions. Often families reform after a family member has died. Sometimes they must learn to function again after an ending of another kind, as when Rahul Mukherjee becomes an alcoholic in *Only Goodness*. However, in addition to these disruptions, which could happen to any family, there are always ripples of culture shock. The gap between India and America, or rather, between traditional India as it was, and America as it is coming to be, is brought vividly to life. The result is a set of lovely and accessible stories that blend the cultural and the individual, the exotic and the strikingly domestic.

WORKS CITED

1. Rushdie, Salman, *Imaginary Homelands*, London: Granta Books, 1991, p.16.
2. Lahiri, Jhumpa, *Interview*, 2004. www.bookbrowse.com.
3. Lahiri, Jhumpa, *Unaccustomed Earth*, India: Random House, 2008. (Subsequent references to the text are from this edition and have been indicated by page numbers in parentheses.)

25

Inheritance and Exile : The Problematics of Diaspora in Jhumpa Lahiri's *The Namesake*

ARTI NIRMAL

Crossing of territories and migratory flow of people from one part of globe to another is an age old phenomena but it assumed diasporic texture with the historic Jewish expulsion in 586 B.C. Indian diaspora, on the other hand emerges as a concentrated phenomenon with the practice of indenture labour by British colonialists in the nineteenth century. The '*girmitiya consciousness*' of diasporic discourse, associated deeply with the sensitive human experiences such as nostalgia, pain, suffering, rootlessness, homesickness and the aching memories of homeland sets a strong background to the postcolonial wave of migration which has been considered as highly fruitful in terms of literary output. The postcolonial configuration of diaspora has raised various serious issues pertaining to 'nation', 'culture' and 'race' which the postcolonial theorists and cultural critics namely Frantz Fanon, Robert Cohen, Stuart Hall, Homi K. Bhabha, Paul Gilroy and Vijay Mishra study in terms of 'combat' or 'combined' culture as represented in literature.

The postcolonial study of Indian diaspora remains incomplete without comprehending the mixing and mingling of boundaries, nations, communities- its people and their ethos. Defining the postcolonial concept of diaspora, the famous Indo- Fijian critic Vijay Mishra aptly writes: "Diasporic epistemology locates itself squarely in the realm of the hybrid, in the domain of the cross cultural and contaminated social and cultural regimes," and therefore "diasporic cultural identity by its very nature is predicated upon the inevitable mixing of castes and peoples" (67-85). Thus, in order to understand the dynamics of diaspora in postcolonial context, "there is need to realise the significance of the cultural encounter which takes place in diasporic writing, the bicultural pulls and the creation of a new culture which finally emerges" (Jain: 15).

The post modernist context of diaspora fundamentally suggests a hybrid and ever changing nature of identity often excluding homogeneity, stability and purity. According to Myria Georgiou "Diasporas' hybridity implies a diversity of culture, that co-exist, compete, merge and emerge in cultures that may be the outcome of a cultural meetings or of suppression, exclusion and domination" (*Thinking Diaspora*). It demonstrates not only the issues of origin and belonging, but of what we refer to as 'transnational identities', 'multi-rootedness' and 'cross-ethnicity' generated through worldwide migration. Jhumpa Lahiri (Nilanjana Sudeshana) of Indo-British origin is one such novelist who poignantly discusses the problematics of Indian diaspora in her writings. Her debut work *The Interpreter of Maladies* dismayed the world by winning Pulitzer Prize for fiction in 1999 and her debut novel *The Namesake* again vibrated the readers with multi-angled deliberation on immigrants' life. Thus, in the light of the foregoing discussion my present paper attempts to study her debut novel *The Namesake* (2003) highlighting some of the vital issues relating to the Indian diaspora.

The Namesake (2003) is an extremely evocative novel by Jhumpa Lahiri, which explores the immigrant experience of the middle class Bengali American couple and their first generation offsprings in the U.S. struggling for survival and assimilation. The treatment of diaspora in this novel is same as that of her *Interpreter of Maladies* (1999) but on a larger canvas. Lahiri in this novel meticulously deals with the life of Ganguli family from India and their attempts to settle in the American culture. But more importantly, the novel speaks about the relationship and rituals of family and country in a simple yet elegant and profoundly controlled manner.

The novel highlights different constructs of diaspora whereby the problem of immigrants get aptly reflected through different characters at different occasion. Lahiri says in one of her interviews: "At the heart, *The Namesake* is about parents and children" and "at the most basic level, this is a story of family that is coming to grips with who they are and where they are under what circumstances" (*India Today*). She employs Gogol for the second generation immigrants, Ashima and Ashoke for the first generation Indian immigrants, Ruth and Maxine for cross-cultural Americans and Moushumi for the third culture with a fine balance. During the course of novel, Lahiri begins with Ashoke Ganguli and finally reaches Gogol via Ashima who is related to Ashoke as wife through "arranged marriage".

The story of the novel is weaved around an immigrant Indian Bengali family living in the United States. The newlywed Ganguli couple - Ashoke and Ashima Ganguli, arrive in the U.S. in 1967, beset with various expectations and dreams. Calcutta born Ashoke and Ashima embrace their new life together in Boston with great enthusiasm and courage in the beginning of their settlement but the 'enigma of arrival' soon dawns upon them. Here, Ashoke easily grows comfortable with the new ambiance, whereas his wife is tormented by the terrible homesickness: "Ashima keeps her ear trained, between the hours of twelve and two, for the sound of the postman's footsteps on the porch, followed by the soft click of the mail slot in the door" (N: 36). Ashima, who is nine months pregnant, misses her family very much and feels thoroughly alone in New England in the late 1960's:

> For being a foreigner Ashima is beginning to realize, is a sort of lifelong pregnancy - a perpetual wait, a constant burden, a continuous feeing out of sorts. It is an ongoing responsibility, a parenthesis in what had once been ordinary life, only to discover that that previous life has vanished, replaced by something more complicated and demanding. Like pregnancy, being a foreigner, Ashima believes, is something that elicits the same curiosity from strangers, the same combination of pity and respect (N: 50).

Everything in America is "a humble approximation" of Ashima's life in India, which she left behind when she married Ashoke -- "hired as an assistant professor" (N: 48) at MIT. By and by the Gangulis learn to adapt to the western culture but at the same time try hard to remain rooted to their homeland and its cultural heritage. Ashima "is terrified to raise a child in a country where she is related to no one, where she knows so little, where life seems so tentative and spare". Therefore she longs for her extended family in Calcutta during her "motherhood in a foreign land" (N: 6). She pathetically says: "I don't want to raise Gogol alone in this country. It is not right. I want to go back" (N: 33). Mira Nair the director of the film based on the novel, speaks about the plot in the following manner:

> It encompasses, in a deep humane way the tale of millions of us who have left one home for another, who have known what it is to combine the old ways with the new world, who have left the shadow of our parents to find ourselves for the first time (*A Conversation*).

Ashima and Ashoke, having no relatives in America plan frequent visits to India with their children in order to remain connected and seek familial comfort: "We have no relatives in this country, that is why we are going to India in the first place" (N: 79). Gradually Ashima learns that "everyone should live on their own at some point" (N: 161). Therefore, thrusted in American way of life Ashima tries to adapt gradually but still finds that "the pages of Bengali type are a perpetual comfort to her" and "voices on the phone, occasionally bearing news of births or weddings, send chills down her spine" (N: 63-64).

As Salman Rushdie in his critical discourse *Imaginary Homelands* writes "Our identity is at once plural and partial" (N: 15). True to this the immigrant Bengali couple attempt to 'fit in' the 'melting pot' of the host country and at the same time make a serious and deliberate effort to cling their roots in the rich Bengali (Indian) culture. For instance, they prefer to make their own circle of Bengali friends such as Maya and Dilip Nandi, Mitras and Banerjees because "they all come from Calcutta, and for this reason alone they are friends" (N: 38). In order to preserve and conserve their cultural heritage and to perpetuate it, they train their children in the Bengali language, literature and history through specially arranged Bengali classes at their home. They organize various Indian festivals and events such as "Navaratras", "Pujo", and "Annaprashan" in order to "expose them to their own family lineage, religious customs, rituals, beliefs, food tastes, habits and mannerisms"(Kaur: 37). Focusing on the common immigrant tendencies, Robert Cohen aptly remarks: "a member's adherence to a diasporic community is demonstrated by an acceptance of the inescapable link with their past migration history" (ix). Despite all this, Ashima teaches her children American lifestyle too, so that they may easily adjust in both the cultures. If she asks them:

> [...] to memorize a four-line children's poem by Tagore, and the names of the deities adorning the ten handed Durga during pujo: Saraswati with her swan and Kartik with his peacock to her left, Laskshmi with her owl and Ganesh with his mouse to her right, [with similar emphasis they are told to watch on television] *Sesame Street* and *The Electric Company* in order to keep up with English they use at nursery school (N: 54).

In this way, the Gangulis' desire to keep their foot in both the cultures for nearly thirty years ultimately leads to the formation of a confused identity. As the novelist herself explains:

> The question of identity is always a difficult one, but especially so for those who are culturally displaced, as immigrants are, or those who grow up in two worlds simultaneously, as in the case for their children. I am aware that I have somehow inherited a sense of exile from my parents, even though in many ways I am not so much more American as they are. In fact it is still very hard to think of myself as an American. Alternatively if I say I'm from India, a place where I was not born and have never lived, this is also inaccurate. It bothers me less now. But it bothered me growing up, the feeling that there was no single place where I fully belonged (*Hinduism*).

Soon, Ashima gives birth to a son who is *accidently* named Gogol by Ashoke because a volume of the Russian writer's (Nikolai Gogol's) work *The Overcoat* had saved his life out of a train wreck. From this episode onwards the narrative moves around the title character Gogol and the significance of name becomes a major theme in *The Namesake.* The novel is an interesting and intriguing meditation on the extent to which our names shape our identity. Reflecting interesting perspectives on the name, Lahiri expresses that unlike West, in India "individual names are sacred, inviolable. They are not meant to be inherited or shared" (N: 28). Apparently, the novel seems to deal with names; "good names", "bad names", and "pet names", but far beyond that Lahiri uses 'name' as a potent metaphor to present existential dilemma and vagaries of cultural dislocation felt by the first and second generation immigrants in the United States. She also reinforces the power of family relations as capable of surmounting all the hurdles in the face of hegemony. Lahiri expresses: "It is almost too perfect a metaphor for the experience of growing up as a child of immigrants, having a divided identity, and divided loyalties" (*Hinduism*).

It is a story of assimilation and generational difference. Unlike Ashoke and Ashima, Gogol and Sonia try to break free from the past of their parents. The offsprings turn away from the inherited customs and cultural values imposed upon them by their parents and enjoy accepting their American heritage at any cost. They prefer "love marriages" to their parent's "arranged marriage" and relish American and continental food more than the "syrupy Bengali dishes". As opposed to Ashima who sits "silently, staring at the clouds, as they journey back to Boston" for Gogol "relief quickly replaces any lingering sadness [...]. With relief he puts on his headset to watch *The Big Chill* and listen to top-forty songs all the way home [Boston]" (N:87). They enjoy the celebration of 'Christmas' and 'Thanksgiving' more than their Bengali festivals, both the children rebel and try desperately to liberate themselves from their past connections so that they may easily assimilate with their American peers. Lahiri elaborates:

> In some sorts he [Gogol] is rejecting them [his parents] at so many levels. And also eventually trying to understand them[his parents].One of the things I wanted to show is that there can be incredibly vast differences between one generation and the next, especially in an immigrant society (*India Today*).

Ashoke and Ashima soon realize that they cannot force their children to follow their way of living and therefore they themselves gradually learn the host culture's lifestyle in order to keep pace with their own children. As Lahiri writes in the novel: "It was for him [Gogol], for Sonia, that his parents had gone to the trouble of learning these customs" (N: 286). Ashima now invites her children's American peers on feast but feels that it is "less stressful" to feed forty Bengali guests "than the task of feeding a handful of American children" (N: 72). In due course of time we notice a remarkable transformation in

Ashima who was young, scared, jobless and dependent woman in the beginning but becomes strong, self-reliant, employed Ashima as the novel proceeds.

The novel basically centers on the title character Gogol, whose name enables Lahiri to illuminate the issues of identity, sense of dislocation, cultural confrontation conflicting loyalties and multiculturalism as well. It is about thirty-two years journey of Gogol Ganguli form his birth in 1968 to a transitional moment in his life in the year 2000 and his ultimate his self-discovery at the end. Lahiri tells that Gogol develops identity issue as a child itself:

> He's come to hate questions pertaining to his name [Gogol], hates having constantly to explain. He hates having to tell people that it doesn't mean anything "in Indian". He even hates signing his name at the bottom of his drawings in art class. He hates that his name is both absurd and obscure, that it has nothing to do with who he is, that it is neither Indian nor American but of all things Russian (N: 75-76).

The name which had immense personal significance as 'survival' and 'rebirth' to his father becomes a burden, a disfigurement, an ugly reminder of the many differences between him and his pals. He wishes to reinvent himself and the first step that he takes in this process is at Yale where he changes his name from Gogol to Nikhil. Gradually his name becomes a symbol to reflect fragmented identity and in this way his life seems to be an attempt to make peace with his divided loyalties:

> At times he feels as if he's cast himself in a play, acting the part of twins, indistinguishable to the naked eye yet fundamentally different. At times he still feels his old name, painfully and without warning, the way his front tooth had unbearably throbbed in recent weeks after a filling, threatening for an instant to sever from his gums when he drunk coffee [...]. (N: 105)

As he grows up, he embarks upon the strange nature of his name and therefore, loathes it, denies it and tries to escape it. He grows up baffled and grappled with strange Russian name and cultural pull in two different directions.

Gogol is the product of time and place. The man can neither connect to the U.S. culture nor to India. He is helplessly torn between the two worlds of Gogol and Nikhil and it is only towards the end of the novel that he comes to realize: "there is no such thing as a perfect name" (N: 245). He shrugs off the name given by his father who loved him immensely and by the time he could realize his fault he finds his father dead. The novel thus talks about those young men who want to shed their inheritance, their heritage and happen to search it impatiently later on. It is the story of coming to terms with one's own identity and origin chiefly in the case of immigrant children who inevitably grow up with confused individuality. Lahiri explains:

> The book is not so much about names per se. It is more about what we inherit from our parents- certain ideas, certain values, certain genes- the whole complex set of things that everyone gets from their parents and the way that, no matters how much we create our own lives and choose what we want out of life, it's very difficult to escape our origins (*Bookpage*).

Gogol abhors his parent's annual trips to India and longs for an independent, autonomous life. "Gogol never thinks of India as *Desh*. He thinks of it as Americans do, as India" and is bored by the talk of "marginality" (N: 118). He spends a lot of time ignoring his culture; and with friends and girlfriends- Ruth, Maxine and wife Moushumi he observes the details of other cultures and compares them to his own. At first he is enchanted by their western lifestyle but soon gets disillusioned after his father's sudden demise. Thus, "his family life [which] feels like a string of accidents, unforeseen, unintended, one incident begetting another" compels him to admit that the life is about attempting "to accept, interpret, and comprehend" the events in our life that shape us into who we are (N: 286-287) Finally, when Gogol comes to appreciate his ethnic background and his family traditions, he learns to accept his identity. Thus, his melancholic journey ends in self-realization and self-acceptance. He realizes the guilt that "his parents carried inside, at being able to do nothing when their parents had died in India, of arriving weeks, sometimes months later, when their was nothing left to do" (N: 179) and accepts that "his immersion in Maxine's family is [was] a betrayal of his own" (N: 141).

We notice considerable change in Gogol as the story moves

toward the end. Gogol who was once fun-loving, enjoying his life to fullest with drinks, discos and parties now bears an "urge to be alone all of a sudden, to be thoroughly passive, to revisit the evening in solitude" (N:199). He confesses to Moushumi that "he still felt guilty at times for changing his name, more so now that his father was dead."(N:244). Finding his father dead and his widow mother Ashima returning back to Calcutta, Gogol regrets:

> Without people in the world to call him Gogol, no matters how long he himself lives, Gogol Ganguli will, once and for all, vanish from the lips of loved ones, and so, cease to exist. Yet the thought of this eventual demise provides no sense of victory, no solace. It provides no solace at all (N: 289).

Highlighting the name issue which disturbs Gogol and which vitally regulates identity formation in general, Ruediger Heinze puts:

> Consequently, the name in transit is a signifier that, leaving the home country but never reaching its destination, remains unknown and unknowable....Gogol's Indian name is therefore at least twice removed and so remains part of realm of the imaginary, with an imaginary connection to the homeland due to its origin and an imaginary connection to its destiny due to its constantly deferred arrival (194).

In *The Namesake* the theme of 'home' has also been discussed in a highly controlled but emphatic manner by Lahiri especially projected through the character of Ashima who is continually shifted from one home to another. At the end, when Ashima decides to return back to India Lahiri writes about her: "True to the meaning of her name, she will be without borders, without a home of her own, a resident everywhere and nowhere" (N: 276). To quote the views of Abdul R. Jan Mohammed on home:

> The notion of exile always emphasizes the absence of "home" of the cultural matrix that formed the individual subject, hence it implied an involuntary or enforced rupture between the collective subject of the original and the individual subject. The nostalgia associated with the exile (a nostalgia i.e. structural

> rather than idiosyncratic) often makes the individual to the values and the characteristics of the host culture the exile chooses if needed s/he has only one choice to live in a context that is least hospitable most like home (101).

The existential dilemma is suffered by almost all the immigrants who for hours "argue about the politics of America, a country in which none of them is eligible to vote" (N: 38).Thus, there are some who quit, some who struggle for their place and some few who try to overcome their pain of political and cultural displacement by opting for a third culture. As is the case of Moushumi:

> Immersing herself in a third language, a third culture, had been her refuge — she approached French, unlike things American or Indian, without guilt, or misgiving, or expectation of any kind. It was easier to turn her back on the two countries that could claim her in favor of one that had no claim whatsoever (N: 214).

Stuart Hall expresses that it is difference not sameness which functions in the determination of diaspora identity: "Diaspora identities are those which are constantly producing and reproducing themselves a new, thorough transformation and difference" (244).

The problematics of diaspora is supplemented by the somber theme of 'death' in the novel. Lahiri seems to consciously harp upon the subject of death which is "inevitable about the world" (N: 14). When Gogol in his childhood visits historic graveyard he apprehends that like other Bengalis (Hindus) "he himself will be burned, not buried, that his body will occupy no plot of earth, that no stone in this country will bear his name beyond life" (N:69). The tone of the narrative grows serious and meditative as the story progresses. After Ashoke's demise, Gogol considers death as the ultimate reality. Contemplating over the futility of *Brain Drain* to earn "security and respect" (N: 105) in a foreign land, Gogol is reminded of her parents "who had forsaken everything to come to this country, to make a better life, only to die here?" (N: 180). It appears as if Lahiri wants to convey a message that death spares no one and no where-Indian or American, black or white, in motherland or in an alien land. She seems to communicate that many of the events in our life are out of control, even random. Contrary to the earlier notion that "names die over time, that they perish just as people do" (N:70) Gogol at the end comprehends \that though death is inevitable, the remnants of departed soul continue to exist in the memory of others.

Jhumpa Lahiri, thus provides an authentic detail of diasporic culture by shedding light on the lives of the characters - Ashoke, Ashima and their son Gogol in her debut novel *The Namesake*. It presents before the readers their emotional struggles, their longings for the origin and the customs, traditions and views through which they comprehend and interpret the world. Lahiri emphasizes the difference between generations and the power of time in bridging this gap. Moreover, she successfully shows how her characters succeed in retaining their values despite all odd circumstances. As a meaningful literary output, the novel reinforces the Indian culture, chiefly Bengali ethnic pattern and presents it in an intimate family garb closely related to social, cultural and psychological norms with respect to 'home'. In general, the novel is a fine discussion on 'names', relations, families, inheritance, cultural assimilation and Russian literature that serves as a raw material to the plot.

WORKS CITED

Cohen, Robert, *Global Diasporas: An Introduction*, UCL Press, 1997.

Georgiou, Myria, *Thinking Diaspora: Why Diaspora is a Key Concept for Understanding Multicultural Europe, The Multicultural Skycraper Newsletter*, Vol.1.4, 4, December, 2001.

Hall, Stuart, *Cultural Identity and Diaspora, Identity: Community, Culture, Difference*, ed., Jonathan Ruthurford, London: Lawrence and Wishart 1990, pp.222-41.

Heinze, Ruediger, *A Diasporic Overcoat, Journal of Postcolonial Writing*, 43:2.2007, www.informaworld.com acc. 29.08.2008, pp.191-202.

Jan Mohammed, *Abdul R. Worldliness - without world, Homelessness-as-Home: Toward a Definition of the Specular Border Intellectual, Edward Said: A Reader*, ed. Michael Sprinker, Cambridge: Blackwell Publishing, 1992, pp.96-120.

Kau Tejinder, *Cultural Dilemmas and Displacements of Immigrants in Jhumpa Lahiri's The Namesake, The Journal of Indian Writing in English*, Vol.32.2, July 2004: 37.

Lahiri, Jhumpa, *The Namesake*, U.S.A.: Harpercollins, 2003: 9th impression, 2005.

Lahiri, Jhumpa, *Interview with Anil Padmanabhan, India Today*, 8 September, 2003.

Lahiri, Jhumpa, *Interview with Alden Mudge*, Bookpage, Sept.2003, 12Nov.2006 http://www.bookpage.com/0309bp/jhumpa_lahiri.html.

Lahiri, Jhumpa, *Interview, Hinduism Online*, a Houghton Miffin Company release, 2003.

Mishra, Vijay, *New Lamps for Old: Diasporas Migrancy Border, Interrogating Post-Colonialism: Theory, Text and Context*, ed. Harish Trivedi and Meenakshi Mukherjee, Shimla: Indian Institute of Advanced Study, 1996, pp.67-85.

Nair, Mira, *A Conversation*, usa.usembassy.de/Classroom/newsletter.

Rushdie, Salman, *Imaginary Homelands*, London: Granta/Vikins, 1991, pp.9-21.

❑❑❑

26

Women and Their Transformations in Bharati Mukherjee's *Jasmine*

D. BALAPRIYADARSHINI

Taking into account the complexity of life, different histories culture and different structures of values, the woman's question despite basic solidarity, needs to be tackled in relation to the socio-cultural situation. The novels of Bharati Mukherjee are self actualizing. Quest for the definition of self and search for identity are the main features of her women who are seen caught in the flux of tradition and modernity. Neither can they completely detach themselves from their part, nor do they have any certitude in the future. Bharati Mukherjee has interceded reworked the study of feminism in her writings. Central to her vision in *The Holder of the World, Wife* and *Jasmine* are issues related to women. Feminism in her works has something of What Caroll Smith Rosen Berg (1979) argues is "the emotional segregation of women and man, which brought about, led to the development of a specifically female world (137)". The network of female world comes to us not only in Mukherjee's novels but also in her collections of Short Stories. She advocates many faces of feminism encompassing agitation for equal opportunity, sexual antonomy and right of self determination.

Mukherjee's fiction convinces us that gender is a multifaceted category open to change and variation, and reinforces, what Anna Lowenhaupt Tsing had suggested-that particular forms of female margirtality must be examined in relation to the conditions of women's lives-as immigrants, minorities, wealthy, poor, black, white, sex workers, maids, or academics (quoted by Rayaprol 135). Mukherjee's depiction of women and their different relationships portrays the dominance of patriarchal practices in traditional society, as well as the forms of liberation and empowerment which are available to women in their diasporic situation. Mukherjee's female characters are real, modern life like. They are typical representatives of young woman particularly of The Third World countries who cherish the dream of emigrating to America for higher education and higher wages, and then after arrival there, aspire to settle there permanently. Their situations and the difficulties they face are also realistically portrayed. In nearly, all stories there is a fixed pattern. In the first part of each story, the focus is on narrating the situation of an immigrant who is in the process of immigration or settling down and in the second part who is in the process of immigration or settling down and in the second part the protagoinst is invariably given to making love with a partner of the opposite sex who is rooted in the American soil.

Bharati Mukerjee is a significant woman novelist. She was born on 27th July 1940, in a Bengali Brahmin family of Calcutta. Her father's name was Sudhir Lal Mukherjee. He was a pharmaceutical chemist. Her mother, Bina Mukherjee was a housewife. Mukherjee spent her first eight years as a member with her parents and two sisters in a joint family. She lived with her parents and two sisters in London for about three years. In 1951 the family returned to Calcutta and she joined the English -speaking Loreto, convent school, run by Irish nuns. Mukherjee and her sisters were chauffeured to the convent school quite, Characteristic of this clash of Bengalis, the family "westernized" in the sense that English education was valued.

In 1958, Mukherjee's father lost her partnership in the factory and moved him family to Baroda. Bharati Mukherjee completed her B.A. (Honours) English at university of Calcutta in 1959. She took her M.A. degree in English from the university of Baroda in 1961. She went to the University of obtained an MFA in creative writing in 1963 and a Ph.D. in English in 1969.

In the University of Iowa Mukherjee met Clark Blaise, a Canadians fellow student at the University of Iowa. She married him in 1963. She lived in Canada from 1966 to 1980. She got Canadian citizenship and lived in Toronto and then in Montreal. She held teaching portions at MC Gill University and Concordia University. She migrated to the U.S.A. in 1980 with her family and become a U.S.A citizen in 1988. She was awarded the "Prestigious Shastri Indo Canadian Institute Grant" during the year 1976-77. She was a recipient of "Guggenhein Foundation Award" in 1978-79 and "Canadian Government Award" in 1982. She also won the first prize from "Periodical Distribution Association" in 1980 for her short story "Isolated Incidents". Mukherjee has also been honoured with the "National Book Critics Circle Award" for her short stories collection, *The Middleman and Other Stories* in 1989. Her creative five novels are: *The Tiger's Daughter* (1972), *Wife* (1975), *Jasmine* (1989), *The Holder of the world* (1993) , *Leave It to me* (1997), *Desirable Daughters* (2002) and *The Tree Bride* (2004) and two collections of short stories: *Darkness* (1985) and *The Middleman and Other Stories* (1988). Her husband, Clark Blaise, helps her in her fiction. He is an American - Canadian author. He teaches also in the English department of Columbia University. She has co-authored with her husband two non-fictional works: first is *Days and Night in Calcutta* in (1977), and second is *The Sorrow and the Terror.*

The major theme of rebirth plays out literally and figuratively in *Jasmine.* In literal language, every word is truthful, whereas figurative language is used for a certain effect. Figurative language might be exaggerated, or embellished, or used to help access otherwise difficult-to-grasp concepts. The opening line, "Lifetimes ago," hints at all the transformations the title character has undergone. Mukherjee consistently highlights this theme, making authorial connections between the fictional action and its significance as a subject under investigation. The narrator says: "There are no harmless, compassionate ways to remake oneself". And "I picked [Sam] up and held him. Truly I had been reborn".

In *Jasmine,* the woman writer shapes female characters who transgress boundaries fixed on them by their gender, race, caste and economic status. Jasmine is determined by strategies of resistance, including shifting names and corresponding identities, escaping from traditional space, using both violence and sexuality in order to move beyond restrictions imposed on her and thus renegotiating the space in which she actually resides. The gendered space underlines the idea of home which remains problematic. The conflation of home, as both security and prison, evokes therefore one's limited identity. Such a division of geographical space would refer to divisions of psychic space including self against non-self.

Jasmine can be read as a feminist novel where the protagonist rebels not only against age-old superstitions and traditions, but also effects a proper balance between tradition and modernity. The novel is a celebration of the strength of a woman, not her weakness. In a language of emotion and meticulous metaphor using images provided by the woman protagonist the novelist has articulated the many sided pathos and rebellion of contemporary Indian Woman, not only in India but also in New World. In Jasmine a woman comes to terms with her own self. As Sumita Roy points out: "Jasmine's search for self-recognition takes her in social and spiritual direction...till she arrives at a time when she can view the future 'greedy with wants and reekless from hope".

From the very beginning Bharati Mukherjee has delineated the Jyoti of Hasanpur (who later on becomes Jasmine, and Jase and Jane) as a rebel against blind beliefs and superstitions. Early in the novel Jyoti tries to raise herself above such blind belief in fate which is adumbrated by the astrologer thus "fate is Fate". While scavenging firewood Jyoti gets a star shaped wound on her forehead. That scar becomes her third eye and through an archetypal image (Shiva's Third Eye) Mukherjee shows that already Jyoti was peering out into invisible words "*Now I am a sage*". The third eye gives her a wide and true perspective on life. She learns to look back to the past not like a coward bunkering herself inside nostalgia, sheathing her heart in a bullet-proof vest. For her, even memories are a sign of disloyalty. Similarly with her third eye she learns to look into the future with pain and hope and when she embarks into her final journey in America she is 'greedy' with wants and reckless with hopes. It is as if like Shiva she was swallowed the cosmos whole. Bharati Mukherjee also shows her woman protagonist repudiating centuries - old ugly Indian tradition of checking the boy's horoscope.

The second archetypal image that Bharati Mukherjee uses to bring out the protagonist's feminist trait is that of Kali, the Goddess of Destruction. But since in Hindu mythology Kali is an incarnation of Durga, the Godess of Strength (Shakti), the image here is more relevant to the strength of a woman like Jasmine who has embarked on a perilous journey to a new world of fulfill her husband's dream. After her husband's death in order to reach USA she stows in a boat captained by half-face. But after landing in America when half-face demands his price (nothing less than the satisfaction of his lustful passions will do) Jasmine in a truly feminist gesture decides to kill the Devil Incarnate and Bharati Mukherjee brilliantly fuses two archetypal image to enact the killing of Kali: The Godess of Destruction and strength and the broken pitcher. This new identity in reality expresses another aspect of the "feminist" in the Indian fiction in English for the true feminist, in my eyes, is the one who has achieved a proper balance between tradition and modernity.

In the beginning in America Jasmine lodges with Prakash's Professorji-Mr. Vadhera. But she feels uncomfortable in Professorji's house which they have converted into a Punjab ghetto. She wants to get away from the claustrophobic traditional 'Indianness' and Bharati Mukherjee brings out this contrast between tradition and modernity through the contrast between Professor's wife Nirmala and the protagonist Jasmine. Nirmala only takes, Jasmine both takes and gives. That is why she can escape the Indian ghetto in flushing and adopt herself to the patterns of dominant. American culture (modernity) but that does not mean she throws to the wind her race, her religion, her beliefs (tradition).

A true feminist Jasmine does not hold fast to nostalgia that is dead but maintains certain basic traits of Indian Culture even after imbibing American Culture. Thus even after Jasmine has become Dulf's day Mummy, a caregiver (not a servant, mind you) in the Taylor household her traditional roots break through again and again. With infinite care Bharati Mukherjee her protagonist's gradual transformation but sometimes there is a conflict between Jasmine's two selves, one still holding fast to traditional Indian Values of life and the other an adventure in a Capitalistic Culture.

But as an apotheosis of true Feminist spirit Jasmine does not hold fast to a "dead nostalgia" and as she tells Taylor about her past, it gets exorcised. She falls hopelessly in love with Taylor but the past comes back to destroy her present when she sees Sukhi, her husband's murderer in the park and she decides to leave Claremont for Iowa. And here in Iowa Budd Ripplemeyer falls in love with her (and she gets a new identity: Jane Ripplemeyer). Budd courts her because for him she is the very embodiment of Eastern mystery. "Budd courts me because I am alien, I am darkness, mystery inscrutability". Bharati Mukherjee passes the final judgement through her mouthpiece, Jasmine;

we are once won over by her scintillating prose, her cadenced rhythm and above all her powerful feminist convictions. "I am caught between the promise of America and old world dutifulness".

Like Bharati Mukherjee herself, Jasmine, the heroine of the novel transforms herself with increasing rapidity. She is Jyoti, Jasmine and Jane. The novel smacks of the autobiography of Bharati Mukherjee. One of the similarities between Jasmine and the author is their drive to go after what they want and to not stop until they get it. Bharati's drive is to become a writer, and Jasmine's is to go to the United States. Like Jasmine, Mukherjee has changed citizenships and cultures with remarkable ease and rapidity.

Jyoti the heroine of the novel, Jasmine is born in a traditional Punjabi family *'eighteen years after the partition riots'*. She was married in her teens to Prakash, but she became a widow within two years. Her husband, Prakash, was shot dead by some terrorist. It was Prakash who first of all wanted to transform Jyoti and it was he who had given the name Jasmine to Jyoti. Jyoti says: "He wanted to break down the Jothi I had been in Hasnapur and makes me a new kind of city woman. To break of the past, he gave me a new name: Jasmine" (77).

Prakash transforms her from village lass into a city bread girl, Jasmine. The traditional woman, Jyoti, now Jasmine, showed the signs of feminism in her when she refused to spend the rest of her life in the robes of a widow. It had always been Prakash's ambition to go to the U.S.A. where his teacher, Prof.Vadehra had migrated. In order to make his dream come true, she seeks the help of her brothers to secure forged documents, and soon she is in her way to the new world and then a series of adventures follow. She is raped in a hotel room by the Half-face, the lecherous Captain of the trawler in which she crosses over to Florida. She is about to commit suicide but the spirit of survival reigns supreme and she determines to punish the evil-doer. Like Kali with her bleeding tongue rolling out she slits open half-face's throat. This marks the death of Jyoti.

Despite the initial horror, the land is not without its saints. Jasmine is rescued from starvation and misery by Lilian Gordan, a kind of Quaker Lady who acts as a saviour of the people in America, who did not possess the proper documents, to be there. Mrs. Gordon helps her search Prof. Vadehra. Prof. Vadehra works for long hours outside and returns home exhausted. Jasmine had to stay there confined for five months. Prof. Vadehra had declared himself to be working as a professor in America. But a certain incident in the novel led to the discovery of the real identity of Prof. Vadehra in America. Jasmine discovered that Devinder Vadehra, who pronounced his name as David O'Hara, was an importer and sorter of human hair, and not a professor as he had declared himself to be. When he discovered that his real identity in America was discovered by Jasmine, he promised to help her acquire a forged Green Card if she promised to keep his secret.

Later in the novel, through her benefactress, Mrs. Gordon, Jasmine becomes a 'care-giver' to Wylie and Taylor, and their little girl, Duff. Jasmine now transforms herself into Jase and falls in love with Taylor. But she leaves him in fear and terror when she spots Prakash's assassin. Her flight to Iowa country on sighting her husband's assassin in New York and living with the Ripplemeyers marks the third phase in her transformation. Jasmine transforms herself into Jane and falls in love with Bud. Jasmine speaks about her these transformations: "I have had a husband for each of the women I have been, Prakash for Jasmine Taylor for Jane, Bud for Jane".

Each stage of Jasmine's life ends in terror, violence and fear. Prakash is shot by the Khalsa terrorists; then there is the violent encounter with the Captain, the rapist, ending in his death; the romance with Taylor ends when she confronts Prakash's assassin. Later Bud is crippled by a shot. In an interview, Bharati Mukherjee has said: "I believe that our souls can be reborn in another body, so the perspective I have about a single character's life is different from that of an American writer who believes that he has only one life" (147).

The transformations in Jasmine's life-beginning in Hasnapur, passing through varied "adventure, risk, transformation" (240), can be read as movement towards the realization of the social and the spiritual dimension of existence. The new literature created by women has both a spiritual and social dimension. It reflects women's struggle to create new ways of living in the world, to go beyond a narrow and constricting mould, to become a complete individual. The protagonist's transformations in 'Jasmine'-Jyoti-Jasmine-Jase-Jane' is her attempt to remake an existence with threatened to end even before it had begun. At the age of seven Jyoti is *'helpless, doomed'* by the shadow of future which holds only *'widowhood and exile'*. But she is not cowed down by fate. Through her various transformations, Jyoti proves herself to be the antithesis of village girls who have no minds of their own, but Jyoti's statement, "I know what I don't want to become" (5), makes clear her early resolve to become what she knows she must. And her search for this self takes her in social and spiritual directions.

Jasmine's transitions are fraught with dangers and challenges. Inspite of fighting against all odds and trying to stand against them, she is strongly conditioned by the society into which she is born. This conditioning expects her to disguise her true self most of the time and live according to images fashioned by others. In this regard Jasmine says: "I wanted to become the person they thought they saw" (171).Thus immigrants are many times born and the assimilation is a spiritual rebirth. Jasmine takes several births namely -- Jyoti, Jasmine, Jase and Jane. Through her character the novelist underlines the proper sity of spiritual metamorphosis as a pre-condition to cultural assimilation.

The sartorial changes we notice in her are symptoms of her inner change. She gets more Americanized. She blooms from a different alien with forged documents into an adventurous Jase: "I became an American in an apartment on Claremont Avenue" (165). But these changes are not without pain. "There are not harmless, compassionate ways to remake oneself. We murder who we were so we can rebirth ourselves" (29). There is an inevitable psychological violence in an immigrant's life which is of positive character and value as it hardens their will to survive. The transformation in them is not smooth but jerky and violent.

The author depicts this transformation and transition as a positive and an optimistic journey. Jasmine creates a new world consisting of new ideas and values, constantly unmasking her past. She tries to establish a new cultural identity by incorporating new desires, skills, and habits. This transition is defined not only in the changes in her attitude, but more significantly in her relationship with men.

Mukherjee's female characters are real, modern life like. They are typical representatives of young woman particularly of The Third World countries who cherish the dream of emigrating to America for higher education and higher wages, and then after arrival there, aspire to settle there permanently. Their situations and the difficulties they face are also realistically portrayed.

WORKS CITED

Mukherjee, Bharati, *Jasmine*, New Delhi: Viking, Penguin, India, 1990.

www.amazines.com/Career/article_detail.cfm/665023?articleid=665023,

www.museindia.com/showcurrent14.asp?id=1304.

www.bookrags.com/studyguide-jasmine/themes.html.

□□□

27

Social Web and Cry of the Self : Some Explorations in Manju Kapur's *Difficult Daughters*

Ashok Kumar

The structure of society and equation of power in it is such that it's difficult for women to get their 'voice' heard. Though they constitute a significant part of population yet one fact remains in general that they have never been considered equal of men. No society or country can ever evolve without a dynamic partaking of women in its overall expansion in terms of development. Though there are quite a few exception when it comes to rendering an equal status to women. In India women must necessarily be righteous, chaste, docile, homely and very much dedicated to her family as she is considered to be an incarnation of sacrifices, silent sufferings, faith and knowledge. Women are expected to seek pleasure only in these domains of life. Men are of thought that being a good wife and a mother is the most important asset of womanhood. Her status is based first and foremost on the simple fact that she is the bearer of children and their concern is her prime responsibility. Her sphere is thus constrained to her familial roles.

Manju Kapur in *Difficult Daughters,*[1] – located primarily in the India of the 1940s – speaks with great narrative eloquence, of the idea of independence[2]. This is the story of a woman torn between family duty, the desire for education, and illicit love. Set around the time of partition, this is the story of Virmati seen through the eyes of her daughter Ida, from whom her mother's past had always been kept a secret. Virmati is a young Punjabi girl belonging to an austere family of Amritsar. A family she defies for the love of a married professor. Because of him, she comes to value education and the higher things in life. She realizes that life's horizons are much wider than those that have been shown to her.

Difficult Daughters is the story of a freedom struggle. While India fights for freedom from the British Raj, Virmati fights for the freedom to live life on her terms. Like so many other Indian girls, she wants to decide what to study and where, whom to marry and when. In the end it appears that she might have achieved all that but it ceases to be important. For in the thorns of the struggle, she loses a part of herself. She is torn in two halves, one of which is on the side she is fighting against. All this when India attains freedom but at the cost of Partition and at the cost of losing half its soul. At the cost of hundreds of thousands of innocent lives, lost in the fire of communal hatred. India's hollow victory is mirrored in Virmati's. In all this the professor (fond of everything English) wields considerable influence, although in a catalytic sort of way. Just as Britain did in the tragedy of Partition[3].

Difficult Daughters is an intense and exciting novel that, to horse between history and the fiction and with a noticeable character of three generations of women of a same resident family in the border zone of the Panjab doing special emphasis in the figure of Virmati, a brave woman, a survivor who in its youth, in the heat of independentista in the sub-conscientious Indian, decided to face by love everything a patriarcal system that decided, without having them, the destiny of women, its women, educated by and for obedience. With an honest prosa and without artifice, reveals a challenging history of love and anxieties of freedom that demonstrates that the personnel always entails political and social implications, because Virmati incarnates with its shut up fight, with its immense sacrifice, to all that that has known the constrictions the responsibilities and impositions of the life, to whatever it has wished to break with them and to dare to choose.

Kapur is a professor of English at Miranda House in Delhi. Having done her graduation from Miranda House, Manju did her M.A. in English from Dalhousie University in Canada. She further did M.Phil. from Delhi University. Her debut novel, *Difficult Daughters* was released in the U.S. in 1998, shortly after Arundhati Roy's *The God of Small Things. Difficult Daughters* is a different kind of book, a quite sober and in some sense deeply conventional story set in Amritsar and Lahore. *Difficult Daughters* received the Commonwealth Award for the Eurasian region. Kapur writes with quiet intelligence and wry, deadpan humour. Set against the bloody backdrop of Partition, this is a powerful portrait of a society where shame is more important than grief; pragmatism goes hand-in-hand with superstition. In contemporary times there is awareness in women regarding themselves. They seek to have an identity of their own 'loud and independent'. Women raised their voice against inequality and oppression in the modern and the post modern era. In the process of evolvement they realize that they can depend a lot on their creative faculty for their development. Betty Freidan writes in *The Feminine Mystique*: "The only way for a woman as for a man to find herself, to know herself as a person, is by her creative work of her own. There is no other way[4].

She suggests that the potential of woman is such that she can be an artist and a mother both simultaneously. In fact the variety in role shall be satisfying to her unlike the common myth that she can't handle the stress of multi-tasking. She writes: "The feeling of creativeness also serves another purpose: it is an outlet for the liberated talents, the better taste, the freer imagination, the greater initiative of the modern woman"[5].

Kapur said, she wrote in a female voice because she "knew no other voice". But she candidly admitted she had difficulty creating likeable male characters. Men in her books, like men in society, came across as negative since they are overly demanding in relationships. "They often hurt women without sometimes knowing they have done so". Women caught in the traditional-versus-modern bind are familiar terrain for Kapur. *Difficult Daughters,* has a rebellious heroine who becomes the second wife of a man she loves, even though her family turns against her. Writing about Indian women provides precious insights on local struggles and grants visibility to subtle sources of tension. Kapur - committed feminist writer - has a very important role to play here by creating sensitivity to women's problems and denouncing the weight of rich traditions whose negative aspects have been deemed acceptable because they have been endured. Kapur's intellectual work is a form of raising awareness, identifying problems, and suggesting forms of resistance and negotiation.

In the case of India, the relationship between women, nation and community is particularly straining. Nationalist movements, usually controlled by high caste members, have tended to revive tradition in rigid, purist ways so as to assert a complex constellation of national/communal cultures. This conservative, repressive mentality has been supported by a pervasive presence of religion which has been interpreted in such a way as to encourage a fatalist and subservient attitude on women. Ania Loomba wisely points out that postcolonial gendered identities are shifting, but "religion plays a key role in defining these shifts" (1998: 226)[6].

Difficult Daughters is mainly about putting the ghosts to rest. The sentences at the very end are: "This book weaves a connection between my mother and me, each word a brick in a mansion I made with my head and my heart. Now live in it, Mama, and leave me be. Do not haunt me any more". Thus, it is not only about difficult daughters but also about difficult mothers. About mothers who do not understand their daughters, about daughters who want to break out into new paths. It starts very well and is quite gripping at the beginning with a daughter going on a quest to understand her mother, after the mother has died.

Kapur's sensuous pages re-create an intimate world where family groups sleep in the open air on the roof and wash themselves in the yard in the dewy cool of morning, where love-making is furtive and urgent because another wife may be listening, and women's lives move to a complex choreography of cooking, washing, weaving and mending, growing, picking, chopping and blending. This offers a completely imagined, aromatic, complex world, a rare thing in first novels. The search for control over one's destiny, surely the key theme of *Difficult Daughters,* refers to the Independence aspired to and obtained by a nation (despite its cruel division by a fateful Partition), but also to the independence yearned after (and finally not obtained) by a woman and member of that same nation (or of one of its rival communities). Virmati, the heroine, seeks human relations that will allow her to be herself and to exercise the degree of control over her life which, as an educated woman, she knows she deserves. Born in Amritsar in the Punjab, the daughter of a father of progressive ideas and a traditionalist mother (Kasturi, obliged to give birth to no less than 11 children), she aspires to a freer life than that offered her by those around her. This aspiration is condemned to failure, thanks to the incomprehension she receives from both her own family and that of the man she marries - but also thanks to her own mistakes, for no-one obliged her to marry who became her husband, and she was free not to make the choice she did.

Virmati, like so many other subcontinental women, is asked to accept a typical arranged marriage. She rebels against that destiny, to the lasting shame of her family, above all of her mother. However she cannot totally shrug off the sense of priorities so deeply embedded in her and doesn't consider herself complete till she has married. Within a span of few years, through her various experiences, she grows up from a naïve girl to a woman matured by suffering. She might have started on a quest for true love, independence and a sense of self, but when almost there, she realizes that things are not always as they appear to be. Or perhaps, they change.

The story-teller is the daughter of Virmati who, as a young woman, is drawn more to the intellectual pursuits of life rather than the political ones some of her schoolmates are drawn to. Virmati has been given the chance to study (though rather reluctantly) by her parents and travels to Lahore to do so. She is a woman ahead of her time and is not keen to be relegated to the kitchen and the bedroom like wives of the time are, and her wish to never marry is somewhat disgraceful to her family.

Nonetheless, she falls in love with an Amritsar teacher known as 'the Professor', a married man who first appears in her life as her parents' tenant. After a number of vicissitudes, including a period as a school principal in a small Himalayan state, she finally marries the man she loves, and returns to Amritsar to live with him. However, he refuses to leave his first wife, and the consequences for Virmati are harsh indeed: she ends up being marginalized by her own family and despised by her husband's. Virmati's tale is told, from a present-day perspective, by Ida, her only daughter, who seeks to reconstruct her late mother's life-story, against the background of the Independence movement of the 1940s and the subsequent trauma of Partition. This marriage results in a complete and total abandonment of Virmati by her family something that wounds her terribly.

We discover that Virmati's daughter, as she seeks out those who can tell her about her mother, has also been a difficult daughter in her own way. Kapur's sensitivity is reflected even in the other issues that she addresses. Whether or not a girl has the right to make her own choices in life is an issue dragged this way and that, for a long time in our country. Facing equal assault from the chauvinists who declare that woman's place is inside the house, and the feminists who condemn the idea of taking the husband's surname after marriage, the idea finds a middle path here. There is after all a difference between possessing and protecting. *Difficult Daughters* deals with the idea of education for a girl for her sake, not just to enable her to land a suitable match.

Difficult Daughters follows the journey of a rebellious woman who chases her dreams at the cost of dishonoring her family name, a time when both India and Virmati (the protagonist) are in a state of turmoil. Virmati, struggles against the traditions that her family would like for her to follow. Virmati's case may be seen as representative up to a point, but not absolutely so. It is well-known that women participated forcefully in the social movements that led up to Independence. Kapur emphasizes the efforts made at that time by numerous women who, while demanding equal opportunities, equal access to education and life-opportunities going beyond convention, were a visible force in the non-violent resistance to the British'[7]. The pages of *Difficult Daughters* speak not only of Virmati, but of other 'difficult daughters', who succeed better than she did in their parallel struggles for independence in their lives. At the centre of the narrative, we are confronted with a woman who fights but falls by the wayside; but at its edges, as no doubt less representative but still symbolic figures, we encounter - as will be seen below - other women, whose relative success points the way to the future. *Difficult Daughter's* linear plot and the stillness of her prose conceal an acute understanding of social hypocrisies. Though Kapur's work is not judgmental in tone, it's uncommonly perceptive about human foibles. She can write lucid, conversation-driven narratives about joint families while also making sharp observations about the inconstancy of people and their relationships, as well as the subtler points of self-deception in a tradition-soaked society[8].

The urge to differ, the daring to defy the society, the family name and its reputation for the sake of one's love is all that are reflected through the character of Virmati. The life of a girl who has the dare and attitude to live her own life is worth admiring. The happiest and most attractive period in Virmati's life is, beyond doubt that which she spends in Nahan, the capital of Sirmaur, the small Himalayan state run by an enlightened Maharaja which gives her refuge for a while as the headmistress of a girl's school. Sirmaur existed in reality, and is now part of the federal state of Himachal Pradesh. It is there that she achieves the greatest degree of control over her life: there are rules she has to obey (and breaking them proves her fall), but she is able to teach inside an ordered framework, and her performance wins her a deserved respect. It is true that the single or widowed lady teacher or headmistress is something of a stock figure in modern Indian literature.

Difficult Daughters is beautifully written and shows the options that women have in Indian society. For a woman to step in or out of the traditional roles there is often a very steep price to pay. Virmati's story is a sad one, but it is a very honest and compelling tale. Virmati's married life with the Professor in Amritsar turns out to be a disaster. She wilts under the implacable and hostile gaze of Ganga, her husband's first wife, with whom she has to live. She loses ali sense of identity: the continuation of her education (she studies for a higher degree in philosophy, but without enthusiasm) feeds no more dreams of independence. In the end, her individual history disappears and becomes all but irrelevant, swallowed up in the greater and more resonant collective tragedy of Partition. Yet, despite all this, Virmati has in her life's path encountered other women, who like her aspired to a different life, and who succeeded better than she did.

Virmati's cousin Shakuntala and Swarna Lata, her roommate in Lahore, both are representatives of a certain female type that recurs in Indian literature: the emancipated woman militant. As we have seen above, no-one should forget the many women who took part in the struggle for Independence and the Gandhian movement: a notable literary testimony to them is Kanthapura, Raja Rao's novel of 1938 in which he tells that story through the prism of a female narrative voice. In post-Independence literature, one may mention such characters as Daisy, the militant of *The Painter of Signs* by R.K. Narayan who prefers to remain single, or Malati Trivedi, the progressive activist of *A Suitable Boy* by Vikram Seth, who first appears in that book as, curiously, also the roommate of the female protagonist, Lata; here too, the convergence of names between Seth's Lata and Kapur's

Swarna Lata may be another detail pointing to a possible inter-textuality. The name Shakuntala, too, has its inter-textual connotations: the Indian reader will think immediately of the eponymous heroine of *The Recognition of Shakuntala,* the play by Kalidasa, and the great classical Sanskrit dramatist – the young girl who, abandoned by her husband the king, finally obtains recognition of her rights and proper treatment.

Difficult Daughters is well-plotted and has truly convincing characterization (like many classic English "rake" stories. Its villain is in some ways more likeable than its heroine). But it is also interesting for reasons that are not just literary; Kapur has an unusual angle on the involvement of women in Gandhi's Swaraj agitations. It's one of those strange, contradictory moments in Indian history. The fact is traditional Indian values had barely modernized at all when, in 1930, Gandhi began to encourage women to participate in civil disobedience actions. By November 1930, 360 out of the 29,000 Indian nationalists imprisoned by the British Raj for expressing their political beliefs were women. The number would grow throughout the 1930s and early 1940s, and a small number of highly educated, independent women were highly visible members of the nationalist movement. Such progress overlapped with a profound backwardness – for the vast majority of Indians, dehumanizing practices such as child marriage, polygamy, and dowry would remain widely practiced (legal until the 1950s). The contradictory progress and non-progress with regards to women and gender roles is one of the great contradictions of Indian modernity, and it's one of Kapur's central preoccupations in *Difficult Daughters* (just as it was Tagore's preoccupation, nearly 90 years earlier, in novels like *The Home and the World* and *Chokher Bali*).

In Virmati's extended family, her cousin Shakuntala appears from the beginning as the exemplar of the 'modern' or 'liberated' women. She studies, teaches, and takes part in the political-Gandhian movement: even after marriage, she keeps a firm grip on her autonomy and her freedom of action and thought. Shakuntala thus becomes a pole of attraction for Virmati: 'Virmati listened…drawn towards Shakuntala, to one whose responsibilities went beyond a husband and children' (17). Nor is she an entirely atypical or isolated figure: she shares her 'liberated' lifestyle with a group of friends, whose activities she explains to her cousin: 'we travel, entertain ourselves in the evenings, follow each other's work, read papers, attend seminars. One of them is even going abroad for higher studies'[9].

Later, in Swarna Lata, Virmati encounters a woman who leads a similar lifestyle; her friend, an ultra-committed activist, takes her to a meeting of the Punjab Women's Student Conference where she shines as an orator: 'Heavy applause broke out as Swarna finished speaking' (145). Swarna continues her political activity post-marriage, expressing herself on the matter to Virmati as follows: 'We have plenty of married women working with us. I'm married, aren't I?' (252). One may draw a parallel between the careers of Shakuntala and Swarna, although here a qualification needs to be made: on the one and only occasion when the two meet, they do not get on – a small narrative irony which points up Kapur's ability to avoid both reductionism and sentimentalism. In the end, the path of political activism does not attract Virmati, as she herself recognizes 'I am not like these women. They are using their minds, organizing, participating in conferences, being politically active, while my time is spent being in love' (142). She chooses – it cannot be said for her own good – the road that leads to the Professor: a road not taken by Swarna, with whom she finally feels obliged to break off relations: 'And Swarna dropped out of her life' (252).[10]

At all events, it may be said that Virmati's frustrated life is, as it were, framed – as if in a triptych – by those two other, much more successful lives: those of Shakuntala and Swarna Lata, both emblematic of the educated, politicized and emancipated woman.[11] In other words, the psychological annihilation of Virmati, at the hands of her own family and her husband's, should not be read as a fatality. What happens to Virmati is no doubt the most representative destiny of the Indian woman (even if educated), quantitatively or statistically, but *Difficult Daughters* shows that other paths also exist, while further stressing that choices are by no means simple.

There are types of female negotiation that work, and others that do not: but nothing is predetermined. One may here invoke, from a comparative viewpoint, another novel by an Indian woman writer; Anita Desai's *Fasting, Feasting,* which appeared in 1999, shortly after *Difficult Daughters.* Here, if Uma, the female protagonist of the novel's Indian part, is unable to get out of the dull mediocrity of her existence as an unmarried daughter – and if the fate of her cousin Anamika, who could have gone to study at Oxford but ends up a victim of the epidemic of bride-burning, is even worse — Uma's sister Aruna appears by contrast as the representative of a different type of Indian woman, the 'socialite' who succeeds in imposing her personality by the skilful pulling of social strings. It may be concluded that, however sadly typical the experiences of Virmati, these also exist paths that lead, with positive effect, to less typical destinations where demands are raised and recognised.

Because *Difficult Daughters* is characterized by a grounded, no-flourishes writing style, I'm surprised to learn that she was quite the experimenter in her early days. "When I first started writing stories and poems," she says, "magic realism was all the rage, thanks in large part to Rushdie. I tried to write like that but in my hands it seemed inauthentic and labored, and so I gave it up. Intuitively, I took the raasta of not standing between the reader and the story — I wanted to make it as transparent and seamless as possible." Her first book originally had footnotes, a story within a story "and lots of other stuff I thought was very innovative — but it all had to go eventually!"[12].

Kapur also has a reputation for being a reticent writer; regulars at the ever-increasing book-launch parties in the capital would have a hard time placing her. Given this, what does she think about the recent developments in Indian publishing, such as the elevation of media-savvy young writers to pop-celebrity status even before their books are out? "It's hard for me to see writing as a social stepping stone," she says:

> It's such a solitary activity, whereas being in society means being gregarious. Of course, younger people have more energy, and if they can party and write, good for them. But if it interferes with your writing, I would say just don't do it. As a writer, you have to serve your art, old-fashioned as it may sound — and personally I do this by not meeting anyone![13].

Difficult Daughters definitely helps to see deep into the psychology of women in love and child bearing. This is not a pure third-person narrative. Virmati's story is told mostly in the third person (with some recourse to the epistolary mode), but is framed by the first-person narration of a search. The search is that of Virmati's daughter, Ida, as she seeks to reconstitute her mother's history. Ida, an educated woman, divorced and childless, apparently leads a freer life than her mother's in external terms; yet inside her she feels, even if not quite so acutely, some of the same anxieties as had plagued her mother: "No matter how I might rationalize otherwise, I feel my existence as a single woman reverberate desolately" (3). It is clear that Ida, the narrator through whose voice Kapur speaks, has achieved more than her mother (and much more than her grandmother): and that this is so even through the simple creative fact of 'writing down' her own family history.

Dora Sales again explores, in *Difficult Daughters* we do not listen to Virmati's voice. She could not speak out, being certainly situated at the juncture of two oppressions: colonialism and patriarchy. What we have is her daughter's reconstruction and representation'.[14] Brave women are not made. They are born. Too much pain, too much tolerance and too much dareness are all reflected in the character of Virmati. Perhaps Kapur has tried to establish the strongness and the dareness of women in love. All in all, the narration is very appealing. As a debutant, Kapur has done the best way it can have been done.

There is, then, a qualitative leap between the life-histories of (narrated) mother and (narrating) daughter. In addition, as another of Kapur's commentators, Gur Pyari Jandial, correctly points out, it would be a mistake to devalue Virmati's struggle because she failed, for what mattered was to have made the attempt: 'What is necessary is to break the patriarchal mould, and for Virmati to have tried to do that in the forties was a great achievement'[15].

Consequently, *Difficult Daughters* is framed by sensitive threads of events. It is so naturally written; that along the way one forgets it is a work of fiction. It feels more like a lifetime unraveling in front of our eyes, with real people in it; experiencing happiness, sorrow, pleasure and pain. And all this comes across with such sensitivity that one is compelled to nod at and understand even the forbidden love affair of Virmati and the professor. *Difficult Daughters* compels one to think wider. We all know about women's emancipation and the serpent called communalism, but Kapur has dealt with both these relatively stale issues in such a manner that we find not just with our eyes but also with our heart. Just the way Kapur has revealed. *Difficult Daughters* spanning three generations, this center on a woman born at the turn of the 20th century into a Punjabi family. It tells of an illicit affair and its wider political and social implications as well as not least the bothered issue, for Indian women, of marriage versus education.

Difficult Daughters is a fascinating insight into many things: into history; into a distant culture; but, most importantly, into human hearts and minds. To an Anglo-Saxon reader, the distance in time and place may, on one level, make this escapist novel; but on another level it does what all the best escapist (or fantasy) novels do. Despite being set during the Indian Partition, this is not an overtly political novel. However, a surprising amount of information about Partition—the political crisis that literally tore apart a nation – is imparted. Moreover, *Difficult Daughters* is a tale of struggle, traditional repression and independence.

Thus, *Difficult Daughters* is, by opposition, a text which does not solve, within the plot, the silences between different generations of women. However, the novel is structured as a biography of a dead mother and the degree of understanding with which it is written is an undirect way of settling disagreements and quarrels. In fact, at the end of the text, Kapur declares the *Difficult Daughters* a sort of exorcism, a last word on disquieting matters. Not surprisingly, one of the main topics of this biography is the troubled relation between the narrator's mother and her own, many years before. According to *Difficult Daughters*, the reasons that make some daughters "difficult" for their families are the rejection of an arranged marriage (which turns an entire and united household against a scared teenager), the incomprehensible ambition to study (which is completely dismissed as irrelevant for women) and the unfortunate display of an independent will. This means that within the logic of the represented culture, the good daughter is "good" because she does everything she is told to and she does not have any ambitions. The tone of the text could have been ironic if it were not for the suffering and sadness that exude from every page.

India women have indeed achieved their successes in half a century of Independence; but if there is to be a true female independence too, much remains to be done. The fight for autonomy remains an unfinished combat; and it is from that perspective that, in her second novel, *A Married Woman*, published five years later, that Kapur, this time from an eminently contemporary viewpoint, returns to the narration of women's issues, deploying an approach that, as in

Difficult Daughters, manages to be, simultaneously, both Indian and universal. And that, too, is 'a great achievement'.

Thus, the brilliant and most fascinating thing about the *Difficult Daughters* is the unresolved dichotomy about the character of Virmati. On one hand she is very strong and has strong will power and can resist all kinds of social and family pressure. On the other hand she is very weak, because she just cannot kick the professor out of her life. The reason for this behavior is not love, but the lack of love. Virmati as a child received very little love. She wanted love and missed it till the professor came with his assurances of love braced with sentences from the English literature. It is another example of a person being in love with the concept of love, rather than with another person. *Difficult Daughters* is both wonderful and terribly sad. Anyone, man or woman, who rails against convention to do what they believe are right for them in their hearts, is bound to be damaged in the process.

WORKS CITED

1. Manju Kapur, *Difficult Daughters*, London: Faber and Faber, 1998. (All subsequent references are from this edition and have been absorbed in the text by giving pages references in parenthesis.)
2. www.seikilos.com.ar/DifficultDaughters_en.html.
3. www.mouthshut.com/review/*Difficult_Daughters*-Manju_Kapur-59806-1.html.
4. Frieden, Betty, *The Feminine Mystique*, New York: Dell Publishing Co. Inc, 1963, p.332.
5. *Ibid.*, p.204
6. Loomba, Ania, *Colonialism/Postcolonialism*, New York and London: Routledge, , 1998.
7. Kapur, Manju, *Hijas dificiles*, translated (with glossary and translator's note) by Dora Sales Salvador, Madrid: Espasa, 2003, p.356.
8. http://ultrabrown.com/posts/a-meeting-with-manju-kapur.
9. The figure of the woman who goes abroad for further study recurs in *A Married Woman*.
10. The path of militancy recurs, once again in a context of meetings and speeches, in *A Married Woman*, where it fuses, albeit for a brief time and in a context that can scarcely be called socially orthodox, with the option of 'being in love': Kapur's second novel presents among its themes, notably, a narrative of intimacy between women

against the backdrop of the 'events of Ayodhya' and Hindu-Muslim conflict.

11. In this sense, both prefigure the impressive Pipee Trivedi, the social militant and intimate friend of the female protagonist of the following novel.
12. http://ultrabrown.com/posts/a-meeting-with-manju-kapur.
13. *Ibid.*
14. Salvador, Dora Sales Salvador, *The Memory of Desire in Manju Kapur's Difficult Daughters: In Past and Future Tense,* in Constanza del Río and Luis M. García Mainar (eds.), *Memory, Imagination and Desire,* Heidelberg: Universitätsverlag C. Winter.
15. Jandial, Gur Pyari, *Evolving a Feminist Tradition: The Novels of Shashi Deshpande and Manju Kapur,* New Delhi: Atlantic Literary Review.

□□□

28

Feministic Visions in the Novels of Manju Kapur

SARIKA DUBEY

Feminist literature in english is certainly not a recent innovation. It has been there ever since perspectives on life were recorded in the medium of literature, though it certainly has come to its own of late of recent origin again is the feminist perception of literature. Feminist criticism in its broadest implication has three distinct subdivisions, each with its own adherents. The first two are well defined and frequently practiced without raising any ideological outrage. These are: The examination and analysis of the portrayal of women characters by themselves or in relationship with their male counterparts, and the appreciation of female authors. What is noteworthy is the fact than in the last few years these commonly accepted critical practices have been overhauled to accommodate the possibility of exclusively feminist perceptions of human relationship. The third direction is that of the so called 'prescriptive criticism' that attempts to set standards for literature that is 'good' from the feminist perspective. Feminism in the Indian context is a by-product of the Western liberalism in general and feminist thought in particular. The indigenous contributing factors have been the legacy of equality of sexes inherited from the freedom struggle, constitutional rights of women, spread of education and the consequent new awareness among women. The Indian woman caught in the flux of tradition and modernity saddled with the burden of the past but both to cast off her aspirations constitutes the crux of aspirations constitutes the crux of feminism in Indian literature. In literary terms it precipitates in a search for identity and a quest for the definition of the self. In critical practice, it boils down to scrutinizing empathetically the plight of women characters at the receiving end of human interaction. Feminist English Literature is a spectrum of many colours and shades - soft, prominent and strident. The voices emanating there from vary from the traditional-but-conscious-of-their-selves to exclusively self-seeking with a seeming vengeance. When clearly articulated, well argued and precisely defined feminist sentiments rather than mere faint echoes thereof can be traced even in early works like Mary Shelley's *Frankenstein* and Jane Austen's *Pride and Prejudice*, one feels chary of dubbing feminism as merely a late twentieth century phenomenon. The feminist perspective on literature- creative or critical - whether in a third world country or elsewhere, has had to confront issues of similar persuasion: male chauvinism, sexist bias, psychological and even physical exploitation, hegemonistic inclinations in not merely the male but also the female sections of society, the utter disregard for the female's psychological, cultural, familial and spiritual quests. Predictably enough the ways out suggested subtly or propagated more avowedly have ranged from mild protest, seeking accommodation through moderation, love and persuasion to carving out of a self-sufficient exclusivist self.

Manju Kapur's novel *A Married Women* (2002) is the story of an educated, upper middle class, working Delhiite women Astha. As a girl 'she was brought up properly, as befits a woman, with large supplements of fear. One ship might find her alone, vulnerable and unprotected. The infinite ways in which she could be harmed were not specified, but Astha absorbed them through her skin, and ever after was drawn to the safe and secure' (p.1). She is her parents' only child. Her education, her character, her health, her marriage are her parents' burdens and liabilities. They are very conscious of them and they never forget Astha to realize it. Like a common teenager school going girl she often imagines of a romantic and handsome young man holding her in his strong manly embrace. In her adolescence she falls in love with Bunty, a boy of her age. 'Day and night the thought of him kept her insides churning; she was unable to eat, sleep or study. Away from him her eyes felt dry and empty. Her ears only registered the sound of his voice. Her mind refused to take seriously anything that was not his face, his body, his feet, his hands, his clothes. Hours were spent in planning accidental meetings how to bump into him...how to die at his doorstep'.

A Married Woman is an honest and seductive story of love, passion, and attachment set at the time of political and religious turmoil in India driven by a powerful physical relationship with a much younger woman, the main character of the novel risks losing the acquisitions of her correctional marriage and safe family. The novel raises the controversial issue of homosexual relationship in a challenging way. After all gay and lesbian relationships are not mere fancies. This is getting more and more visible in modern societies though we may or may not accept it. Various elements of feminism are clearly visible in the novel *A Married Woman*; Astha faces biological subjugation in her relationship with the mother in the childhood and with husband in her married life. Her inability to buy an art piece in Goa exhibits her economic dependence in spite of being an earning member of the family. Her mother and father constantly remind her that she is vulnerable and unprotected and so is their liability. Later her husband and in-laws also make her realize that as a bride, wife and mother she is not independent and any act of her is challengeable is family life. All these circumstances force her to make a lesbian relationship with the widow of the man. She loves unconsciously. The last decade of the twentieth century witnessed a sudden spurt in feminist writing in Indian English fiction. A group of Indian women novelists in their in between's, hybridist of thought and multicultural, multi-lingual and multi- religious social dimensions have contextualized the women problems in general and middle-class and upper class women in particular. While the gynocrities think that too many women in too many countries speak the same language of silence, some Indian women novelists like Gita Hariharan, Shashi Deshpande, Arundhati Roy, Meena Alexander and Manju Kapur have tried with sincerity and honesty to deal with the physical, psychological and emotional stress syndrome of women. Manju Kapur, a Reader in English literature at Miranda House, University of Delhi, is the winner of the 1999 Common wealth Writers Prize for the socio-political scenario in our country with insight and precision. While her first novel is a family saga against the historical backdrop of partition, her second novel *A Married Woman* (2002) is a work of investigative reporting on the most controversial and political issue of the demolition of Babri Masjid and a woman's obsession with love and lesbianism. The novel is a kind of narrative on a woman's incompatible marriage and resultant frustration and the contemporary political turmoil in its historical context. Like premarital relationship in Nayantara Sahgal's *Storm in Chandigarh* (1969), adulterous relationship in Shashi Deshpande's *Roots and Shadows* (1983), second marriage for biganous relationship in Sahgal's *Rich Like Us* (1985) or Alan Sealy's *The Trotter- Nama* (1988) and in her own novel *Difficult Daughters*, Kapur's second novel *A Married Woman* deals with lesbianism. In the novel, Kapur has taken writing as a protest, a way of mapping from the point of a woman's experience. Kapur negotiates different issues emerging out of a socio- political upheaval in her country. In a realistic way, she has described the Indian male perception of woman as a holy cow even though women are not very interested in history and those in power trying to twist and turn historical facts to serve their own purposes. As a writer of new generation in an atmosphere of the nation's socio-political flux, Kapur has recorded the truth in her fictive narrative. With zeal to change the Indian male perception, she describes the traumas of her female protagonists from which they suffer, and perish in for their triumph. She is shocked at the growth of fundamentalism and the rise of religious zealots to uplift and elevate the country by a crusade and establish paranoia by presenting evil as a historical necessity. Kapur describes these polities of genocide as an important fabric in India's unique experience of democracy. She is sincere and naive as a sociologist in exposing the bizarre paradox of rationality that underlines a sentiment of antipathy sheltered under political support and social approval. She resonates with her feminine assertion, hatred for violence, blood, death and ill-feeling in the name of God and religion, and her feminine assertions remain untouched by history, politics and human interpretations. *A Married Woman* is a novel with a social purpose. It deals with three issues - reinterpretation of history, political ideologies and feminist views in the present context. The pointed references to life and delicate dealing with political activities of the time are presented with the historical backdrop of Babri Masjid- Ram Janambhoomi episode. This gives the story a tangible shape with the articulation of emotional issues, communal hatred and women concerns. While the political backdrop is controversial and no conducive for the secularists, the demolition of Babri Masjid adds substance to the novel. The main ideas conceived in the novel are based on family life, sexual relationship, gender discrimination, socio-political upheaval and the desire for peaceful co-existence. The purpose of the novelist seems to be uni-dimensional with the idea of love what can really drive a woman into such a relationship. In her interview with Nivedita Mukherjee, Kapur says:

> It is an attempt to inject an element of artistic and emotional coherence. Actually a relationship with a woman does not threaten a marriage as much as a relationship with a man". The novel exposes the domestic terrain where woman explores the space in her domestic relationship. Kapur has remained very truthful in presenting the women and the challenges they face in their personal, professional, religious and socio-political levels.

Taking into account the complexity of life, different histories, cultures and different structures of values, the Woman's Question, despite basic solidarity, needs to be tackled in relation to the socio-cultural situation. The impact of patriarchy of the Indian society varies...and therefore ...stream of feminism grounded in reality. Kapur the socialist conveys the message that communal riot is a terrible disease that kills God in man and commits murder in the cathedral while Kapur the feminist refers to three forms of mysogyny, sexism or discrimination against women, patriarchy or male supremacy at institutional and individual level, and phallocentrism or discrimination at the conceptual level. She desires to prove through her woman protagonist that "A woman should be aware, self-controlled, strong-willed, self-reliant and rational having faith in the inner strength of womanhood. A meaningful change can be brought only from within by being free in the deeper psychic sense. She seems to bring out the implicit fallacy in Aristotle's dictum, "Man is a social animal", in the present socio-cultural context of India in which people fail to realize the futility of violence, and the necessity of peaceful of-existence for all. She apprehends the approach of an apocalyptic social climate with the rise of the fundamentalists and fanatics in nation's spurious polities who take religion to be ultra-patriotic. Like *Difficult Daughters, A Married Woman* "has a sophisticated plot". The story of love is honest. Set at a time of political and religious upheaval it is narrated with sympathy and intelligence for anyone who has known life's responsibilities. The novel is a sincere confession of a woman about her personality cult in the personal allegory of a bad marriage. Astha the sensitive daughter of an enlightened father and orthodox mother has grown in a middle-class educated family in South Delhi and becomes a housewife, teacher, painter, and a lesbian in her status of a married woman she fights for her self-assertions. Unlike many unmarried girls she had her infatuations of adolescent love for Bunty, a boy of another colony and for Rohan who left for overseas for a better career. But her real story of love and marriage started with Hemant, the son of a successful government official in Delhi. Soon after marriage, Astha gets disillusioned about human nature in general and politics of the country in particular. She is fed up with the politicians who, in the guise of democrats and socialists, attempt to organize different yatras for their vote banks under the pseudo-secular banner of national unity. On the other hand, these yatras have become inauspicious for the nation. Sharing her feelings "we should struggle with her, agonize together with her about her choices, and weep with her once she's made them". Astha's family affairs are not good and nothing is right with her. Hemant doesn't prove a suitable boy nor does she become a desirable daughter-in-law in her in-law's house. In the Kosher world of Saas bahu social dynamics, she does not want only to be heavily sindoored, bejeweled and walk around the tulsi plant every morning and offer a mandatory pooja. As a married woman she becomes an enduring wife and sacrificing mother. Her temperamental incompatibility with her corporate thinking husband compels her to play the role of "mother and father" for her children. This denies her self fulfilment and leads to the collapse of the institution of marriage. Discontentment leads her to defiance and restlessness. Her anxiety, discomfort, loneliness and isolation do not encourage her to give voice to her unhappiness over her troubled relationship, rather it prompts her to develop the feelings of guilt, negativity and lack of self- esteem in facing the challenges of her life. Restlessness drives her to enjoy absolute loneliness, a sort of entrapment by the family, its commitments, its subtle oppression and she yearns for freedom. In the midst of a family and its vast minefield of income, expenditure, rights, responsibilities, knowledge, discontent, restlessness and dependency, Astha enjoys the fate of the poorest. She is suffocated with the growing needs of her family and "always adjusting to everybody's needs" (227). Astha understands a married woman's place in the family to be that of an unpaid servant or a slave and the thought of divorce brings social and economic death in her Indian status. She feels for herself: "A willingly body at night, a willing pair of hands and feet in the day and an obedient mouth" (231), are the necessary prerequisites of a married woman. She contemplates marriage a terrible decision as it puts her in a lot to enjoy bouts of rage, pain and indecision. Judging the male impression of woman she thinks that a married woman is an object of "mind fucking" (218). She does not think "marriage is just sex" (275) rather it provides interest, togetherness and respect. Being torn between her duty and responsibility, faith and fact, history and contemporaneity, public ethos and personal ethics she thinks "a tired woman cannot make good wives", (154) and struggles for an emotional freedom from the scourge of the nation. She develops psychosomatic symptoms of stress and depression balancing between existing and living. Astha's slow discovery of her differences with her husband, her change from a tender and hopeful bride to a battered wife and her meeting with Pipeelika Trivedi lead her to realize the other state of woman in their "familiar distress" (188) This leads her to an immoral, rather amoral, guilt consciousness of lesbian love rationalizing her outmoded morality. Being marginalized by the affluence of her family, vicious social atmosphere, sheer hysteria of communalism and quarrel of two communities for god over a small thing, she is disillusioned in the empirical study of man's nature and his framing of social values. There is the evolution of a romantic fantasy in her lesbophobic imagination for her definition and self reliance. Astha's marriage to a Pan-American and Pan-Indian husband in her parents' choice is a miscalculation. Hemant's foreign education, banking profession and money minting addiction do not make Astha happy for a long time. Hemant's resignation from the banking job and joining in T.V. manufacturing business, Astha's joining as a teacher, her giving birth to Anuradha and Himanshu bring enough change in her life. Her impression that "with good job comes independence" (4) is proved wrong and she "seemed very pedestrian" (47). By giving birth to a son on the one hand, she proves herself no "socially inferior" and enjoys the gratitude of her family members for whom "The family is complete at last" (68) and on the other she expresses commitment to her profession. Like every married woman, no doubt she has a liking for motherhood but she does not like the sex-subjugation of her in laws. She is surprised at the reaction of the family and society when they remain cypheric of Anuradha's birth but gets an overwhelming approval of motherhood after the birth of Himanshu. In her feminist assertion Astha does not appreciate superstition, sex-subjugation and pride and prejudices of having children just for their discriminated sex in the Indian perception. Being "caught up in the web of daily life" (84) she develops restlessness, anxiety and tension, "the disease of modern life" (76), She remembers her mother's words "woman is earth", (69) and that, duties, responsibilities and obligations help a married woman to understand the grandeur of Hinduism. *Vasudha ev Kutumbkum*. She does not believe that only a woman can bring purity and peace to the family. She becomes serious for man's ignorance at woman's suffering and asserts her rights with the knowledge that "Religion a choice as much as other things" (89). She differs from the male perception of woman as a holy cow that must be a secular food. The inhospitable family and hostile social atmosphere due to Babri Masjid- Ram Janambhoomi issue have made her realize the other state of a woman's life. Pipeelika, a Hindu Brahmin Girl, had married a Muslim Aijaz Akhtar Khan, a sensitive, socially committed history lecturer, painter, theatre activist and founder of Street Theatre Troupe. Astha appreciates them for the ideals of their conjugal life and their secularist vision. Like a modern feminist she appreciates Aijaz's aesthetic and creative genius and for his working on slum life and sufferings of underage girls. She admires Pipee's asserting her rights to marry against her mother's desire and against society's recommendation. Astha, like Virmati in *Difficult Daughters*, desires to have a break from "dependence syndrome" and proceeds on the path of full human status that poses a threat to Hemant and his male superiority. She is, not a lesser mortal for her sex and like her male counterpart takes interest in political activism and fundamental issues of human life. Although she finds herself trapped between the pressures of the modern developing society and shackles of ancient biases she sets.

Home (2006) is the third novel of Manju Kapur. This is a fast moving story which makes an ordinary middle class family's life in Delhi. The patriarch of this family is Banwari Lal, a cloth businessman who lives with his family in New Delhi neighbourhood of Karol Bagh. Banwari Lal has two sons and one daughter. Elder is Yashpal, younger is Pyare Lal and daughter's name is Sunita who is already married to a person named Murli before the beginning of the novel. Who is married to Murli a person beyond the status of Banwari Lal in views as well as in money? It seems that Sunita likes the boy that's why she is married to him. The Banwari Lal family belongs to a class whose skills have been honed over generations to ensure prosperity in the market place. From an early age children are trained to maintain the foundation on which these homes rested. The education they received, the values they imbibed, the alliances they made has everything to do with protecting the steady stream of gold and silver that burnished their lives. Banwari Lal is a believer in the old ways. Men work out of the home, women within. Men carry forward the family line, women enable their mission. His two sons unquestioningly follow their father in business and in life but their wives do not. Neither does his grand daughter who makes choices considered unavailable to the women to the family. At the beginning of the story Sona Lal and Rupa Gupta both sisters are childless. Sona is the wife of Yashpal who falls in love while Sona with her mother comes from Meerut to match a blouse in preparing to attend an uncle's wedding. Sona's mother considers that it is necessary for marriageable girls to blossom during such occasions, it being likely that among the guests a boy, or better still his parents, can cast a glance and held it steadily upon her person. With this in mind, the mother with her daughters is shopping in Karol Bagh determines that her daughters should look their best for every function. Yashpal falls in love and enquires all necessary details. Next morning he puts the address on his father's hand and says he should go and talk to the family without delay. If he could not marry her he would leave the shop and spend the rest of his life celibate, by the bank of the Ganges. Banwari Lal consults to a holy man, a Baba and settles the matter. Although Sona's family is not as rich as Yashpal's family. In marriage they can offer nothing but their daughter whose heart is golden like her name. Their marriage is performed. But her mother-in-law is not pleased and she passes taunts. This makes Sona unhappy but Yashpal consoles her saying that when we have children, mother will forget all this. But unfortunately Sona could not conceive for a long time. By this time Pyare Lal is also married to Sushila who gives birth to a boy within one year of the marriage. Sona feels very bad and thinks that it may be the result of her past Karma, Sona keeps fast but it is of no use. During this period Yashpal's sister burns herself and dies. As the family receives the news, they leave for Bareilly. Here Sona's mother-in-law mourns, Sona tries to consols her. 'Sleep now, Maji, sleep you will make yourself ill if you cry like this, and it will not bring her back. The old woman glared at Sona and spat out, you think sleep is possible? What can you know of a mother's feelings? All you do is enjoy life, no children, no sorrow, only a husband to dance around you, Sona is already mentally disturb to hear the taunt of her. Her father-in-law comes back with Vicky ten years old. The Boy is pushed towards Sona. Sona has to take care of Vicky Sona discusses her matters to Rupa and tells that her life has become unbearable ever since Sushila has entered in the house. 'Ever since that woman has come, my life has been a misery' (p.24.) Yashpal feels that Sona is not feeling well so he makes plan to visit a shrine at Chitai, near Almora Though the shrine is small it is famous, the Devi of these hills is said to have miraculous powers. Rupa & Premnath also joins them. After two mothers Sona discovers that she has conceived. Sona feels it is because of Devi. Later on Sona gives birth to a girl. Nisha is declaring as a Mangli. Nisha grows up as a beautiful girl and after Nisha, Sona gives birth to Raju. Now Vickey starts going to shop and there is some relax for Sona. Who does not like Vickey's activities? By the time Vickey is fifteen and he begins to take interest in Nisha. Nisha cannot understand his intension. Nisha becomes mentally disturbed and nobody could understand why she is not eating, sleeping. So she is sent to Rupa's Home for a change. Here she has no problem at all. Rupa & her husband Premnath understand all that there is a hand of Vicky behind Nisha's miserable condition. Nisha now finds herself in an atmosphere very different from the one she has lived in. As the only child she is the centre of interest, concern and attention. The pattern of Nisha's next ten years is not set. She passes all week with her aunt and uncle. Premnath teaches her and brings a lot of things. Here Nisha flourishes as the most beautiful girl. On the other hand Vicky passes class X with third Division & Yashpal argues that he should go back to his father. So Banwari Lal with Vickey visits Bareilly but his father refuses to keep him pretending so many reasons. Now Banwari Lal thinks about his marriage and performs it with Asha. Soon Asha gives birth to Virat. After a long illness Banwari Lal also dies and the whole burden comes to Yashpal, being the elder one. Nisha also returns her home to accompany her grand mother. Ajay's marriage takes place a year after his grandfather's death and after it Vijay Marriage. The Board results are out Raju in Class X has barely scraped through with a 45 percent overall aggregate. Nisha was a mangli. A mangli, destined to marry unfortunately, destined for misery, unless a similar mangli could be found, with a similar fate and horoscope. To do this would take time, and during that time perhaps an education? Not too much just a bit

& Nisha enters in Durga Bai College for doing English Honours. In College Nisha's best friend is Pratibha. Soon Nisha meets a boy Suresh who is studying in Khalsa College of Engineering. They become friendly within two or three meetings. Both fall in love and wonder here and there in each other's company. She now totally changes. 'Who gave you permission to cut your hair, suddenly you have become so independent, you decide things on your own, where did you find the money, the time, the beauty parlour, where did you find all these things?' (p.150). The academic session is coming to close. Nisha has had a difficult year and now she feels nervous. 'I can't meet you, I have to study, I have to get a second division at least', she told Suresh, 'Arre yaar, what does it matter? It's impossible to do badly in English' (p.152). Suresh purchases St. Stephen's tutorials from Daryaganj at Sunday bazaar and gives to Nisha. Nisha with the help of these notes gets success and gets first division. Nisha and Suresh continue their routine in next year also. As for Nisha, her uncle's training has stood her in good stead. With family wedding, she has still been able to obtain a 70 percent in Humanities. The uncle is thanked profusely for the care he has taken of his niece. By this time Pyare Lal has two daughters-in-law so he feels uncomfortable in the house where there is no separate bathroom for them. So he consults his brother to reconstruct the home again. Yashpal says nothing at the moment. Her wife also does not like the reconstruction. Yashpal says: "It was not his fault. He was the youngest, what could he do by himself? Now he had sons, daughter in law and grand children, now he was a patriarch in his own right" (p.170). So they all move out of the house Hotel Palace Heights in Karol Bagh. Nisha enjoys in company of Suresh. He takes her to the room in Vijay Nagar where he tries to make sexual relation with her but could not successes. On the way back Nisha remarks if he is so keen to do all this, why does not he make his parents talk to her parents? Let the whole thing be clear. Towards the end of Nisha's third year her parents receives a letter from the college authorities. Their daughter is short of attendance, and will not be allowed to sit for exams. Now parents enquire the reason, but Nisha does not tell directly and sent Suresh to meet at the shop. Now all things become clear & Yashpal enquires all things. Finally he declares him unfit for the girl. All day she remains in the house, a prisoner of her deed, a prisoner of their words. Once she gets a chance to go with her masi Rupa & arranges to meet him. Here Suresh finally declares that he cannot marry her

& leaves her. Nisha's nights are now ones of restlessness. After three years of thinking that Suresh is her future, Nisha will have adjust to the idea of another man in his place. Later on she badly suffers from eczema. This disease affects her a lot. This period had very important for Nisha's coming future but it had passed in this fatal eczema. This condition of Nisha remains same for a long period. Parents have been worrying; daughter getting older by the minute, son's future blocks because of this, good matches will pass over because of this. One day a proposal comes from a richer branch of Rekha's family showrooms in Karol Bagh and South Extension. Pyare Lal tells his brother that this type of proposal does not come daily so without any delay he should make up his mind. So they all go to Babaji. Babaji tells: "I have good news, continued Babaji. The boy and the girl's horoscopes are perfectly matched. This girl will be good for the family and even Nisha's future will open after her sister-in-law comes to the house" (p.248). So marriage is performed and Raju & Pooja go for a honeymoon in Europe. They return after one month and Pooja proves quite opposite. Sona complains to Raju that Pooja is not behaving like a daughter-in-law. Pooja spends no time with the rest of the family, no time with Nisha. Raju responses 'Pooja is right: you don't like her, why did you marry me to her, then? Was I in such a hurry? snapped Raju before returning to his lair, leaving Sona to tearfully narrate the conversation word for bitter word to Nisha and later to Rupa' (p.259). Sona things that her son has become the slave of his wife and is bent on stabbing his mother in heart. Condition is getting worse day by day and there is a great dispute among the family. Pooja goes and comes without anyone's permission. Parents think that it is very bad for Nisha to remain at home all the time. She should join a school so that she feels better. She starts going to school to teach. After seven months of the marriage Raju announces that Pooja is pregnant. Soon she gives birth to a boy. Parents are continuously searching a mangli boy to match for Nisha, but they are not getting success in it. Soon Nisha feds up of the teaching job and plans to start a business. She consults to her father. Yashpal at the time of dinner says to Nisha 'Beti' he started, 'business is not an easy thing' (p. 291). I will help you in the beginning, but the responsibility, profit and loss all are yours. In teaching no matter what you do, you get your salary. This is different Nisha starts business and it flourishes day by day. Demands of suits increase in the Market. During this period Yeshpal finds a mangoli boy for Nisha, soon boy and his mother came to see Nisha and pass her. Although boy is a widow and aggres on Nisha's condition. 'I cannot give it up' she confided this was the only thing she could visualise in any marriage, that she had to come to the basement everyday' (p.303). Arvinds lives in Daryaganj and have a business there. He accepts that Nisha need not to stop her business and he will hire a room near Karol Bagh so she will not feel any problem to continue it. Only one thing Arvind wants a registry marriage. All agree and the preparison of marriage begins after a long period. They have an eleven o'clock appointment with the registrar at Tees Hazari. In evening there will be the reception at the Sartaj Hotel. All family members with Nisha reach at Tees Hazari. Finally they collect in front of a magistrate in the nicest room. Here Arvind and Nisha sign their names in several places. Pooja takes out a box from her hand bag and unnrapes the paper covering to reveal fat white squares of cashew barfi. She firmly holds a piece out to Arvind. 'Now you are married: She says laughing 'You should be the first to sweeten the mouth of your bride' (p.312). Their marriage performs happily from the court they drive straight to the Sartaj Hotel in Karol Bagh. Here all family and relatives of both side enjoy the reception and bless the couple. Next morning Arvind takes Nisha to his home & they pass their time happily. Nisha continues her business and comes regularly to see the work of tailors. This routine does not continue for long due to the pregnancy of Nisha. Her mother in-law advises her not to go daily otherwise it will create big problem so Nisha have to stop it. After ten months she gives birth to twins, girl and boy. Nisha feels that God has shown mercy on her and now her duty is over. Thus novel ends with the naming ceremony of twins and everybody looks happy and satisfied.

The concept of feminism in Indian society varies from the one in the West and therefore, Manju Kapur has tried to evolve her own stream of feminism grounded in reality. She has her own concerns, priorities as well as her own ways of dealing with the predicament of her women protagonists. Her novels make a significant contribution in this direction.

Feminism, as a concept, emerges as a protest against male domination and the marginalization of woman. Man has subjugated woman to his will, used her to promote his sexual gratification but never has he desired to elevate her to her genuine rank. What is gratification for a man is a sin for a woman, what is desire for one is a disgrace for the other, what is amusement for one is a scandal for the other. Characters of Manju Kapur, Astha and Nisha too move into this forbidden territory. Astha is disillusioned with her rich family setup and finds solace in the company of another woman while Nisha has to wait for a very long time in spite of all her physical and mental attainments due to astrological reasons.

WORKS CITED

Beauvoir, Simon de, *The Second Sex*, tran H.M. Parshley, Harmondsworth 1971, London: Pan Books, 1988.

Bhatnagar, K.C., *Realism in Major Indo-English Fiction*, Bareilly: Prakash Book Depot, 1980.

Brunton, T.D., *India in Fiction: The Heritage of Indiannes, Critical Essays on Indian Writing in English*, Nork, Desai Amur, Dharwar: Karnataka University, 1968.

Chaman Nahal, *Feminism in Indian English Fiction, Indian Women Novelestsed*, R.K. Dhawan, New Delhi: Prestige, 1991.

Dhawan, R.K., ed., *Explorations in Modern Indo-English Fictions*, New Delhi: Bahri Publication, 1982.

Forster, E.M., *Aspects of Novel*, London: Penguim Books, 1979.

Gokak, Y.K., *English in India Its Present and Future*, Bombay: Asia Pub House 1964.

Grimke, Sarah, *Letters on the Equality of the Sexes and the Condition of Woman*, New York: Burt Franklin, 1970.

Iyenger, K.R.S., *Indian Writing In English*, New Delhi: Sterling Publication, 1984.

Kalimnni Kova, Elena, J., *Indian English Literature: A Perspective*, Ghaziabad; Vimal Publication, 1982.

Kapur, Manju, *A Married Woman*, Pub. Roli Books Pvt. Ltd. ND – 48, 2002.

Kapur, Manju, *Home*, Pub. Random House, India, 2006.

Klein, Viola, *The Feminine Character*, London: Routledge, 1989.

Mehta, P.P., *Indo-Anglion Fiction: An Assessment*, Bareilly: Prakash Book Depot, 1968.

Millett, Kate, *Sexual Politics'*, Garden City, New York: Double Day, 1970.

Naik, M.K., *Aspects of Indian Writing in English*, New Delhi: Macmillan, 1979.

Sinha, K.N., *An Indian Writing in English*, The University of Bihar, Muzaffarpur.

❒❒❒

29

The Novels of Nayantara Sahgal : A Study in the Feminist Perspective

P. MADHURIMA AND V. SARAVANAN

'Novel' until the seventeenth century, if at all used as a literary form, meant a short narrative in prose. It was only in the early eighteenth century, the word, acquired its present meaning and significance. The novel today is defined as a fictitious prose narrative of considerable length in which characters and actions represent the ongoing reality. Modern novelist is greatly concerned with socio-political, cultural and psychological crises in the society in transition.

The Indian novelist is linguistically handicapped and the Indian writer in English in general has to evolve a language flexible and varied enough to suit different fictitious characters drawn from most varied professions and strata of society, for authenticity and to attract Indian readership. Mulk Raj Anand has tried to Indianize English by literal translation into English of Indian expressions, proverbs etc. Raja Rao does not write 'Baboo English' but successfully transmutes into English, the idiom, the rhythm and the tone of the natural speech of his characters. R.K. Narayan writes 'admirably clean English' perfectly adapted to communicate Indian sensibility.

Novel as a literary form emerges out of prevailing social conditions in the country. In India, during the period of British rule in 1792, Charles Grant put forth the idea of making English a channel to transmit western ideas. This prompted many Indian thinkers and writers to use English to express their views and respect their problems to the administration. The political panorama was a perennial source of inspiration to many writers.

In the changing situation today, with more immediate social, economic political crisis, novel has come to mean, not a story of time against the Smug pattern of permeance as the traditional novel now rightly seems to have been- but a story of time against a background of contingency. The traditional role of the novelist, as story teller has metamorphosed into that of a prophet or a visionary and consequently moral and ultimately apocalyptic meaning has got imperceptibly blended in the writer's craft. Life being circumscribed in an historical matrix, all his creative efforts cannot be seen in their historical and cultural facets. Consequently it is legitimate as well as desirable to direct not merely critical evaluation of art but also the creative imagination. A truly great litterateur is one who speaks about the phenomenon of living as well as the very possibilities of life. And fiction should be read in the context of and with primary regard for the social and the political views of the novelist. In Fiction, the genre most in-extricably intertwinced with the times wherein it is written, this reawakened recognition of the relevance of the socio-political context of literature assumes all the more significance.

The novel, infact, more than any other form of literature, has become a political and social barometer of the times. On the other hand it embraces a multitude of characters, feelings and incidents and holds a great appeal it is not a mere story in prose. It is the "prose of human life It is the first arm to comprehend and represent the total man". It presents an entirely new vision of life. Poetry, drama, cinema, painting or music might catch parts of human existence outside the reach of novel but "Only novel can fully portray the life of a man, woman or a child" And thus as chronicler of human life, the novelist is "Superior to the Saint, the scientist, he philosopher and the poet." The subject matter of novel is man Novel is the epic of man's struggle against society, against nature, against his own self".

And novel prospers but in circumstances where the inner equilibrium among things has got snapped. The novel though opens itself to questions about the inner dynamics of society, political consciousness ideology, social conflict and fragmentation therein, the novelist in so far as he is an artist and not merely social historian or an ideologue, must feel committed in his intimate practical relationship with his material to deal in specifics with particular dramatic situations and concrete instances of the experiences he wishes to represent.

The novelist can legitimately generalize and create a picture of an entire society, a political system or mankind as a whole. He commits himself to a belief in the priority of the individual person and in the primacy of individual experience over collective experience, experiential individual human truth over social doctrine. The seminal thoughts of women's emancipation made some of the great thinkers of 19th century Europe transmute their thought into works of art. Ibsen in Norway, Hauptmann in Germany and Zola in France, with their powerful and lurid realism, recorded the fortunes of women in the society of their times. Infact, Ibsen became critical of the hypocrisy of the people in masculine society. Commenting on the dubiety of the man he says: "There are two kinds of Spiritual laws; two kinds of consciences; one in man and another altogether different in women. They do not understand each other but in practical life the woman is judged by man's law as though she were not a woman but a man". This draws our attention to the plight of a woman, who can not be herself in the society of present day which is an exclusively masculine society with laws framed by men and with a judicial system that judges feminine conduct from a masculine point of view.

Ibsen's Nora, who is bound to her husband, feels that her trust in her husband is shattered and she decides that there is no point in staying with him. She takes a momentous decision of leaving her husband to himself. The slamming of the door behind her, not surprisingly, Chimed with the Zolaist temper of the younger generation of Europe in the 19th century.

In the same way women affort Hauptman and Zola, specimens of humanity particularly trammeled by their conventional disabilities in the struggle for personal emancipation. Hauptmann's Before Dawn, Zola's Nana, depict powerfully and realistically the problems encountered by the women in society. An increasing awareness of injustice done to women pervades the works of the writers and thinkers like Bernard Shaw, James Joyce, and Lawrence. But Indian fiction in English evolved historically as an effect of Britain's role in India for about two centuries. The contact between India and Great Britain led to a considerable body of fiction writing, thereby producing quite a good number of Indian novelists in English. In the words of

F.W. Bain: "India a withered trunk: Suddenly shot out with foreign foliage".

The influence of language and literature of England proved fruitful in the creation of fiction in India. Bankim Chandra Chatterji with his powerful novels like Raj Mohan's wife, Durgesh Nandini and Ananda Matt, achieved considerable success in the realm of fiction writing. The early 20th century India witnessed many changes, which gave a stimulus to creative artists. The rapidity of National Movement, the growing awareness of people to socio-economic problems and the Satyagraha Movement influenced the Indo-English novelists. The writers in India did not hesitate to record the harassed and the exploited women in Indian society. Rabindranath Tagore came out with Vinodini, his first successful novel. He was primarily a poet, incarnating the spirit of India, a prophet of the religion of Man. Though he was a poet, he wrote quite a few novels in English, which almost present a traditional type of the woman.

Saratchandra, another powerful creative artist from Bengal produced great works like *Sreekantha, Grihadaha Pathardabi, Bipradas* and *Ses Prasna*. He portrayed in his works the tears and the sweat of women. Thus the novel in India was fostered at the hands of the Bengali Trio, Bankim, Tagore and Sarat. Fiction as a form of creative literature found its place in the hands of Mulk Raj Anand, Raja Rao and R.K. Narayan. They bore a deep impress on the later novelists like Bhabani Battacharya, Kushwant Singh, Manohar Malgonkar, Nayantara Sahgal, Ruth Prawar Jabwala and Anita Desai.

Feminism has been subtly handled in the massive work of English novels in India. Feminism is defined as cultural, economic and political movements that are focused towards establishing legal protection and complete equality for the women. In Indian writing feminism has been used as a modest attempt for evaluating the real social scenario as far as women are concerned. The Indian English novelists use oriental approaches of feminism. There are several novels in English literature of India that aptly portrays the actual status of the women in Indian societies. Throughout the world, feminism has generated interest amongst the people and India is no exception. Feminism is thoroughly accomplished through the work of the Indian English novelists.

Feminism does not particularly talk of equality and rights of woman but it is more about compassion, respect and understanding from the male counterparts. The main cause for the dissatisfaction of the women in today's society is the superior attitude of the men. Throughout, the women have suffered in silence and feminism talks exactly about that. Women have affirmed their fundamental rights and have realized where they exactly went wrong. Indian English novelists have frankly highlighted this concept. Authors like Anita Desai, Shashi Deshpande and Kamala Markandaya have actually used the various aspects of the male dominated society as their main theme. However, the concept of feminism is handled in restricted conditions by the authors. Today, Indian societies have broadly accepted feminism keeping aside the patriarchal predomination to an extent.

Feminism as a clearly and precisely defined concept relating to sociological and literary studies is a phenomenon of recent development. No doubt in the past women like Nora in Ibsen's *A Doll's House* came out boldly against convention. In the 20th century, 'Feminism' as a concept developed and fostered by quite a few creative artists in the west, particularly in France. Simone de Beavoure's Second Sex, a French model of Feminism, takes into account the greater sexual expression. In the same way the American and the Canadian Feminists like Karson Maculler lay stress upon the strong expression of self assertion by a woman. Creative artists like Kate Millet explored the problem of woman in a patriarchal society. Chaman Nahal makes the following observations on feminism.

I define Feminism as a mode of existence in which the woman is free of the dependence Syndrome. There is a dependence syndrome whether it is the husband or the father or the community or whether it is a religious group, ethnic group. When women are free themselves of the dependence Syndrome and lead a normal life my idea of feminism materializes

There are several Indian novelists who produced novels that revealed the truth of Indian societies and how women are being treated here. They present the aspects of feminism with authentic and impressive language. The struggle of an Indian woman for her true identity clearly emerges in the Indian English novels. Rama Mehta's *Inside the Haveli*, Nayantara Sahgal's *Rich Like Us*, Gita Hariharan's *The Thousand Faces of Night* are some of the novels that uses this theme of feminism and highlights the statue of a woman in Indian societies. Anita Desai's *Cry, the Peacock, Where Shall We Go This Summer*? or

Voices in the City are some of the examples of feministic theory based English novels. More authors like Gita Mehta, Shama Futehally and Nisha Da Cunha work exclusively on feminine themes and emotional crisis faced by a woman. Kamala Markandaya and Kamala Das are two well renowned feminist writers of India. Some more examples of female subjective oriented English novels of India are Ruth Prawar Jhabvala's *To Whom She Will,* Kamala Markandaya's *Two Virgins* and Santha Rama Rau's *Remember the House.*

The Indian English novels based on Feminism and its different aspects depict the position of a woman in general. She has been portrayed as the key figure of Indian families and at the same time she has been projected as the subject of suffering, domestic slavery and suppression. The hidden thoughts, feelings and the realization of a woman are found in the feministic oriented English novels of India.

Indian novelist and short story writer especially noted for her sensitive portrayal of the inner life of her female characters. Several of Desai's novels explore tensions between family members and the alienation of middle-class women. In her later novels Desai has dealt with such themes as German anti-Semitism, the demise of traditions, and Western stereotypical views of India. Kamala Markandaya (1924-May 16, 2004) was a pseudonym used by Kamala Purnaiya Taylor, an Indian novelist and journalist. A native of Mysore, India, Markandaya was a graduate of Madras University, and afterwards published several short stories in Indian newspapers. After India declared its independence, Markandaya moved to Britain, though she still labeled herself an Indian expatriate long afterwards. Known for writing about culture clash between Indian urban and rural societies, Markandaya's first published novel, *Nectar in a Sieve,* was a bestseller and named a notable book of 1955 by the American Library Association. Kamala Markandaya belonged to that pioneering group of Indian women writers who made their mark not just through their subject matter, but also through their fluid, polished literary style. Nectar in a Sieve was her first published work, and its depiction of rural India and the suffering of farmers made it popular in the west. This was followed by other fiction that dramatized the Quit India movement in 1942, the clash between East and West and the tragedy that resulted from it, or the problems facing ordinary middle-class Indians making a living, finding inner peace, coping with modern technology and its effects on the poor.

Shashi Deshpande (born in 1938 in Dharwad, Karnataka, India) is a well known name in the field of Indian literature. She was born as the daughter of the renowned Kannada dramatist as well as a great Sanskrit scholar Sriranga. During her stay in Mumbai, she decided to pursue a course in Journalism. So, she took up a job as a journalist in the magazine *Onlooker*. While working in the magazine, she began writing and the first short story that she wrote got published in 1970. Her short stories headed their way in popular magazines like *Femina, Eve's Weekly* etc. she had written a novel titled *That Long Silence*, which brought her lot of praise and appreciation. Infact, for her fabulous work in this novel, she received the Sahitya Akademi award and Nanjangud Thirumalamba award. She has been actively involved in writing books for children. In her novels she dealt with the sufferings of women.

Nayantara Sahgal hails from the illustrious and erudite Nehru family. She was born in 1927 as a second daughter of Ranjit Sitaram Pandit and Vijaya Lakshmi Pandit. Her childhood was spent at Anandha Bhavan in Allahabad, where most of the major decisions pertaining to the fate of India were taken. In course of time the family home of Nehru's Ananda Bhavan became Swaraj Bhavan, which gave shelter to many veteran freedom fighters and social workers. Nayantara lived in Swaraj Bhavan along with her parents whose distinguished intellectual concerns and liberal minded views deeply touched the mental proclivities of the young Nayantara. In her own words: "Her father was a man with abundant love and understanding, refinement and restraint besides a healthy zest for life both physical and intellectual. From this intelligent and liberal minded father, Nayantara Sahgal imbibed the spirit of understanding others, particularly women with utmost sympathy and latitude". Even her mother was a woman with abundant domesticity and involvement in the political life of India under the leadership of Nehru. In the words of Isabel Pollard: "Here is a woman (Madam Pandit) who confounds all theories about clever career women, working mothers through her daughter". Nayantara sahgal with more than 30yrs of literary career occupies a significant place in the history of Indo-English novel. Sahgal as a responsible writer takes special care to keep track of the stream of national consciousness. Having eight novels to her credit she personally believes in the 'Power of pen'. She herself has admitted that: "Nayantara Sahgal has stressed the need for more writers having the courage of their convictions who could help people through their works, to question existing ideologies and not to merely the line". She opines that it is not merely the policies of a government that can steer a nation clear of its difficulties, but the people too should be equally aware of their duties. In all her novels, she emphasizes the value of freedom so essential to inner and outer development of individual entrapped in trying situations but being honest to themselves.

Sahgal's first five novels are more situational than character study, while her later three are mainly character-oriented. Out of these characters, emerges the emancipated woman, one who harbors adequate courage to walk out of her suffocating and infra-dig circumstances. She is the liberated woman who is virtuous, moral upright, self-respecting, though she appears to deviate from age-hold tradition she asserts her right as a human-being and as an individual who can endure suffering to a certain extent.

The historical consciousness in her novels is intermixed with socio-political scenario of Indian melieu. Sahgal interprets segments of history according to her perception and India comes alive, troubling with energy struggling to shake off shackles of failure created by some mistakes and take a new birth. Her novels inculcate the value of loving one's roots. One's identity and taking pride in one's motherland. A clever intermingling of history and fiction can be discerned in Sahgal, gradually journeying from her first novel, *A Time to be Happy* up to her latest one Mistaken Identity. She believes in the reorientation of values for survival in the face of new challenges. Her novels seem to reflect her views on womanhood, the value of freedom of individual and of nation and futility of violence. Among the women novelists in Indian English literature, Nayantara Sahgal is one writer who is: "Preoccupied with the modern Indian Women's search for sexual freedom and self realization".

The literary career of Nayantara Sahgal ranges from 1954 to 1988. Her *Prison and Chacolake Cake* that appeared in 1954 is her first book of auto-biography. She dedicated this to her beloved parents. In this work, she recorded her own experiences of childhood and adolescence culminating in her graduation from an American college. It ably illustrates her superb narrative skill, power of reminiscential concentration, meticulous observation and effective articulation combined with imaginative descriptions. As A.V. Krishna Rao rightly observes: "Its theme appears to be the growth of consciousness,

Individual as well as national and its concern essentially with the problem of freedom and its fundamental significance". Her first novel *A Time to be Happy* appeared in 1956. The chief concern of this novel is with the women of three generations, some of whom adopt traditional way of life while others seek freedom within the confines of their marital life. Next appeared her second novel, *This Time of Morning*, the central theme of which is the suffering of woman within marriage and also the conditioning of her to a position next to man. Sahgal's third novel *Storm in Chandigarh* deals with complex human relationships in both private and public life. The two themes in this novel run alongside to each other. The political theme deals with the crisis in the newly divided states of Punjab and Haryana. The second theme concerns itself with the crisis in the lives of three young married couple. Her fourth novel, *The Day in Shadow*, dwells upon not only on the release and recognition of individual conscience but also with its growth and maturation. Here she brings into sharp focus the diversity of the human life and enacts its variety. This novel reflects much of the author's stand on divorce and traditional Hindu society's attitude to marriage and womanhood.

Infact, Sahgal's article entitled *Of Divorce and Hindu Woman* that appeared in *Hindustan Times* illustrates her own concept of Indian womanhood. She fervently puts forth her views on woman thus:

> She stands for new morality according to which a Woman is not to be taken as a mere toy, an object of lust and momentary pleasure but man's equal and honoured partner, in word and deed as against the inhuman traditional posture.

This shows her undoubted concern for the gender oppression and he marginalized and repressed position of woman in a male dominant society.

Sahgal's fifth novel, *A Situation* in New Delhi deals with the problems of alienation and frustration of the younger generation of Indians in the light of opportunistic politics pursued in New Delhi. The problems that confront the younger men and women of free India.

Sahgal's *Rich like Us* won the prestigious 'Sinclair Prize' for fiction. In this novel, she depicts the woman, who is made subservient to man at all costs and is also dispossessed of her soul, mind and self. It portrays her unconventional and feministic view that the entire social setup in India supports male domination and that women are exploited and victimized in marriage, in sexual relationships and even in child birth.

Sahgal's next novel *Plans for Departure* has been awarded the common wealth writers prize for Eurasia Region. The primary concern of this novel is with the problems confronted by women and also with woman's socio- personal predicament. It deals with the story of Anna Hansen, a Danish girl who postponed her marriage to an English Diplomat, Nicholas because of her desire for self realization. In the words of the novelist this novel left her: with the feeling that there are all kinds of fresh pastures ahead and that in essence I have only just begun to write.

Mistaken Identity portrays two parallel themes: The political theme about the colonial attitudes of the rulers towards the natives and the theme of man-woman relationship in a man dominant society. Bhushan Singh's mother, the protagonist in the novel is unorthodox, unconventional rebellious and an ardent feminist daringly breaks all traditional taboos and steps out of the palace for over to live openly with the Urban Yusuf.

Besides the above mentioned major works of fiction, Nayantara Sahgal has been writing since her childhood filling up diaries and note books with passages from her uncle. She wrote a poem *The Awakening* (1952) followed by *You are not alone* (1953) and *Afternoon Magic* (1953). As a freelance writer, she wrote regularly on national and international topics of current interest to Indian Express, India Today, London Magazine, Indo Asia and Hemisphere. She wrote another book of her autobiography *From Fear Set Fee* (1962) which takes up the broken thread of her story as narrated in Prison and Chacolate cake. She wrote her political work *A Voice for Freedom* (1977), which records grippingly the events in India during emergency.

Her Indira Gandhi's *Emergency and Style* (1977), a study of Mrs. Gandhi's years in power from 1966 to 1977, presents a refreshingly and seemingly caustic view of Indian policy. She also brings out the attitudes and practices combined with strong personal tendencies that led to the authoritarian trend of affairs during Mrs. Gandhi's regime. Besides being a poet, freelance writer and a novelist, Nayantara Sahgal has a few short stories to her credit. Her short stories like The promising young woman, The Golden afternoon appeared in the illustrated weekly of India while stories like: *Marthand, The Nakalit, The Girl in the book shop, Gucify,* found a place in Indian and foreign magazines like London Magazine, Hemisphere, Indian Horizon, Cosmopolitan. Even in her book reviewing, she makes it a point to strive for the cause of woman only.

WORKS CITED

Archer, Willion, ed., *The Collected works of Henry Ibsen,* London: William Heinemann, 1912, pp.91-92.

Bhatnagar, K.C., *Indo-English Approach in Realism, Realism in Indo-English Fiction,* Barcilly: Prakash Book Depot, 1970, p.120.

Fox, Ralph, *Novel and the people,* New York: International Publishers, 1937, p.36.

Iyengar, K.R. Srinivas, *Indian Writing in English,* New Delhi: Sterling Publishers, Pvt.Ltd, 1984, p.317.

Nahal, Chaman, *Feminism in English Fiction 'Forms and Variations',* ed. Susheela Singh, *Feminism and Recent Fiction in English,* New Delhi: Prestige Books, 1991, p.17.

Naik, M.K., *A History of Indian English Literature,* New Delhi: Sahitya Akademi, 1982, p.239.

Pontes, H., *Nayantara Sahgal,* New Delhi: Concept Publishing Company, 1970, p.4.

http://pib.nic.in/release/release.asp?relid=46983.

www.contemporary writers.com/authors/?p=auth 124.

www.hrc.utexas.edu/research/fa/desai.html.

www.sawnet.org/books/authors.php?Markandaya+Kamala.

www.loc.gov/acq/ovop/delhi/salrp/nayantarasahgal.html.

❑❑❑

30

An Examination of Feminism in the Select Novels of Kiran Desai, Kamala Markandaya and Shobha De

N. Jaishree

Women writers in India are moving forward with their strong and sure strides, matching the pace of the world. We see them bursting out in full bloom spreading their own individual fragrances. They are recognized for their originality, versatility and the indigenous flavor of the soil that they bring to their work. Yes, they are our women writers. Writers first, I must insist. Gender is only incidental...but, one must admit, it does spice up their work.

Women are an integral part of human civilization. No society or country can ever progress without an active participation of women in its overall development. Although the place of woman in society has differed from culture to culture and from age to age yet one fact common to almost all societies is that woman have never been considered equal to men. Women are held in great esteem in India. The feminist writers dwell on tortured womanhood. The present paper explores the feministic perspectives of three great writers Kamala Markandaya, Kiran Desai and Shoba De.

Kamala Markandaya another great feminist, is a housewife in real life and is very much conscious of gender differences when she enters her journalistic career. She underlines the traditional attitude to women in her novels. In her early novels she draws our attention to the secondary and insignificant role of women in ancient India.

But in her later novels we find her moving from this female self analysis to a feminine protest. The importance of domestic life and the integrity of the family formed an important part of her fiction. She believes that the truth about human relations can be best expressed in terms of social situations such as marriage and family. Rukmani in *Nectar in a Sieve* is the best example to illustrate the novelist's stance. Rukmani seems to be the legendary archetype of an ideal housewife, but we find that she also rises against the social forces confronting her, remaining within the sanctity of her home. Rukmani in her assertions against the social forces emerges as an assertive woman. Kamala Markandaya's heroines do not adore of worship their husbands, though their respect and love them.

Pramila in *Some Inner Fury* is a representative of Kamala Markandaya's feminist view of life. Pramila, brought up in the conventional Hindi tradition, is married to the westernized Kit. What Pramila wants out of life is apparently so different from what Kit wants out of life is apparently so different from what Kit wants her to be Kit's conception of the wife as an equal and a companion is rarely translated into action. This double attitude and his distaste for the Indian way of life, particularly in the area of family relationships, turn him into a bully and a sadist. His later negligence of Pramila can be rationalized as a desperate attempt to evoke responses but it is actually an expression of his disenchantment and regret. Under these circumstances Pramila's attempts to adjust herself to her husband fail.

Kamala Markandaya pays an important attention on the mother-childood bondage, in all her novels. Mothers are often depicted as self-sacrificing, and protective towards their children. In A *Handful of Rice*, Ravi's mother, though heart broken at the departure of her sons, does not openly come in their way to happiness. Ravi also cherishes deep regard for her even during his criminal days. Ravi also regards his mother with the core of his heart. We hear deep rooted love and regard for his birth giver when he tells Jayamma that if he could lie to her, he would lie to his own mother. In all her fiction she gives importance to this close relationship. In her fiction women find fulfilment in becoming the mother of a son. Nalini, also considers herself supremely blessed when Raju, her son is born.Nalini's mother keeps a protective watch on her. She does not trust the young girl alone even in the company of Ravi. The novelist also presents in the novel the nature of jealously of women. Thangam, another character fills with jealously when Nalini is expecting her first child.

Women's struggle is one ranging from survival at the sheer physical level to the quest for identity. Most women have to struggle with conflicting situations at home and also outside. In Kamala Markandaya wide range of women characters ranging from the harassed, victimized peasant woman to the princess, we discern the plight of Indian woman crippled by sex, society and economic condition. Her women, though victims of nature and society, never give in completely. Beneath the covering of fragility and weakness lies an inherent strength. They are like leaves of grass - the humblest. Her fictional canvas portrays certain social conventions and attitudes that victimize women. Yet neither the struggle for survival nor the social inequalities can defeat them completely.

Kiran Desai's *The Inheritance of Loss* opens with a teenage Indian girl, an orphan called Sai, living with her Cambridge - educated Anglophile grandfather, a retired judge, in the town of Kalimpong on the Indian side of the Himalayas. Sai is romantically involved with her math tutor, Gyan, the descendant of a Nepali Gurkha mercenary, but he eventually recoils from her obvious privilege and falls in with a group of ethnic Nepalese insurgents. In a parallel narrative, we are shown the life of Biju, the son of Sai's grandfather's cook, who belongs to the "shadow class" of illegal immigrants in New York and spends much of his time dodging the authorities, moving from one ill-paid job to another.

What binds these seemingly disparate characters is a shared historical legacy and a common experience of impotence and humiliation. "Certain moves made long ago had produced all of them," Desai writes, referring to centuries of subjection by the economic and cultural power of the West. But the beginnings of an apparently leveled field in a late-20th century global economy serve merely to scratch those wounds rather than heal them.

Almost all of Desai's characters have been stunted by their encounters with the West. As a student, isolated in racist England, the future judge feels "barely human at all" and leaps "when touched on the arm as if from an unbearable intimacy". Yet on his return to India, he finds himself despising his apparently backward Indian wife.

The judge is one of those "ridiculous Indians," as the novel puts it, "who couldn't rid themselves of what they had broken their souls to learn" and whose Anglophilia can only turn into self-hatred. These Indians are also an unwanted anachronism in postcolonial India, where long-suppressed peoples have begun to awaken to their dereliction, to express their anger and despair. For some of Desai's characters, including one of the judge's neighbours in Kalimpong, this comes as a distinct shock: "Just when Lola had thought it would continue, a hundred years like the one past – Trollope, BBC, a burst of hilarity at Christmas – all of a sudden, all that they had claimed innocent, fun, funny, not really to matter, was proven wrong".

There is no mistaking the literary influences on Desai's exploration of postcolonial chaos and despair. Early in the novel, she sets two Anglophilic Indian women to discussing *A Bend in the River*, V.S. Naipaul's powerfully bleak novel about traditional Africa's encounter with the modern world. Lola, whose clothesline sags "under a load of Marks and Spencer's panties," thinks Naipaul is "strange. Stuck in the past... He has not progressed. Colonial neurosis, he's never freed himself from it". Lola goes on to accuse Naipaul of ignoring the fact that there is a "new England," a "completely cosmopolitan society" where "chicken tikka masala has replaced fish and chips as the No.1 takeout dinner". As further evidence, she mentions her own daughter, a newsreader for BBC radio, who "doesn't have a chip on her shoulder".

Desai takes a skeptical view of the West's consumer-driven multiculturalism, noting the "sanitized elegance" of Lola's daughter's British-accented voice, which is "triumphant over any horrors the world might thrust upon others". At such moments, Desai seems far from writers like Zadie Smith and Hari Kunzru, whose fiction takes a generally optimistic view of what Salman Rushdie has called "hybridity, impurity, intermingling, the transformation that comes of new and unexpected combinations of human beings, cultures, ideas, politics, movies, songs".

In fact, Desai's novel seems to argue that such multiculturalism, confined to the Western metropolis and academe, doesn't begin to address the causes of extremism and violence in the modern world. Nor, it suggests, can economic globalization become a route to prosperity for the downtrodden. "Profit," Desai observes at one point, "could only be harvested in the gap between nations, working one against the other".

In the novels of Shobha De, most of her protagonists are from middle class background who move upward to socialite society and all of them find marriage dull. The men portrayed are unromantic, overwhelming acquisitive and slightly ridiculous as in *Second Thought, Starry Nights* and *Socialite Evenings.* The women of Shobha De reject their husbands because heroines are romantic, sensual and sensitive. Her heroines find themselves trapped in their marriageand take their husband as a thing of pleasure. In all her novels we notice that the heroines established extramarital relationships. In her novel *Socialite Evenings* she explored the lives of the bored housewives and their loveless life of the rich industrialist families. The woman characters of her novel are shown madly in love with the male characters.

In the *Second Thought* it seems like the perfect match. Maya is pretty, young, eager to escape her dull, middle-class home in Calcutta and plunge into the whirl of Bombay, where she moves after her marriage. Ranjan, handsome, hard-driving and ambitious, has all the glamour of an American university degree and a wealthy family background. Maya is determined to be the ideal wife. Instead, she finds herself trapped and stifled by the confines of an arranged marriage to a man who, she discovers, is rigidly conservative and completely indifferent to her desires. She begins to experience, too, the utter loneliness of a stranger in suburban Bombay. And then she strikes up a friendship with Nikhil, her charming, college-going neighbour, and the stage is set for an explosive tale of love, betrayal and paths not taken. Shobha De has left the reader impressed and entirely captivated by her sketch of characters and her beautiful crafted English that leaves the dumbstruck.

Starry Nights is an illustrious novel where the pungent ink of the writer illustrates the various facets of woman. The painful sores of the society are explored in the novel while making Starry nights a matchless anecdote of the society. It portrays the story of Aasha Rani and Akshay that is based on real life love story of two celluloid stars. The central character Aasha Rani is a dark sweet girl form Chennai aspiring to become a film star. Her amma instigated her to be in the film world by hook or by crook. When she was fifteen years she has to sleep with kishenbai, a film producer to get a chance. He assisted her in getting her roles and sponsored a film for her. In this process he falls in love with her but it was too late as she has already gets engaged with Akshay arora, a famous Bollywood star. In later days

Akshay gets bored with Aasha and leaves her. In one of the magazine he reveals her as "pornographic actress'. Eventually she gets attached to Sheth Amirchand, a Member of Parliament and starts working under his control. Then she moves to Chennai to do an art film, but still she has love for Akshay and she tries to rekindle it. When she realizes that his love for her is only because of stardom, she gets frustrated and attempts suicide and fails in it. In the process she marries a New Zealander and begets a child. Eventually Akshay gets AIDS because of his lifestyle. Asha returns to India and makes sasha, her daughter a prosperous film star.

Socialite Evenings is set at the backdrop of Mumbai high society. This story is all about the lives of bored housewives of rich families whose husbands remain busy with their work and their wives choose the option of extra marital affair. Their marriages are often seen as loveless ones. Their husbands are often seeing as their wives with respectability rather than their life partners. Karuna, the central character of the story is bored with the life with her husband and she wants to get rid of her boredom by writing a memoir. Her memoirs become successful and achieves a lot of name and pride in her new venture. She becomes a socialite and uses this prominence to get a job of advertising copyrighter or a creator of television channel. This novel was critically acclaimed and but truly a masterpiece. Many woman of the society get accustomed with the story. The story is partially an autobiography of the author.

These women writers, Kamala Markandaya, Kiran Desai and Shobha De have given literary work in India an unmistakable edge. They are able to sensitively portray a world that has in it women rich in substance. Their women are real flesh-and- blood protagonists who make you look at them with awe with their relationships to their surroundings, their society, their men, their children, their families; their mental make-ups and themselves.

Indian woman whose badge has been that of silent-suffering and who is an upholder of Indian culture is an oft-repeated type in Indian English fiction. She is shown to be enacting various roles of a mother, wife, a daughter and a sister - a cog in the family machines but never as an individual claiming her life to be her own, wherein she could seek personal gratification and self fulfillment. This is mainly due to the patriarchal pattern of society where the authority emanates from the eldest male in the family. In the male dominated society, the inflated male tends to dominate and neglect the female who is his partner. Historical and sociological aspects seem to have contributed their share in keeping behind curtain.

Thus we find that contemporary novelists have taken up the feminist issue as major themes of their novels. Woman, in their novels, has been depicted as emerging from her stereotyped roles. She is being shows as searching for an identity of her own and striving to create space for herself. She is rejecting patriarchal domination. She is marching ahead searching for fulfillment as an individual asserting herself. The price that she has to pay may be psychological or emotional ostracism but she does not see, to recede her steps.

WORKS CITED

Agarwal, Krishna Avtar, *Post Colonial Indian English Literature,* Jaipur: Book Enclave, 2007.

Iyengar, K.R. Srinivas, *Indian Writing in English,* New Delhi: Asia Publishing House, 1973.

Kamala, Markandaya, *A Handful of Rice,* New Delhi, Paperbacks, 1985.

Kamala, Markandaya, *Some Inner Fury,* New York: The John Day Co.1956.

Kumar, Shiv K., *Tradition and Change in the Novels of Markandaya,* Books Abroad, 1969.

□□□

Books of Similar Interest

Critical Studies on Indian English Literature (3 Volumes Set)

M.F. Patel **978-81-7132-630-3 (Set) 2010 Rs. 2500.00 (Set)**

Indian English literature is very resonant and elegant literature among regional literatures in India and among other literatures around the globe. The rapid growth of this literature is amazingly wonderful. Some literary legends and all time great writers like R.N. Tagore. R.K. Narayan, M.R. Anand, Raja Rao, Anita Desai etc. are prettiest feathers in the cap of Indo-Anglian literature. This progress has been a saga of a colourful procession in the field of fiction, poetry and drama.

In this critical anthology several scholars have tried to explore and detect this odyssey of Indian English literature. There are a good number of articles in the present anthology contributed by writers from different walks of life-professors, lecturers, poets, critics, and research scholars etc. Some of the writers analysed are Mulk Raj Anand, Amitav Ghosh, Salman Rushdie, Mahesh Dattani, Girish Karnad, Arun Joshi, Jayanta Mahapatra, Kamla Das, Shashi Deshpande, Namita Gokhale, Bharati Mukherjee, Taslima Nasrin, Kiran Desai, Nayantara Sahgal, Anita Desai and D.C. Chambial. It is hoped that the book will be of great help to the students, researchers and teachers of English literature and will even appeal to those interested in Indian English literature.

Dr. M.F. Patel (b. 1974) achieved Bachelor Degree in English from Shri. & Smt. P.K. Kotawala Arts College, Patan in 1994 and Master Degree from Department of English, North Gujarat University, Patan in 1996. Presently he is discharging his duties as Prinicipal of Smt. C.C. Mahila Arts & Sheth C.N. Commerce College, Visnagar, Gujarat. He had also served as a NCC Officer with the rank of Lieutenant. He obtained his Ph.D. Degree from Hemchandracharya North Gujarat University, Patan. Dr Patel's twenty articles have been published in books and various national & International journals. He has presented papers in State, National & International Level Seminars and participated in various workshops and International Symposium as well as International Writers Festival. His area of special interest is Indian Writing in English. He has to his credit seventeen voluminous books till date.

Mulk Raj Anand : His Vision and Work

Raj Vir Singh **978-81-7132-636-5** **2010** **Rs. 595.00**

This book studies in depth and detail of Mulk Raj Anand's all major novels which are truly representative of his creative, artistic and literary genius. Mulk Raj Anand enjoyed his childhood in the idyllic world. Later on he came in touch with the urban atmosphere. He enjoyed most of his years of life in cities but his nostalgic past always remained in his mind. That is reflected in most of his novels. He combined in his fictional work his vision of the rural world with that of the urban world. We find in him Henry Fielding and Charles Dickens rolled into one as it were, encompassing the rural and urban conditions. But at heart, he is like Rousseau, pleading for return to the naturalness of nature, simplicity and innocence of the countryside contrasted with the stiffness and callousness of the city.

Undoubtedly, the book makes an interesting and meaningful reading. It keeps the reader thrilled by the new vision of life in to the works of Anand and offers fresh interpretations. It will certainly be very useful to the teachers, researchers and students of Indian writing in English, particularly those having keen interest in the fictional world of Mulk Raj Anand in broad perspective.

Raj Vir Singh obtained his M. A. in 1987 from St. John's College, Agra and Ph. D. from the same institution in 1992 on the topic entitled: The Fiction of Katherine Anne Porter, "A Study in Themes, Symbols and Techniques." He was conferred on a degree of D. Litt.on the topic entitled, "The Idyllic Vis-A-Vis Urban Vision of Life in Mulk Raj Anand's Fiction" from Dr. Bhimrao Ambedkar University (Formerly: Agra University) Agra. He was selected as a lecturer in English in 1996 through Rajasthan Public Service Commission. Since then he has been working in M. S. J. Government Post-graduate College, Bharatpur, Rajasthan. He has a research experience of almost two decades, especially in the field of American fiction and Indian writing in English. At present he has been working on a U.G.C. sanctioned project on Mulk Raj Anand's novels. He has attended various conferences, seminars and workshops of National and International standard and published many research papers in various reputed journals.